# Building the Young Reader's Brain, Birth Through Age 8

# Building the Young Reader's Brain, Birth Through Age 8

## Third Edition

Pamela Nevills

**FOR INFORMATION:**

Corwin
A SAGE Company
2455 Teller Road
Thousand Oaks, California 91320
(800) 233-9936
www.corwin.com

SAGE Publications Ltd.
1 Oliver's Yard
55 City Road
London EC1Y 1SP
United Kingdom

SAGE Publications India Pvt. Ltd.
Unit No 323-333, Third Floor, F-Block
International Trade Tower Nehru Place
New Delhi 110 019
India

SAGE Publications Asia-Pacific Pte. Ltd.
18 Cross Street #10-10/11/12
China Square Central
Singapore 048423

Vice President and Editorial
 Director:  Monica Eckman
Publisher:  Jessica Allan
Content Development Editor:
 Mia Rodriguez
Senior Editorial Assistant:
 Natalie Delpino
Editorial Intern:  Lex Nunez
Production Editor:  Melanie Birdsall
Copy Editor:  Melinda Masson
Typesetter:  Exeter Premedia Services
Proofreader:  Jeff Bryant
Indexer:  Integra
Cover Designer:  Candice Harman
Marketing Manager:  Olivia Bartlett



*Library of Congress Cataloging-in-Publication Data*

Names: Nevills, Pamela, author.
Title: Building the young reader's brain, birth through age 8 / Pamela Nevills.
Other titles: Building the reading brain, PreK-3
Description: Third edition. | Thousand Oaks, California : Corwin, 2024. | Revised edition of: Building the reading brain, PreK-3 / Pamela Nevills, Patricia Wolfe. 2nd ed. ©2009. | Includes bibliographical references and index.
Identifiers: LCCN 2023010563 (print) | LCCN 2023010564 (ebook) | ISBN 9781071888780 (paperback) | ISBN 9781071888759 (ebook)
Subjects: LCSH: Reading (Early childhood) | Reading, Psychology of.
Classification: LCC LB1139.5.R43 W65 2024 (print) | LCC LB1139.5.R43 (ebook) | DDC 372.4--dc23/eng/20230403
LC record available at https://lccn.loc.gov/2023010563
LC ebook record available at https://lccn.loc.gov/2023010564

# Contents

Visit the companion website at
https://resources.corwin.com/BuildingtheYoungReadersBrain3E
for downloadable resources.

# Preface

As I approached writing the third edition of *Building the Young Reader's Brain, Birth Through Age 8*, I looked at the previous introduction. A positive, upbeat dialog followed the book's development and assured the reader of all that would be found in the second edition. The book's co-author, Dr. Pat Wolfe, and I realized there was so much excitement in 2009 about the potential for reading instruction that could benefit from the advances and information in neuroscience. The introduction finished with this statement:

> Finally it is acknowledged that it takes talented teachers, who understand how children learn to read, to orchestrate a delicate balance of instruction, student engagement, conversation, and reading practice so their students are able to read with a natural amount of effort and with obvious enjoyment.

The end of the previous introduction provides a beginning for the third edition of this book. Much has changed for our schools, for the education profession, and for parents. We continue to have talented teachers who are knowledgeable and sensitive about the learning needs of children, but the professional conditions educators work under have changed. An update on the "state of education" is a most appropriate introduction. Recent history of education in our schools is the foundation for teachers and students as they strive to master reading. The stage is set for a book to understand the whole child, specifically with a focus on neurology and on "WHAT IS HAPPENING IN THERE?"

## ABOUT THIS THIRD EDITION

This third edition, with a new title, is a practical guide to teaching the way the brain learns, specifically how children's brains are innately designed for oral language, and not naturally intended to learn reading. Other deep topics include the brain's memory systems, along with developmental stages of benchmark development for very young children, and for developing readers, priming skills of attention, concentration, remembering, and organization, culminating with cognitive development.

In many ways it is a book grounded upon cumulative practices from many educational experts, who base their recommendations on strong educational research.

While the science of reading (National Reading Panel, 2000) is the backbone of most educational practices for teaching reading, researchers continue to provide new insights to influence effective teaching practices. This book is a showcase of those practices as they relate to brain building for reading. The reader is invited to review the expansive list of references that back the scientific review of brain structures and their functions. Note that the reading instructional practices that are included were selected based on their relevance to how the brain processes information, and on an extensive review of current literature.

## BACKGROUND AND A BIT OF HISTORY

Learning to read has had powerful attention for the last 30 years or more. Everyone knows the statistics. Children who learn to read, and learn to read well, are more likely to be successful in life, according to society's standards. A predominance of people who break laws and go to prison are poor readers. The education system gets a low grade when a high number of students graduate from high school without reading proficiency, or if dropout rates are high, most likely because reading is too hard. There was a time, not so long ago, when educators started to "get it together" and publishers were producing teacher's manuals and reading texts that accounted for and addressed the reading needs of all children.

I remember the year 2008 when California's textbook selection committee had completed its work. Recommended publishers were selected, and their names were announced to school districts. The materials truly represented what was known about the best available reading practices. Most importantly, the materials reflected the National Reading Panel's (2000) findings. Conclusions in this report resulted from a rigorous set of research methodologies through a review of over 300 studies, which were selected from two databases, PsycINFO and ERIC. In textbooks and teacher's manuals, all areas for reading instruction were covered including practices that were compatible with the cognitive (brain) aspects of reading:

> This Report is organized into sections to provide an overview of the major findings and determinations achieved by the NRP in the areas of alphabetics (phonemic awareness instruction and phonics instruction), fluency,

comprehension (vocabulary instruction, text comprehension instruction, and teacher preparation and comprehension strategies instruction), teacher education
and reading instruction, computer technology and reading instruction, and next steps. (National Institute of
Child Health and Human Development, 2019)

Don't be deceived by the date of this abstract. The National
Reading Panel's findings were publicized in 2000, but remain
applicable and continually acknowledged today. What is known
about the science of reading is based on this report from the
turn of the century. It continues to provide the most current
information about the science of reading.

*Build the Brain the Common Core Way* (Nevills, 2014) was produced
as a response to the Common Core State Standards Initiative
(2010). The nationwide project was influenced by the National
Reading Panel's (2000) report. The initiative furthered the
panel's findings by defining high-quality academic standards
presented as goals for English language arts (ELA) and mathematics, with an outline for student achievement at the completion of each grade level. In 2010, the Common Core State
Standards (CCSS) were approved by the federal Department
of Education. Performance goals and to-be-developed standardized assessments were designed for use across the nation.
In 2014, response to the CCSS was questionably positive, but
critical implementation supports were lacking.

With a focus on ELA, the question is, "What did *not* accompany the CCSS?" First, curriculum with instructional materials
aligned to the standards was nonexistent. Previous textbooks
with accompanying teacher's manuals were mostly discarded,
as they did not match terminology with the nationwide standards. Teachers scrambled to develop or find materials to
use for their day-to-day instruction. District decision makers
questioned how they could provide standards-based materials. Educators also lost some of the formative reading assessments they had relied upon to direct student instruction.
National standardized assessments were under development,
but not yet available. Retooling through staff development was
requested, but not yet available. Parents and caregivers were
glaringly absent during the development of the CCSS. However,
the standards directed schools and their districts to acquaint
and involve families during implementation efforts. And, if all
those voids were not enough, the CCSS did not address students
with reading disabilities, who required special education services. At this time, 2014–2019, teachers, who are early imple-
menters, found or developed new instructional programs, but

many were still in a day-to-day response mode for student needs when COVID-19 came and schools closed and moved to an online presence.

Two years followed with educators, parents, and children adapting to a "new normal" for education. What an incredible job all areas of education accomplished as the system closed down for in-person classroom teaching! Almost instantaneously, schools revamped themselves for a totally different online school experience. Educators hardly skipped a beat while operating in extremely harsh and unpredictable situations. Parents adjusted and did what they could to maintain a learning environment for their children. Without any preparation, parents dealt with dramatic changes in their day-to-day lives during the following two years. Still, there remained a mostly unresolved issue of how to teach reading according to the CCSS, in whatever form the standards had been adopted state by state.

An article published by EdSource in early 2022, about six months after children returned to their classrooms following the COVID-19 mandates, reported that the literacy crisis had deepened.

> [A] cluster of new studies shows that about a third of children in the youngest grades are missing reading benchmarks, as the New York Times reported, which was up significantly from before the pandemic.
>
> One study found that early reading skills were at a 20-year low this fall, a situation the researchers described as "alarming." In another study, 60% of students at some impoverished schools have been identified as at high risk for reading problems—twice the number of students as before the pandemic. (D'Souza, 2022a)

Studies from around the states were equally alarming (D'Souza, 2022b; Nation's Report Card, 2022). Fortunately, teachers now receive more support from their districts, counties, and state departments of education. Educators are diving into the teaching of reading with new vigor, equipped with vastly improved instructional materials and armed with knowledge, including brain (cognitive) awareness of how children learn.

Research and reporting centers, including the Center for Applied Linguistics, EdSource, APM Reports, the Hechinger Report, and the National Center for Education Statistics, along with hundreds of other agencies, provide prolific research and reports. Teacher training through podcasts, webinars, and blogs is readily available, and many provide continuing education credits at no cost. The blast of information was paired with extensive online resources to help and support education at all levels, including subject areas beyond the CCSS-targeted areas of ELA and mathematics. Publishers scrapped previous textbooks and materials and reworked their publications for a national audience. State education agencies revised their documents and online presence. There is so much information and yet a limited time to digest the abundance of usable resources.

## THE THIRD EDITION

The pandemic exacerbated an already existing situation, identified as the need to provide teaching of phonological processing, which includes phonemic awareness with the addition of phonics instruction. Along with this sequence are the myriad of other reading skills that demand development, which are addressed in this book.

The third edition of *Building the Reading Brain, PreK–3*, now called *Building the Young Reader's Brain, Birth Through Age 8*, is poised to respond to the issues of the here and now, as well as to provide a solid reading foundation for the field of education in years to come. Curriculum and instructional materials to teach reading are developed and revised. Educators once again can collaborate, retool, and be supported by research-substantiated published materials. The foundation that cements it all together is research information that verifies how a child's brain is programmed to learn efficiently and effectively.

Children are equipped with a powerful learning instrument that we call the human brain. It is preset to learn. It is resilient. It is reprogrammable. Children are naturally curious and innovative. The students of today and tomorrow have the brain stuff to survive and thrive. Their teachers and parents do also. Readers can look to the summary of each chapter and recognize that this is a "must read it all" book.

## CHAPTER SUMMARY

**Chapter 1**—A child's brain, even before birth, begins to develop the five senses and motor skills. The miniscule brain of a developing fetus directs the formation of the nervous system and the child's body. Language experiences, such as talking, singing, and interacting with a newborn through the developmental years, are of extreme importance. Parents and caregivers quite naturally provide an environment that starts learning right during the first two years of their child's life.

**Chapter 2**—Different structures inside the youngster's brain rapidly develop for children to listen to and speak their native language. What are developmental benchmarks for young children? What are the cognitive aspects of learning? Why is information from neuroscience important? A language explosion is going on, and adults can join its progress with excitement.

**Chapter 3**—Oral language and social development are key for 4-year-olds as they approach or attend preschool. Are they ready? Developmental benchmarks continue to be listed for parents and teachers to follow language and social development. Information about the nerve cells (neurons) of the body and how they become mature is gleaned through an understanding of the awesome term *neuroplasticity*. Memory means more than remembering. Some learning does happen spontaneously, but as language systems become more complex, so do the ways children remember. Going back to the five senses, we learn how input from the senses is received and acknowledged, or not. We all know how important play is to 3- and 4-year-olds, but is it known that play equates to learning and brain development in addition to how much fun it is?

**Chapter 4**—Playtime is addressed again with other benefits for preK and kindergarten children. A dive into neuroscience this time looks at the structures of the limbic system and why this primitive part of the brain is important to understand. Memory system information builds on working memory and what is worthy of a child's attention. This chapter concludes with a discussion of habits of mind, also called priming skills.

**Chapter 5**—The oral language pathway is defined including areas of the brain that support speech. The reading pathway is different and difficult to build. Teachers respond by teaching explicit lessons for sounds to letters and then to words. Print awareness, functions, conventions, and form are learned for encoding words. The cognitive skills children need to support them along the way to becoming readers are also a part of this chapter.

**Chapter 6**—This chapter is a must-read to understand the major overhaul that is occurring nationally and internationally in English-speaking countries. All readers, even those who appear to learn on their own, will be better readers with a strong foundation in decoding and encoding through phonological processing. Premier teaching practices described will support learning the way a child's brain by design will respond efficiently.

**Chapter 7**—The memory systems in the brain, when understood, make sense of all aspects of learning to read. Objectives from the CCSS can be addressed with memory-specific instruction.

Research from the science of reading is validated. Neuroscience once again provides answers, along with best teaching practices, to lingering questions about how children learn to read.

**Chapter 8**—This chapter is loaded with ways students are supported to read with fluency, automaticity, and prosody. All-out strategies prepare students to progress from "learning to read" to "reading to learn." As in previous chapters, the role of the developing brain is a key feature. A cognitive skills continuum, which began in Chapter 2 featuring 1- and 2-year-olds, is concluded in this chapter with students at ages 8 and 9.

**Chapter 9**—Early assessment is vindicated. In-depth discussions feature responses for children with reading deficits through cognitive, brain-specific interventions. This chapter opens with a wide range of possible reasons and solutions for students who are challenged readers. Special considerations are provided for English language learners (ELLs), also identified as English learners (ELs). The concern for overabundance of special education placements for children who are racially or ethnically different is also a topic. Finally, there is a question about learning two languages—is it beneficial? That topic can be found in this chapter.

**Chapter 10**—The seriousness of the preceding chapters is gone, as this chapter looks at the enjoyable and engaging practice of partnering with students to teach them about their brains. Teachers take on the role of providing "what" students learn and "how" it can be learned. The emphasis changes when students are invited to be responsible for learning strategies that are productive *and* unique to how each one learns best.

**Chapter 11**—Responses to the pivotal questions in the first chapter are the focus of this final chapter. A challenge question from Chapter 5 is also addressed. Readers are invited to the cognitive world of children and their abilities for reading. This book concludes with a tapestry of woven information about the human brain as students train, build, and fortify their own brains to become successful at reading.

The reader is invited to match the science of reading, as well as the CCSS or other adopted standards, with the science of neurology. What sounds like an unimaginable assignment can come together in a nice package. The intricacies of the human brain—its micro and macro systems, how it builds a reading pathway, and how memory works for comprehension, recall, and telling—can relate and intermix with all areas of instruction to give a clear pathway for building a young child's brain for reading.

# Acknowledgments

Corwin gratefully acknowledges the contributions of the following reviewers:

Annika Barton
Assistant Director of Early Childhood Assessments
Douglas County School District Early Childhood Department
Castle Rock, CO

Catherine Cloran
Second-Grade Teacher
Los Alamos Public Schools
Los Alamos, NM

Rebecca Dennis-Canges
Associate Professor
Metropolitan State University of Denver
Denver, CO

Brian E. Fernandes
Reading Specialist
Barrington Public Schools
Barrington, RI

Carol Gallegos
ELA Curriculum Specialist, Retired
Hanford Elementary School District
Hanford, CA

Lisa Sousa
Educator
San Diego Unified School District
San Diego, CA

Lauren A. Sousa-Coladonato
Graduate Student
Alliant International University
San Diego, CA

# About the Author

**Pamela Nevills** is first and foremost a teacher of children and adults. Her passion for teaching includes a full range of educator experiences from teaching in the primary grades, to teaching middle and high school, to being a teacher supervisor and instructor in university undergraduate, graduate, and doctoral programs. She participates in local, state, and national educational committees in the area of special education. As a two-time member of the instructional textbook selection committee for reading in the state of California, she brings expert knowledge of how children learn to read, and the materials teachers can use to follow the science of reading.

Her passion for the cognitive and neurological aspects of reading stems from interactions with Dr. Pat Wolfe. Nevills is a national and international speaker and consultant on topics that include reading standards according to the Common Core; brain development from infancy to adulthood; all aspects of cognitive, neurological involvement for reading; and school management and design for teaching reading. Writing became a part of Nevills's work as she published for newsletters, the state of California, the *Journal of Staff Development*, and Corwin. Her involvement also includes research and studies for church organizations and an advisory board position for preschool.

To contact Pamela Nevills, please email panevills@earthlink.net.

# CHAPTER 1

# Learning From Birth to 2 Years

All children are learners. Learning to read can be especially hard. To determine why learning to read is so difficult, the human brain that accomplishes the task of becoming a reader is the focus of this book.

In this beginning chapter the infant brain is explored. Even in utero the miniature brain is functioning and directing activities of an ever-so-tiny, forming embryo. Immediately after birth there is rapid firing of individual or sets of neurons (nerve cells) as they connect to each other. Neurons fire when they are roused by sensory stimulation from the infant's environment. Maturation of the motor and somatosensory cortex, which will be explained later in this chapter, allows the developing brain to gain control of muscles throughout the body from top to bottom. Development of the five senses is of particular interest. It is essential for the infant to receive information from the environment to stimulate the connections needed for each sense to establish itself.

Parents and caregivers are encouraged to be aware of their important roles. Much of what parents do with their babies happens naturally: holding, swaying and patting, talking with elongated words, feeding, and making eye contact, to mention a few. If parents are inexperienced or unaware of the infant's environmental needs, training classes may be attended at child care centers or public schools. A continuum of developmental benchmarks from birth to age 2, located at the end of this chapter, provides support to teachers as they help parents and caregivers to follow an anticipated sequence for their child's growth and benchmark development.

Language begins with babbling and results in a recognizable word or two at 12 months of age. Phonemes, the sounds from a word when voiced in its smallest parts, and the language a child hears are practiced prior to 10 months. Repetition and reinforcement of sounds determine which sounds a baby learns. At 18 months many children begin adding recognized vocabulary at a rate of one new word every two hours or so. At this stage of brain development metabolic activity and neural connections are higher than at any other time during life.

Parents who are aware of the important role they play in their children's eminent reading ability make a conscious effort to "talk, talk, talk" to their infants. They encourage vocabulary development and build background information critical for comprehension through conversation and story reading. Nursery rhymes are valued for the development of abstract phonological sounds. Oral language development in early childhood is so important, along with genetic influences, that research reports there is a causal or continuing relationship with the forthcoming ability to read (Dickinson et al., 2010; Hope Abilitation Medical Center, 2019).

##  SOME PIVOTAL QUESTIONS

### SUMMARY QUESTIONS

Before learning to read can be understood in neurological terms, it must be acknowledged that children are born as learning creatures. Children begin learning at birth or earlier. Realizing the learning capacity that is present at birth allows for a gateway of questions about building the reading brain. The questions identified here represent big-picture understandings that are addressed throughout the book's chapters, not necessarily in the following order, and are summarized in Chapter 11.

1. Children learn to speak naturally, so why is learning to read so difficult?

2. How do a baby's experiences shape the brain?

3. How can potential reading success be determined when a child is only 3 years old?

4. Why is there interest in cognitive skills for focus, concentration, and attention even for very young children at 1 and 2 years of age?

5. What is the importance of sounds, called *phonemes*, in terms of the child's cognitive development for reading?

6. Why are some teaching strategies for decoding less effective than others?

7. Why is there so much interest in teaching children to read in kindergarten? What helps to determine if a young child is ready to learn to read?

8. Why do some children experience difficulties when they try to read?

9. What is happening in the brain when children read with fluency and comprehension?

10. How do children move from "learning to read" to "reading to learn"?

11. How do students develop an understanding of word vocabulary?

12. What proficiency for reading is expected at the end of third grade? How do children's brains function during proficient reading?

Each of these questions has a comprehensible response. When the cognitive aspects of learning are understood, teachers can add this information to their ever-progressing wealth of methodologies and materials. Understanding a child's brain function provides answers to questions teachers have about how much time to spend on a teaching skill, how much repetition is needed, or what ways the material can be presented to hold students' attention. The reader of this book is invited to start at the very beginning of a child's life, and to follow the progression of brain development needed for students to become proficient, skilled readers as 8-year-olds.

## CHAPTER QUESTIONS

Reflective questions are located at the end of each chapter. Readers may want to review these questions prior to reading the chapter to direct their thinking, and also to develop their own inquiries.

# WHAT IS KNOWN FROM NEUROSCIENCE?

An infant is already becoming a learner as the brain rapidly builds itself. This is known, but the development cannot be seen without sophisticated imaging techniques. Advances have been made with systems that are noninvasive even for children under the age of 12 months. For example, electrical field changes are measured through event-related potentials (ERPs), a noiseless, inexpensive measure of temporal resolution to allow studies of early speech and language processing in young children. Another technique has a horrendously long name, magnetoencephalography (MEG). This magnetic field test, which is safe and noiseless, allows for head movement while it records phonetic discrimination in newborns and infants as they listen to speech. Neuroscientists have recorded lexicosemantic word meaning in the left frontotemporal brain areas. Lexicosemantics is the study to describe the meanings of words and how to account for the variability of meaning from one context to another. The fact that scientists are intent on obtaining measures through this type of sophisticated measurement and with several other available imaging devices validates the importance of social interactions and language advancement for very young children, even as infants (Kuhl, 2012; Reynolds et al., 2010).

Each child is progressing through developmental stages during the years from the womb along a pathway that culminates with adulthood. Every child has a story to be told. One by one they contribute to a family and to the community. Eventually, as they come to a classroom, each is unique and comes packaged with an unimaginable potential for creativity. The entire education community scrambles to find answers about the neurological process behind learning, particularly, "What happens in children's brains as they learn to read?" It is discovered not only that children are programmed to learn, but also that with specific instruction their brains can be coaxed and trained for proficient reading. Educators in all the various roles, caring parents, and involved caregivers embrace with a passion the goal of reading for all children.

## THE HUMAN BRAIN AT ITS BEGINNING

The beginning is not birth; rather, it is conception. What happens to a fetus's brain during pregnancy can impact the success a child has in school. It is known that pregnancy can be labeled by trimesters. Realize that at the end of merely four weeks of development in the first trimester the **nervous**

**system** has already begun to form. The nervous system is the brain, the spinal column, and the complete network of nerves that connect the brain to all parts of the body. That means the brain is developed enough to direct the spinal cord, the heart, and the arms and legs, which are beginning to bud (Mayo Clinic Staff, 2022b). The embryo is 1/25 of an inch long. The brain is functioning (Targonskaya, 2020).

At the eighth week of the first trimester, all major organs have started to form. The heart is beating and pumping needed nutrients to the arms and legs, which now have fingers and toes. Even the tiny face has the beginnings of features. At this point in development, the baby is called a fetus at almost an inch long and weighing less than 1/8 of an ounce. At the end of the first trimester, which is about 12 weeks, the baby is able to use muscles and nerves together to form a fist. Eyelids close at this time to protect the developing eyes. They will not reopen until the 28th week. Although the head has been growing to keep up with the expansion of the brain, it will slow at this time to allow growth of the rest of the body parts. At this stage the baby is slightly less than 3 inches long and weighs about ½ of an ounce (Mayo Clinic Staff, 2022b).

It seems unimaginable that a living being can be so small and still have most of its body parts developing under the direction of such a tiny brain. Certainly, the second and third trimesters are equally interesting. Curious readers can find a continuation of conception-to-birth details from OnHealth in the list of references (Stoppler, 2022). The first trimester is provided as the most dramatic example of the human brain's unimaginable administrative functioning and its capabilities. Although incredibly small, the brain becomes the CEO, or chief executive officer, of the miniature body as it develops itself according to the coded instructions of a unique individualized set of genes and chromosomes. In the womb, the brain interprets complex DNA information to direct all the body's development and growth at the beginning of and throughout life (Thomas et al., 1995).

## MICROSTRUCTURES OF LEARNING

It is asked, "When does a child start learning?" The answer is illusive, as even those versed in education may have a variety of responses as they define learning. A dictionary description from Oxford University Press (2023) reads like this: "the acquisition of knowledge or skills through experience, study, or by being taught." It is known that a child at birth is ready to learn. Additionally, at the time of a natural birthing process an infant's reflexes and motor development are stimulated (Stanford Medicine Children's Health, 2023a). At this early stage the brain itself is wired sparsely, but it is expansive in its number of nerve cells. A baby's brain has about as many brain cells, or **neurons**, as there are stars in the Milky Way. That is a huge, unimaginable number, 100 billion neurons. A look at a single neuron gives meaning to what is happening microscopically in the brain (see Figure 1.1). Neurons develop during the fetal stage at a rate of up to 250,000 per minute when the neural tube closes at about 7 weeks and then throughout the next 21 weeks prior to birth (Graham & Forstadt, 2011; RakicNational Academy of Sciences, 1992).

Connections between nerve cells occur as **dendrites** spread from a neuron cell body seeking other neurons (see Figure 1.2). Dendrites, short, hair-like input fibers, pursue an **axon** branch to make a connection. One elongated axon, the output fiber, goes forth from each neuron's cell body sending impulses to other neurons. Each axon develops many branches to search for a dendrite from a neuron in the same general area of the brain. Neurons communicate by an electrical shock from the nucleus of an axon that flows down the axon to a **synapse**, a small space, where it spews its chemicals. A nearby dendrite uptakes the chemicals and sends them to the receiving neuron.

**FIGURE 1.1** ● Neurons vary in shape and size depending on their location in the central nervous system. Neurons have distinct parts: a cell body with a nucleus, and appendages. Here is a neuron with appendages: axon branches and a large number of dendrites.

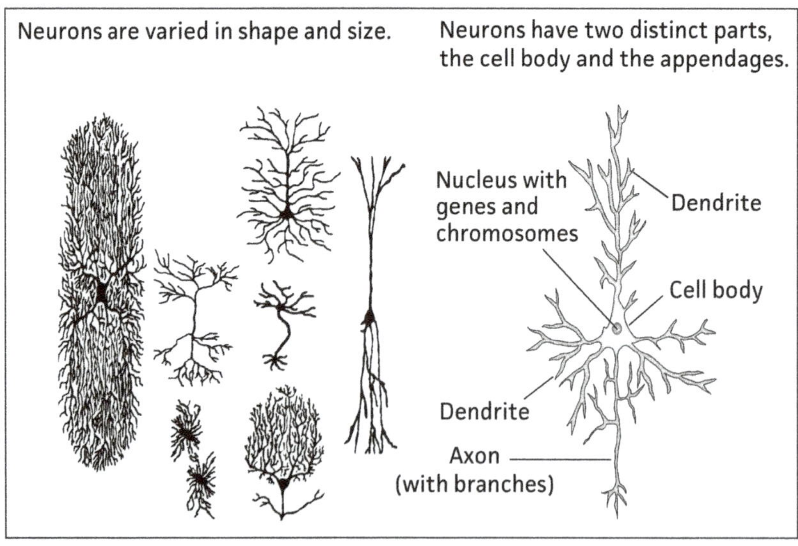


**Source:** Created by Herb Higashi. Reprinted from Nevills (2014).

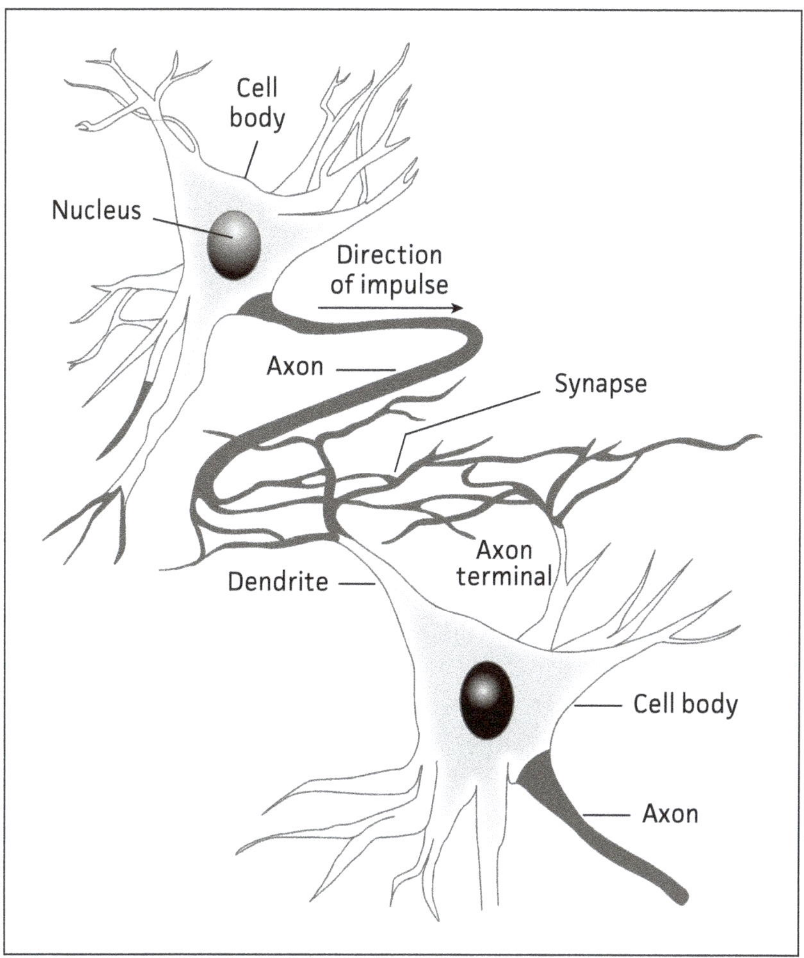


Source: Created by Herb Higashi. Reprinted from Nevills (2014).

Here the receiving neuron's nucleus responds again with an electrical charge that continues the journey down its axon. The process continues from one neuron's axon to another neuron's dendrite, until it loses its electrical and chemical responses. This is the complex process for one neuron to connect to another. Imagine the fireworks in the brain when tens of thousands of these connections are occurring at once. The strength and reoccurance of the reaction determines the potential for learning and remembering.

A microscopic look inside any area of the brain soon after birth would reveal a rapid expansion of nerve cell networks. Recall from Figure 1.1 that neurons are differently shaped, depending on where they are found in the central nervous system. During a child's growth years the number of neurons remains relatively stable, but each neuron grows more dense and heavier with a proliferation of dendrites and an expansion of synaptic connections.

## THE DEVELOPING FIVE SENSES

An infant's brain is busy making sense of the space that surrounds it by receiving information from the five senses. Think about it this way: If a young child did not have environmental input from the senses, there would be no need to respond, no brain development would occur, and access to learning would be not only blocked, but also nonexistent.

As a child gains control over different body parts, the senses are emerging: first smell and taste, followed by clearer vision, sharper hearing, and understanding the pressure or pain of touch. Everything is awakening. The child's brain is rapidly developing connections to make sense out of the child's new world.

### SMELL

Scientists have studied the five senses as they develop. It is well known that the sense of smell is completely functional at a full-term birth. Colleen de Bellefonds (2021) reports that during the third trimester of pregnancy a baby can smell almost everything the mother eats or inhales. The early maturation of the sense of smell is a survival issue, as it is observed that a full-term baby merely hours old will turn toward the scent of mother's milk or a bottle and begin to suck. The infant has been practicing in utero to pucker the tiny lips and to draw in the life-sustaining milk. This sense is so vital to the baby's feelings of security that parents and caregivers are advised to "keep the scents baby smells consistent." This means to avoid changing personal soap or lotions, and to refrain from washing the baby's blankets or stuffed toys unnecessarily. The olfactory environment is best for a newborn baby when it is as stable, pleasant, and comforting as possible. A place where the odors smelled are predictable during the early months supports child–parent bonding and feelings of emotional security. Hedonics, the distinction between good and bad smells, does not complete development until around 3 years of age.

### TASTE

There is a very early preference in taste also. It is believed that flavors from the food the expectant mother eats are passed through the amniotic fluid, the life source for nutrition of the developing baby. Young children learn the "tastes of the culture" very early. Taste is terribly important for an infant, not only for its nutritional significance but also as other senses and motor abilities are relatively underdeveloped. Chemical detectors on the tongue, roof of mouth, soft palate, and upper throat area detect four categories—sweet, salty, bitter, and sour. The tongue alone has about 4,500 taste buds, and each taste bud can have as many as 40 taste receptor cells. Taste stimulation to the medulla at the top of the spinal cord unconsciously (no frontal lobe action from the brain required) activates salivation, swallowing, and tongue movements. Taste information controls motivation to eat and drink (Forestell & Mennella, 2017). Taste and smell combined allow the full appreciation of taste. Note that if sensations of smell are blocked, up to 90% of the refined sense of taste can be lost.

## VISION

At birth an infant's vision is of a relatively dark world with movement appearing through a long narrow tunnel centered on a line of sight. Eye movements are uncoordinated. A newborn can detect the difference between light and dark, but is unable to see colors. Some infant books include black-and-white patterns to represent this stage of visual maturation (Coby, 2021; duopress labs & Mora, 2016). Visual resolution for a child at birth is 1/40 of that of a normal adult, which equates to about 8 to 10 inches from the eyes out into space. From being able to focus on a human face, when held as a newborn, the infant's brain rapidly adjusts to environmental stimuli and can see almost as well as an adult by the first birthday. Without environmental stimuli, which could be the result of low vision or no vision, neurons predetermined to build the visual system will atrophy or migrate to another area of the brain to help development of a different sense. This added neural support will mitigate the loss of one sense to make another sensory system more powerful (University of California–Los Angeles, 2009).

Recognizing seen objects begins as neurons naturally migrate to different areas of the brain for visual interpretation. The process is complete through the formation of a refined map of neural wiring. The connections happen through seeing, which is determined by the nurture of the environment. There are sensitive periods in children's lives when specific systems are developed. Neurons for vision begin sending messages back and forth with rapidity during the second and fourth months of a baby's life, and peak with intensity by the eighth month. At around the second month of age the baby develops obligatory looking, which becomes a "gaze fest" between an adult and the child as they fixate on one another. Fixation engagement can be emotionally charged as love is fostered between child and parent or caregiver.

Depth perception, color vision, fine acuity, and well-controlled eye movements are in place at the sixth month of age. The child's brain is tasked to convert light information into electrical signals that map each color, shape, and point in a visual field. Images are a series of dots that are filed, organized, and stored in the brain for interpretation. Different areas of each side of the brain are devoted to recording and saving the parallel process of visual stimuli for color, motion, shape, and depth.

## HEARING

During pregnancy mothers notice that the fetus may kick or jump as a response to unusual or loud noises. The child may settle down after a time of activity upon hearing somewhat muffled soft voices, music, or calming humming. Hearing in utero begins about 12 weeks before birth and develops a definite preference for the mother's voice. Hearing is routinely tested in the hospital prior to the baby's release. Infants need input from many different sounds in the home environment to stimulate the pathway from the ears to the auditory interpretation area. They prefer to hear language called "parentese," which is speaking with slower, higher-pitched words and strong intonation. Further described later in this chapter, this type of speech is naturally used by parents and caregivers in all cultures. Hearing is likely the most important sense for development of early reading skills. The variation of sounds allows an infant to experience the language of words, rhythm, rhyme, and music, which may be provided through singing, all of which stimulate the brain as it develops for both cognitive and emotional growth.

A small percentage of children are born with an inability to hear. If the loss is present at birth, it is called a congenital hearing loss (American Speech–Language–Hearing Association [ASHA], 2023). There are various causes for hearing loss including premature birth or genetic factors. Genetic factors can be present at birth or develop later in life. Both hearing and deaf parents can have a child with a hearing disability (ASHA, 2023). The Centers for Disease Control and Prevention (CDC, 2022) indicate the prevalence of hearing loss in babies was 1.7 per 1,000 of those tested for hearing loss in the United States in 2019. Over 98% of newborns were screened for hearing loss in 2019 (CDC, 2022). Most babies develop normal hearing during the first year of their lives.

The all-important touch sensation runs from the body parts via the spinal cord to the base of the brain where the thalamus routes the signal to the somatosensory cortex. The thalamus, which is located in the center of the brain and acts as a relay station, is described in Chapter 4. After this instantaneous relay the baby can feel pressure, pain, heat, or coldness. Remember there are many, many more sensory receptors for human babies and adults around the mouth, hands, and fingers than are in the rest of the body.

Touching babies is an innately programmed parental behavior, a natural and loving activity that promotes health and normal growth. Newborn babies are comforted when a hand is placed on their belly or they are wrapped tightly (swaddled) or cuddled. A caveat is that pediatricians warn about swaddling infants after 2 months of age, as they need freedom to build the ability of rolling from the back to the stomach (WebMD Editorial Contributors, 2021). Because the sense of touch is so prominent, babies respond to being in a sling or a carrier, which allows them to perceive closeness to another person.

The five senses become alert and activated, and the young one responds in new and advancing ways through the months leading to the end of the first year. Through the five senses, very young children are always learning something.

## MACROSTRUCTURES OF THE MOTOR CORTEX AND THE SOMATOSENSORY CORTEX

During the first few years of life, the brain is wiring itself at a tremendous pace to learn to speak, move body parts, and understand the setting surrounding the child. Trillions of connections are formed as the infant (*in fantis*, meaning "not speaking") attempts to understand sounds, particularly those from people, and uses information from the five senses to comprehend the importance of the space around the small body.

In the brain the **motor cortex** and the **somatosensory cortex**, also called the sensory cortex, are macrostructures that are located next to each other, forming a headband at the top of the brain. The motor cortex follows a highly specific order of growth and development. First, it develops ability for head movement, followed by the arms and hands, and then connections become coordinated throughout the body. The movement extends to all four limbs. The legs and feet are the last to respond. It makes sense that a child has good control of the hands long before walking is accomplished.

## THE MOTOR CORTEX

The motor cortex, as noted, is adjacent to the somatosensory cortex. As an infant takes in information through the senses, the motor area is stimulated to mature and respond. A look at Figure 1.3 provides an image of the outermost part of the human brain, the cerebral cortex, with its physical shape. Of specific interest is the motor cortex and the somatosensory cortex, which stretch across the top of the brain from ear to ear. The motor cortex controls all movement functions, which involve planning, muscle control, and execution. An exception is reflex actions, such as sneezing, blinking, and shivering, which are automatic responses from an area at the top of the spinal cord, where the brain stem is located. Of added importance is the location of the motor cortex directly behind the frontal lobes. The frontal lobes, the brain's CEO, were mentioned earlier during the discussion of brain development in pregnancy. The brain's frontal area, addressed in detail in Chapter 2, directs cognitive thinking by drawing information

**FIGURE 1.3** ● The cerebral cortex is the outermost portion of the brain located under the skull. This figure shows the areas where the motor and somatosensory cortices are located.

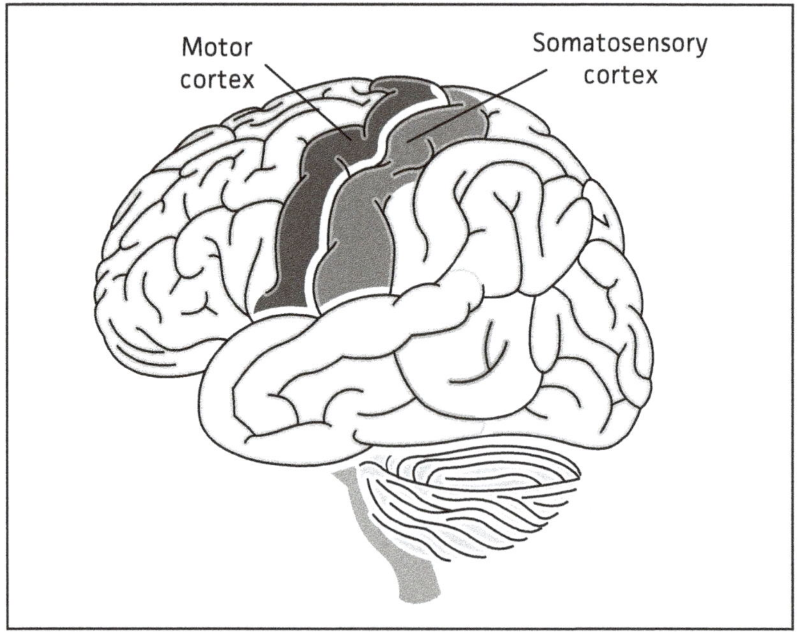


**Source:** Reprinted from Nevills & Wolfe (2009).

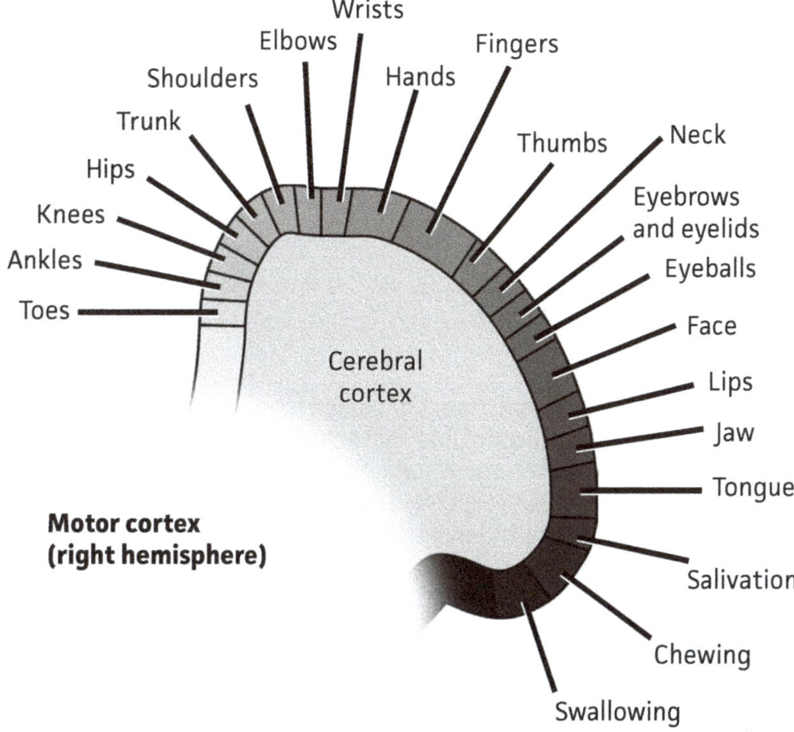


Source: CNX OpenStax. https://creativecommons.org/licenses/by/4.0/deed.en

from all parts of the brain to make executive decisions and provide direction for movement. From this location behind the frontal lobes, different sections of the motor cortex can govern the movements of specific muscles in different areas of the body as seen in Figure 1.4.

Maturation of the motor cortex is noticeable as the infant begins to reach, move, and eventually become mobile through turning over, crawling, and then walking. The first part of the motor cortex to mature is in the center with movement of the head and neck. The sequence previously stated follows on both the right and left sides of the body.

Parents and other adults can see this development with infants. Match what is physically possible with the continuum of developmental benchmarks provided later in this chapter.

## THE SOMATOSENSORY CORTEX

Immediately behind the motor cortex lies the somatosensory cortex. While the motor cortex sends messages to the various muscles in the body about how and when to move, the somato-sensory cortex receives information from the environment through the baby's rapidly developing senses and interprets the information with help from the **parietal lobe**, which is introduced in Chapter 2. Infants develop feeling and elicit responses to temperature, hunger, pressure, or pain. Also, developing is knowledge of where the limbs are in relation to the rest of the body. As with the motor cortex, each part of the body is represented by a specific area on the surface of the somatosensory cortex, and maturation of bodily sensations follows a developmental sequence. Figure 1.5 gives the areas of the body as they are represented in the somatosensory cortex (Human Physiology Academy, 2020).

**FIGURE 1.5** ● The somatosensory cortex labeled for the body areas responsible for receiving signals and sending signals to the thinking areas of the brain for interpretation. Also represented are body parts to indicate the oversensitivity of nerve cells in these specific areas of the developing infant.

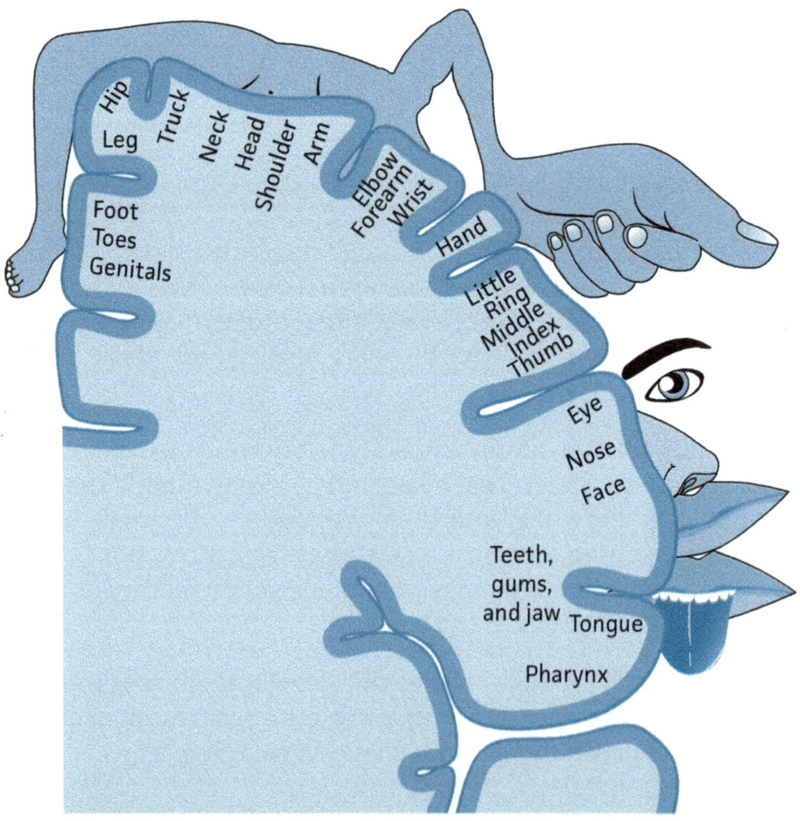


Source: Anatomy & Physiology, Connexions Web site. http://cnx.org/content/col11496/1.6/. https://creativecommons.org/licenses/by/3.0/

Notice the oddly shaped body parts in Figure 1.5. Upon careful observation the reader will recognize these overemphasized areas of the body are most populated with nerves in the very young child. Certainly, the size of the head, particularly the mouth area, and the enlarged hands give a good indication where the strongest sensations are experienced by the baby and sent to the somatosensory cortex for interpretation.

##  COGNITIVE DEVELOPMENT

Developmental benchmarks are observable; however, cognition is not as easily identified. What happens in the human brain is more difficult to assess, but dynamic in process. Cognitive skills allow a child to think, explore, or solve problems. Consider the fields of cognitive psychology and cognitive neuroscience. Although they are intimately related, the way they are measured and their terminology differ. Cognitive psychology, according to Usha Goswami (2020), a professor of cognitive developmental neuroscience, can be identified by defining **mindfulness**. Mindfulness allows a young child to hold thinking concepts in the brain for consideration. To assess cognitive concepts a psychologist presents a task and then measures the infant's accuracy or response time. These measurements provide insights into abilities of attention, concentration, memory, and organization (concept development), which are increasingly important as the child approaches school age. In later chapters they are referred to as **priming skills**.

In contrast, cognitive neuroscience involves the observation of blood flow or electrical activity in the human brain with sophisticated laboratory devices. In this instance a task is given, such as pointing to objects or listening for sounds or words. Brain activity is measured before the task, as the child's brain is at rest, and then during the activity. This type of measurement becomes useful as neuroscience partners with education. Goswami (2020) asserts that together the two cognitive fields can determine what is happening in the brain when a child is unsuccessful with a developmentally appropriate task. Neuroscience can explain how a selected neural pathway can lead to successful reading, for example, and become nonproductive when those brain areas are not activated. This information becomes useful when educators are determining a course of study for reading with school-aged children and will be addressed in most of the following chapters.

# COGNITIVE GROWTH: LEARNING LANGUAGE

Even for children at an early age, environment can encourage formation of cognitive skills. Families can encourage their children to make choices, which will prompt thoughtful decisions with questions like "Do you want this frog?" or "Would you like to hold this toy?" Putting two or three different items in separate places, away from a crawling child, allows the child to decide which one to pursue. A child who watches an adult hide an object can be encouraged to find it. These examples can be expanded to develop cognitive skills of attention, self-control, and problem solving.

Everyday interactions for most infants pose a world rich with opportunities to explore and subsequently to stimulate cognitive growth. There are faces to recognize and voices to imitate, sights and sounds to remember, and problems to solve, such as "How do I get this big person to notice that I am hungry?"

The mechanism that allows an infant, who is quickly becoming a toddler, to learn a language is a sensitivity to **prosody**. The emotional qualities of speech, such as intonation and rhythm, which define prosody, occur discretely and rapidly. For the curious baby, as well as for all people, meaning is captured from conversations by tracing the rhythm and intonations of spoken language. In fact, these prosodic cues are probably more important to meaning than the actual words. The phrase "That's great" or "Look at you," for example, can be either positive or negative, based on how the comment is expressed. Humans determine meaning by reading facial cues and the intonation of the speaker. Infants develop the ability to recognize these cues as young as 3 months.

## A CHILD'S BRAIN AND LANGUAGE

At 2 to 3 months, the areas of the motor cortex that control the larynx and vocal cords have matured sufficiently to allow babies to begin vocalization with what sounds like babbling. In babbling, babies appear to be experimenting with various ways of making sounds. Even when there are no listeners, they babble to themselves. While they make many different sounds, babies seem to show a preference for the sounds they experience repeatedly. Sounds that are not reinforced by the environment are pruned or experience atrophy in the brain to allow a child to focus on the language heard repeatedly. Babies who are born deaf also babble for a period of time. Ultimately, when the sounds are not reinforced, the babbling ceases.

## PARENTESE

The language and accompanying emotional emphasis used by parents and caregivers as they talk to infants is often called parentese. This language, with its elongated vowels, repetitions, and overpronounced syllables, appears to be just what the baby needs to develop language skills. It models and reinforces the prosody and sound structure—the **phonology**, syntax, and lexicon of the family's native language. Parentese may be more grammatically correct than normal speech. It is interesting that parentese is apparently innate, and is used quite naturally in virtually all of the world's languages (Eckart, 2020). Studies to advance children's language achievement through coaching parents in parentese have not had long-term benefits. The process of speaking slowly and succinctly generally happens naturally as adults speak to babies in any language.

## BABY SIGNS

Infants comprehend words and phrases long before they are able to say much of anything. Baby Signs is a system designed by psychologists Linda Acredolo and Susan Goodwyn (1996) for babies to communicate before their brains develop the ability to produce oral speech. Through this program, babies as young as 5 months old are able to convey what they need through simple hand gestures or sign language. Baby Signs developers Acredelo and Goodwyn conducted many studies regarding the advantages of using Baby Signs as they followed children well beyond the age of 3. The results of their studies indicate that when parents use a systematic plan with hand signals or signs with very young children, there is a lasting impact. The children tested had measurable advantages over children who did not learn Baby Signs in the areas of language and cognitive skills. In subsequent years, however, the long-term benefit of implementing Baby Signs was questioned; studies by Fitzpatrick et al. (2014), Kirk et al. (2012), and Seal and DePaolis (2014) used stringent controls and found no evidence that babies whose parents had been trained in Baby Signs benefited in a lasting way beyond age 3. Consequently, parents who use Baby Signs with or without training have an increased advantage of improved communication with their very young children. The use of Baby Signs with children who are deaf is an understandable advantage.

Parents can relax; young, normally developing children will learn to speak and communicate successfully with or without parenting classes for speaking with parentese or communicating with Baby Signs. Children learn language as their brains are powerfully programmed to do so in an environment that is full of positive language opportunities. Families are encouraged to follow their natural inclinations of interacting with their young children.

## A LANGUAGE EXPLOSION AT YEARS 1 AND 2

Around the age of 12 months, children begin to speak their first words. Although they are beginning to produce speech, they do not understand linguistic rules. They are essentially parroting what others say. However, by 18 months, language comprehension begins to develop. The toddler can understand many statements, such as "Let's put on your shoes" or "It is time to get in the car." Between ages 1 and 2, a rapid progression of receptive language occurs, due to maturation in the brain's left hemisphere. The auditory brain area (temporal lobe) forms neural connections with other lobes of the brain, located in the upper and frontal brain areas. These areas of the brain are explained in Chapter 2. Simultaneously, vocabulary explodes with children being exposed to a new word at the astounding rate of one word every two hours or so. Realize that pronunciation may be only 25% intelligible. This period of rapidly expanding language development coincides with synapse formation and metabolic activity, which are at their highest rate for connections among neurons in the brain.

## WHAT CAN PARENTS AND CAREGIVERS DO?

Those who care for infants are encouraged to know about infant development. Consider how the young child's environment is structured to stimulate and support all the tremendous work that is being orchestrated by the infant brain. A parent or caregiver bonds with the infant through holding, cuddling, feeding, eye contact, elongated language, and even keeping scents consistent. Parents are reminded that vision is limited for several months while at the same time smell is completely developed. Infants sense the primary adult in their life initially by the sense of smell.

As described, all parts of the small child's body are developing and responding to touch. It all begins at the head, next goes down the arms, and finally reaches the hands and fingers. Soon the baby is acknowledging legs and feet. Notice at several months of age tiny hands reach for the baby's own feet and explore the little toes by touching. Parents hold babies close and often sway back and forth while lightly patting and comforting the baby. That is all natural. Babies soon learn to roll, push up with their arms, roll over, sit, crawl, walk, and then run. To prop a child on one side or the other, or support and place the little one in a device or seat to hold them in a sitting position before the child is ready, is contrary to the natural developmental sequence. Holding the little one in the lap in a sitting position, as the child is ready, is an entirely natural thing to do. Remember: *There is no way to hurry through nurture the plan that is set up by nature.*

Parents are encouraged to listen to the sound environment in their home. Are people talking, singing, or yelling? Is a television screen on? Human voices are best for a young child to hear as the sense of hearing is becoming fine-tuned. The environment does not have to be perfect, but families can be aware of the sounds the baby is hearing. Children need to hear all kinds of sounds. They also need to be exposed to lots of human conversation with some of it directed toward them.

Vision takes about a year to become focused for distance viewing. Child development experts almost unanimously agree that young children should not be looking at a screen, any screen, prior to age 2, and even then restrictions should be put in place. Make certain digital media is high in quality, such as music, movement stimulating, or stories (Mayo Clinic Staff, 2022a). Parents who wonder about this recommendation might try this. Turn on a screen or television to a familiar program. Notice what is happening on the screen both with and without the sound, and think about how these images appear to the child under 2 years of age, knowing vision and oral language is underdeveloped. Neuroscience tells us that babies do not learn from voices that are not from actual people (Kuhl, 2012). Digital media cannot be a substitute for personal attention, individual play, or exploration time. Children sleep a lot due to the amount of energy they are using during this critical developmental time. Parents and caregivers are encouraged to make the baby's waking time as meaningful as possible.

A child's environment can contain different views and a variety of objects. Mobiles hung on a crib or infant seat can hold a baby's interest for a period of time. Toys can be changed and used in different ways—adults and siblings can make stuffed animals talk, and have hand toys or plastic and wooden blocks for holding or stacking. Babies put toys to their mouths, but adults are advised to make certain these objects are too big to fit inside. This action of toys to the mouth is a precursor to self-feeding. Books with items commonly seen by the child can be used over and over. Accompanying these suggestions and cautions, a continuum of developmental benchmarks has been collected to define how infants advance from birth to 2 years of age.

## CONTINUUM OF DEVELOPMENTAL BENCHMARKS: BIRTH TO AGE 2

Infants and toddlers follow particular developmental benchmarks during the first two years of life. The following chart describes what is expected from birth to age 2. Parents and families may use this benchmark list to support their young ones as they attain new skills. Note that the activities are cumulative, built one upon another.

Many, many sources were consulted to develop this continuum. These resources, among them the CDC's (2022a) developmental milestones, are located in the reference section at the end of the book. The developmental characteristics also represent observations by the author, parents, grandparents, and child care providers. The benchmarks are predictive, not based on scientific evidence. Variance will be discovered even at this very young age, as children develop according to their own unique, predetermined timeline. Developmental benchmarks will be added to the continuum in following chapters. A complete continuum for ages 1 month to 5 years is located in Appendix A at the end of this book.

Developmental Benchmarks: Birth to Age 2

| 1 month | Watches objects and faces at 12 inches or more, even when moving. Moves by arching back, kicking legs, or flailing arms when startled by noises. Hearing is developing. Sense of smell is the only sense that is fully developed. Turns head toward mother's breast. Recognizes scents such as handwashing fragrance. |
|---|---|
| 2 months | Eyes follow an object. Begins to recognize familiar people. Becomes fussy when awake and is unstimulated. Seems happy when parent approaches. Makes sounds other than crying. Holds head up when on tummy. Moves both arms and legs. Opens hands briefly. Looks at a toy for several seconds. Sense of vision is becoming more acute. |

| 3 months | Recognizes source of food: bottle or breast. Beginning to develop interest in taste. Turns head to identify sounds. Tries to push up when on tummy. |
|---|---|
| 4 months | Communicates if happy, sad, or irritated. Watches faces, particularly during feeding. Good head control. Pushes up onto elbows/forearms when on tummy. Reaches for toys and can bring a toy to the mouth (sense of taste). Better motor control and the sense of touch is developing. Chuckles when others laugh. Opens mouth if hungry and sees food source (breast or bottle). Brings hands to mouth. Makes sounds back when talked to. |
| 6 months | Good control of hands and hand-to-mouth activities. Moves items from one hand to the other. Reaches for items that are out of reach. Knows familiar people. Looks at self in a mirror. Takes turns at making sounds with another. Makes the "raspberry" sound. Closes lips when does not want food. Rolls from tummy to back. Leans on hands to support when sitting. |
| 9 months | Plays peekaboo. Can pick up small items with precision. Turns pages of a book. Watches as an item is hidden and seeks it. Able to move arms and limbs to hold body in crawl position or picks self up when holding on to a table or chair. Is shy around strangers. Looks when name is called. Reacts when care provider or parent leaves and reaches for the person. Makes a lot of different sounds, such as "mamamama" and "babababababa." Lifts arms to be picked up. Can move into a sitting position and sits without support. |
| 12 months | Moves items from container to container. Points to pictures of words known and stored in long-term memory. Claps and bangs items together. Can drink from a cup, pick up a book, brush own hair, and poke with index finger. Can pick things up with thumb and pointer finger, like small pieces of food to eat or a crayon to make marks. Stands upright alone or with support. May be able to navigate walking or moving from one object to another. Waves "bye-bye," and understands "no." |
| 15 months | Copies other children. Claps when excited. Hugs dolls or other stuffed toys. Shows signs of affection with hugs, cuddles, or kisses. Tries to say one or two words for common items. Follows simple directions, such as "Clap your hands." Attempts to use common items, such as a phone, cup, or book. Can walk somewhat on own. Uses fingers to eat finger food, such as Cheerios. Scribbling and coloring may include blocks of color and more definite marks and patterns. Stacks at least two things or blocks. |
| 18 months | Holds a crayon or pencil to scribble. Begins to identify body parts. Can follow one oral direction. For example, if an adult says, "Stop," the child ceases the activity. Can identify by pointing to common objects: cup, spoon, brush, book, phone, and so on. Enjoys singing, following stories in a book, and listening to simple stories without a book. Is interested in toys and can pretend play with a stuffed toy. Puts hands out to be washed. Walks without holding on. Climbs up on a chair or couch. Can drink from a cup without a lid. Tries to use a spoon. Crayon strokes represent something to the child. Swirly loops may be a puppy, or bold lines may be Daddy. May have a tantrum when does not get what is wanted. (Respond or not to tantrums, but be at eye level if a tantrum is addressed.) |

# CONCLUDING THOUGHTS ABOUT INFANTS TO AGE 2

Children can be stimulated when they are very young with activities and experiences that ultimately support them to become good readers in the years that follow. A most important activity for very young children is lots of family talk, and engagement with everyday language experiences, even if it is simply about what the family is doing. Babies love the sounds of words that they make, and how their mouths feel when they make sounds. Suggestions for parents and caregivers include talking; communicating language through picture and other simple books; making words come alive through dance, gestures, and songs; and playing games with sounds.

The way children learn language—any language—is very predictable. Deeply rooted language is in human biological makeup. As emphasized repeatedly, children are born with a brain programmed for language learning. Humans can't help but talk; it is the primary means of social interaction for a lifetime of learning. How do parents start their infants off on the right track to become a child who reads well? There is no formal program; rather, families are encouraged to follow natural inclinations to talk to infants, smile at them, and express affection in positive ways. A very young child's mastery of language proceeds right on course with steady dialog from parents, other involved adults, and siblings.

As noted, the developmental benchmarks presented in Chapter 1 will be expanded upon in subsequent chapters to follow the dynamic growth of children's skills and abilities. The maturation of the infant's brain and the accompanying body development initiate a story that continues to amaze and delight families and caregivers alike.

# Reflective Questions

1. Neuroscientists are using scanning devices on children under the age of 12 months. What information are they seeking to discover?

**2.** As you study with a group or individually, keep a list of the pivotal questions from the start of this chapter handy and record answers during reading of the chapters. Take the challenge to fill in as many answers as you can to compare with the responses of the author in Chapter 11.

**3.** Give an "aha" statement about the brain's capabilities, even at birth.

**4.** How would you explain the microscopic development of neurons and their connections to a parent? What might parents care to know about neurons?

**5.** What is new to you about the development of the baby's five senses?

**6.** The developmental benchmarks as a whole might be overwhelming to parents. How could this information be provided to parents in a way that is useful? Describe also how it could be a benefit for educators.

**7.** Talk and write about the explosion of language between birth and age 2. What advice would you give new parents about how to stimulate their baby in the family's environment?

# CHAPTER 2

# Rapid Learning for 2- and 3-Year-Olds

Since the 1980s, there has been a tremendous explosion of research from neurology about human brain structures and their functions. The breathtaking progress of scientific developments can be seen in brain-imaging techniques, which identify brain activity when an individual is engaged in various learning activities. This chapter has been redesigned from *Building the Reading Brain*, second edition, to describe the rapid expansion of the very young human neurological system. The reader is encouraged to look for the *big* picture of brain development for the oral language pathway. Another name for this chapter could be "Understanding the Human Brain." An overabundance of brain terminology is necessary. Although some will want this level of explanation, other readers may decide to grasp and understand the generalities of the human brain as it builds itself for receptive oral language. The chapter's emphasis is on the toddler and the prior-to-school years.

Another focus is on the adults who surround these children—what can they do? For adults, it is easy to become immersed in the excitement and fun that accompanies the abundance of new developments for toddlers. Parents and caregivers find that the spontaneity of play and the joy of learning appear to come so easily. What is witnessed on the outside, however, is no indication of what is happening in a child's brain.

The continuum of developmental benchmarks is extended in this chapter to ages 2 and 3. Additionally, the reader will find a list of skills for cognitive brain development. These areas of development are more difficult to observe but equally important to understand as parents and educators support a child's developing brain. Areas of attention for visual and auditory input and discrimination for phonemic awareness are defined in a chart format. Note the cognitive aspects of brain development are directed at the 3-year-old. Now is the time in this chapter for serious discernment of how the *nature* of the human brain designs itself through the *nurture* of the environment, to operate with effectiveness and efficiency for the continuation of the child's life.

## LANGUAGE DEVELOPMENT FOR 2- AND 3-YEAR-OLDS

By age 2, nearly all children have between 100 and 300 words in their vocabulary. Between the second and third birthday, youngsters learn two to three words a day (Johnson, 2019). They begin to combine words to form simple phrases. These phrases are usually word sequences they hear frequently in the speech of others. The words are spoken in what is called **telegraphic speech**—short phrases containing basic information such as "All gone" or "Daddy play ball." Children's neural pathways for language develop rapidly, and between 24 and 30 months, their sentences become longer and more complete. The child's brain is going through not only a language explosion, but a grammar explosion as well. Children at this stage are beginning to analyze the longer patterns of words they hear, and are experimenting with some rules. For example, they figure out that you add an *s* for plurals and *ed* for past tense. Parents and other adults are advised not to correct, but rather to accept children's language use during this time, as children are very good at finding their own errors and matching their language to those around them. Correcting them could actually discourage the young ones from trying new words and phrases (McPherson, 2023).

### THE IMPORTANCE OF LEARNING TO TALK

There is no way to underestimate the importance of learning to talk and communicate through language. As previously emphasized, building a strong foundation at the toddler age is critical to reading success during the school years. As 2-year-olds advance with a rapidly expanding number of words in their vocabulary, they begin to combine words to express simple phrases. Next their sentences become longer, and the ideas they convey are more complete and complex.

As exposure to books increases, young children observe how others enjoy and even cherish their books. They learn how to hold a book and turn the pages. An amazing thing happens when a child can identify a flat, colored picture with lines and shapes as a ball or teddy bear, for instance, or more amazingly an image of a child or parent. Can you envision how many parts of the young brain must be activated to identify a real thing from a flat illustration? This activity is important, and a similar outcome is expected later when a written word, a noun, is identified with an actual object.

## A RECENT STUDY ABOUT ATTENTION

A study was conducted to examine the function of infant attention and the education level of their mothers, to find out if either had an influence on receptive vocabulary development (a priming and cognitive skill). Madeleine Bruce and colleagues (2022) conducted a study with 313 children. These researchers measured visual attention beginning at 10 months with a dynamic puppet task. The assessment continued with children at ages 3, 4, 6, and 9 years with the Peabody Picture Vocabulary Test, which measures listening and understanding of single-word vocabulary. Results showed that both child attention and higher levels of maternal education are predictors of receptive vocabulary progress from early preschool through the elementary years. Boys demonstrated a slightly faster rate of receptive language development as compared to girls. Interestingly, these findings more importantly indicate that without accounting for the assigned sex of the child or the education level of the mother, for children up to age 9 the *ability to attend was the most important factor*. To focus or concentrate on pictures and pay attention to verbal cues is indicative of ability for receptive oral language. Children who are able to attend are working on building a strong oral language pathway in their brains. Attention is the first of the priming skills that will be identified and connected with cognitive skill development.

Evidence continues to support prompting youngsters with a rich environment of language and visual stimulation. Being able to sustain attention to what is going on in the child's environment is a key to learning. Neuroscience research gives a clear understanding of how language develops cognitively; the science of reading explains how best instructional practices and instructional methodology provide the process for teaching reading.

# CONTINUUM OF DEVELOPMENTAL BENCHMARKS: AGES 2 TO 3

The initial developmental benchmarks for youngsters beginning at birth are extended here for the second and third years. Developmental benchmarks are apparent from children's actions and can be observed by others. Remember these descriptors are from a variety of sources and have importance for their suggestive/predictive activities. They are not based on scientific study. Appendix A at the end of the book provides a complete chart of benchmarks from birth through age 5.

Developmental Benchmarks: Ages 2 to 3

| | |
|---|---|
| 2 Years | Builds with blocks. Explores how toys work. Can follow simple two-step directions, such as "Pick up the blocks and put them in the box." Plays make-believe games. Can name pictures in a book. (*Side note:* This is a complex task to recognize an abstract picture of a physical item.) Speaks in simple sentences and recites rhymes. Kicks a ball, runs, and walks up a few stairs without help. Eats with a spoon. Can point to at least two body parts. Increases the number of gestures like blowing a kiss or nodding yes. Notices when others are upset. Recognizes books by their cover. |
| 3 Years | Can fit three to four pieces to complete a puzzle. Enters into make-believe play. Has the concept of one and two items. Sorts objects by shape and/or color. Can identify common colors. Can open a door using the handle. Plays next to other children and sometimes with them. Follows simple routines. Pretend plays, like reading a book, flying like a bird, or feeding a doll. Turns the pages of a book one at a time. Handles books a specific way. Can label known objects in books, including characters. Looks at specific print, such as letters in a name. Occasionally distinguishes between drawing and writing. Talks well enough for others to understand. Can identify animals, their actions, and sounds they make. Draws a circle with instruction. Can help with getting dressed. |

These guidelines can be applied to young children as a model for families and other caregivers.

# WHAT IS KNOWN FROM NEUROSCIENCE?

An explanation of the structures of the human brain, with identification of some of its important functions, makes language development explicitly understandable. The human brain is no longer considered "a black box." Educators communicate with

**TABLE 2.1** ● Definitions of Neuroanatomy and Neurophysiology

| NEUROSCIENCE | |
| --- | --- |
| Neuroanatomy | Study of the *structure and organization* of the central nervous system |
| Neurophysiology | Study of the *function* of the central nervous system |

neuroscientists, and the two disciplines have found common ground. Education draws from two different aspects of **neuroscience**, which is an understanding of the nervous system. As noted in Table 2.1, **neuroanatomy** is the branch of neuroscience focused on the *structures* of the system, while the *functions* of the system are the focus of **neurophysiology**. Working together and uniquely separate, these two systems of study focus on the human **central nervous system** (the brain and spinal cord) and peripheral nervous system (the cranial and spinal nerves, which carry information from the body via the spinal cord to the brain for interpretation).

Imaging machines, while available and noninvasive even for use with infants, are not required for information from neuroscience to be applicable to home and classroom practices. Although these two very different fields do not speak a common language, educators interpret and apply information from neurological science for instructional purposes. The insights about brain structure, brain organization, and brain function can be deciphered. This information helps to explain what educators and parents observe as children build their brains during childhood. Observation of children's behavior is boosted by knowing the difficult tasks the brain performs to build the circuitry supporting listening, understanding, and speaking. Cooperation between these two professions provides valued and essential information about cognition and learning. The significance of understanding the human brain is for parents, caregivers, and teachers to be informed of *what they can do, why they do it,* and *how the emerging young reader will benefit.*

## A CHILD'S BRAIN AT AGES 2 AND 3

The discipline of neurology explains how information is known about the very young brain and also about the adult brain. At this early point in the book, a deep delve into all that is happening in the toddler brain is needed. The reader is encouraged to think through the following sections, not being overly concerned with the terminology but rather focusing on the brain's structures and systems.

The human brain controls conscious parts of the central nervous system. Children think to direct their movements as they walk and speak, but they also are able to breathe, digest food, and blink their eyes without any conscious thought. Knowing the basic design of the human brain is essential to understanding the complex gyrations the brain undergoes to progress from a child capable of speaking to a child who possesses a brain for reading. The reader is directed to the Glossary at the end of the book for neurological or technical terms for reading, as needed.

## THREE DISTINCT BRAIN PARTS

As shown in Figure 2.1, a child's brain can be depicted with three major areas of development. First, the main structure, and also the largest, is the **cerebral cortex**, where signals from the senses are received for interpretation. Activity in the cerebral cortex allows one to learn, think, solve problems, interact, and remember. There may be confusion between the cerebral cortex and the cerebrum. Note the **cerebrum** is the largest part of the entire brain including both hemispheres, the lobes, and the cortices depicted in Figure 2.2. It also includes the innermost part of the brain called the limbic system. The cerebral cortex, while occupying a large portion of the brain, is the outer layer of the cerebrum.

The **cerebellum** is at the back of the cerebral cortex and may be called the "little brain." Neuroscientists continue to learn new attributes for this structure. For the purposes of this book, it

**FIGURE 2.1** ● Three distinct parts of the brain: The cerebral cortex, the cerebellum, and the brain stem.

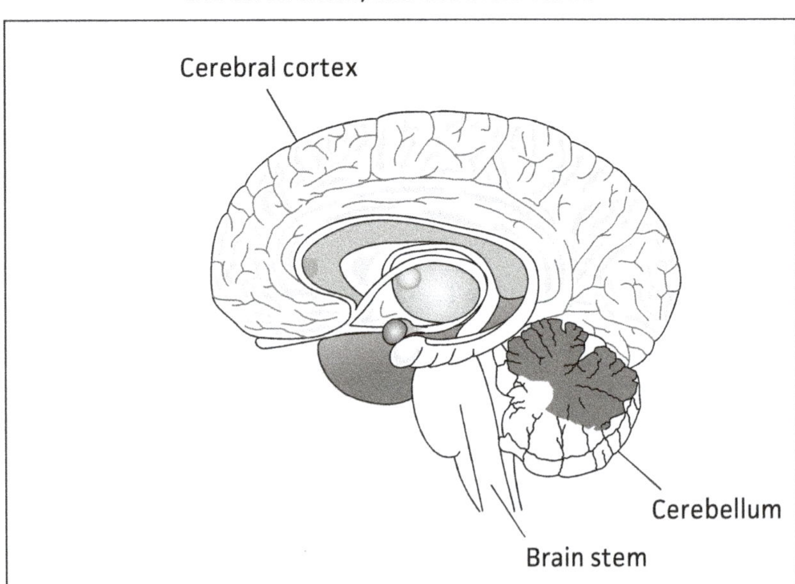


**Source:** Created by Herb Higashi. Adapted from Nevills (2014).

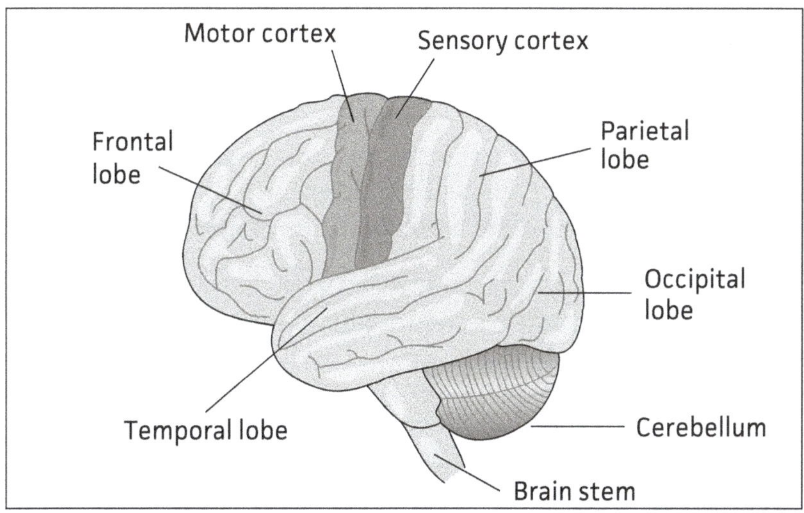


Source: Created by Herb Higashi. Adapted from Nevills (2014).

is known that this structure is called into action when something is learned to a proficient or automatic level, thus freeing the cerebral cortex from directing the activity. A toddler who walks easily no longer has to concentrate on the work of walking; it happens naturally through the coordinated movements of the cerebellum. Likewise, after practice a young child can turn the pages of a book with **automaticity**, giving way for the child to look pensively at the pictures. Humans can only concentrate on one thing at a time. If it appears otherwise, it is because the individual is good at rapidly switching from one thing to another, or even to a variety of things, while holding each in conscious memory. The cerebellum allows a person to do one or more things unconsciously, while focusing on something else that is mentally attractive. Scientists continue to discover other ways the cerebellum is involved with learning processes.

The third part of the brain's central nervous system is the **brain stem**, which is the stalk-like feature that connects the cerebral cortex with the spinal cord. The brain stem has three parts: the *midbrain*, *pons*, and *medulla*. For the purpose of this chapter, the explanation of this third part of the brain is limited. Simply put, it unconsciously regulates many of the body's vital functions, like breathing, heart rate, balance, coordination, and reflexes.

## THE CEREBRAL CORTEX'S TWO HEMISPHERES AND FOUR LOBES

The **cerebral cortex** is divided into two distinct parts, a *right* and a *left hemisphere* (see Figure 2.2). The two parts of the brain are connected by the **corpus callosum**, which is a bundle of nerve fibers that allows the corresponding regions of the two hemispheres to communicate. Although this connection between the hemispheres is minimally functional at this young age, it will not completely mature and be totally effective until adulthood. Communication between the two parts of the brain is important. Both hemispheres are needed to understand the messages that come to the toddler's brain through the five senses.

Each hemisphere in the cerebral cortex has four lobes—the **frontal, parietal, temporal,** and **occipital lobes**—along with the motor and somatosensory areas. The first chapter identified the motor and somatosensory cortices and their important role for early movement and for *receiving input* from the environment through the five senses. Now the understanding of the brain and its design goes a step further. The lobes are where *the stimuli from the environment are interpreted*. Table 2.2 provides a summary statement for each of the four lobes.

For readers who want to take a deeper dive into brain terminology, an expanded explanation of each of the fourdivisions follows.

- **Occipital lobes**—Starting at the very back of the human brain are the occipital lobes, which are primarily responsible for receiving and interpreting visual stimuli. The cortex covering the occipital lobes is called the **visual cortex**. The occipital lobes take visual images from the eyes to interpret and identify what the individual is seeing.

- **Parietal lobes**—Between the occipital lobes at the back of the brain and the frontal lobes at the front of the brain,

**TABLE 2.2** ● The Cerebral Cortex Divided Into Four Lobes

| | |
|---|---|
| **Occipital Lobes** | Located at the back of the brain; responsible for the processing of visual stimuli. (Vision) |
| **Parietal Lobes** | Located between the occipital lobes and frontal cortex; integrate information from the senses and determine well-being or danger. (Feelings) |
| **Temporal Lobes** | Located near the ears; process auditory information and some aspects of memory. (Hearing) |
| **Frontal Lobes** | The largest of the brain's lobes, located at the front of the brain; directly involved with every other functional unit for response and complex thinking. (Thinking) |

and behind the motor and somatosensory cortices, described in Chapter 1, are the parietal lobes. This pair of lobes additionally is located directly above the thalamus, which is defined, and further discussed in Chapter 4, as the human brain's information relay system. The ideal placement of the parietal lobes allows them to receive tactile (pressure, temperature, pain) and other (visual and auditory) sensory information. The parietal lobes are responsible for integrating all this information with the executive functions of the frontal lobes through working memory. In this case, information is maintained in the mind (mindfulness) while the individual reacts to or ignores the feelings experienced (Pence & Justice, 2008). Additional functions of the parietal lobes determine a general sense of well-being, safety, discomfort, or potential danger. All of these interpretive reactions have potential to determine a state of readiness for paying attention and learning.

- **Temporal lobes**—Located on the sides of the brain above the ears are the hearing parts, the temporal lobes. The cortex covering them is called the **auditory cortex**. The temporal lobes are responsible for receiving and interpreting auditory stimuli, more commonly understood as "noise" in the environment. Structures within the temporal lobes also control the production of speech and many aspects of memory. Notice how the temporal lobes for the habits of listening are located next to the ears.

- **Frontal lobes**—Right at the forehead and extending back over the top of the brain are the frontal lobes. This frontal area of the human brain encompasses slightly less than half (between 38.5% and 41%) of the cerebral cortex and is involved with conscious decisions and behaviors. Referred to as the chief executive officer, or CEO, of the brain, the frontal lobes are responsible for problem solving, dealing with abstractions from sensory information, and future planning. An older child or an adult will access the frontal lobes for other higher-order thinking skills including association, comprehension, evaluation, analysis, and synthesis.

When school-age children are engaged in demanding cognitive tasks, neuroscientists see images of heightened activity in the frontal lobe areas of the brain. Due to this intense activity, science refers to the area covering the frontal lobes as the **association cortex**.

# THE ORAL LANGUAGE PATHWAY

Realizing a young child is able to understand and act upon hearing a command while also producing recognizable words is cause for excitement. Although all this occurs spontaneously, what is happening in the child's brain is nothing short of brilliance. The story of the oral language pathway is best understood by reviewing Figure 2.3a.

Once again, there are many areas of the brain that need to be described for this figure to be understood—*Broca's area*, *Heschl's gyrus*, and *Wernicke's area*, to name a few. As demonstrated in Figure 2.3b, these areas, in conjunction with the *auditory cortex*, *motor cortex*, and *thalamus*, work together to refine listening and speaking. Know here that what the brain has accomplished to prepare the young one to listen and speak is unimaginably intricate. *The purpose of presenting the oral language pathway for listening and speaking is not for the reader of this book to remember all the technical terms*, though they are defined in more detail as follows for those who may be interested in an expanded explanation. Rather, it is

**FIGURE 2.3A** ● The oral language pathway in the brain.

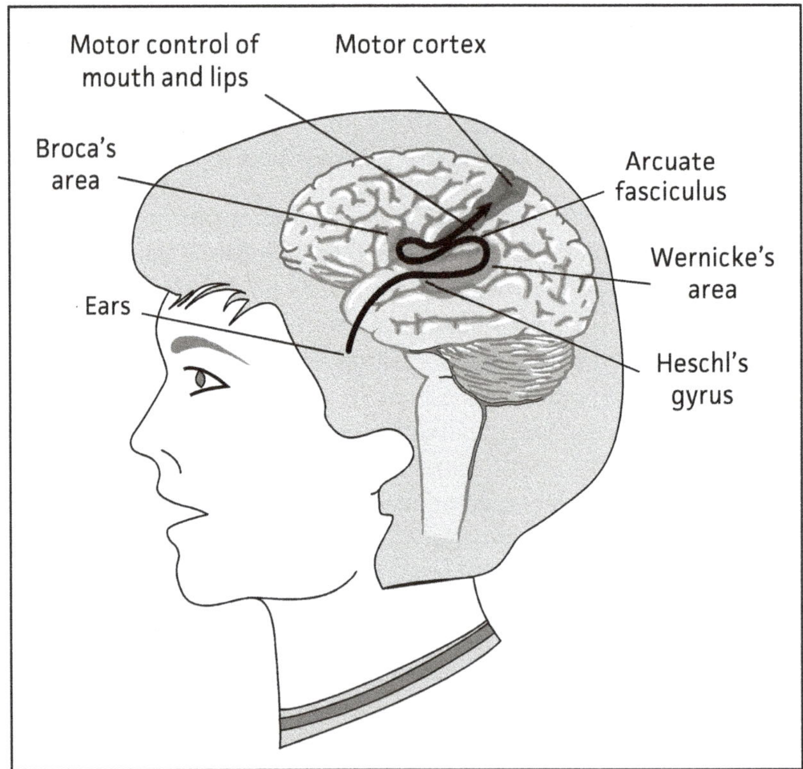


**Source:** Reprinted from Nevills & Wolfe (2009).

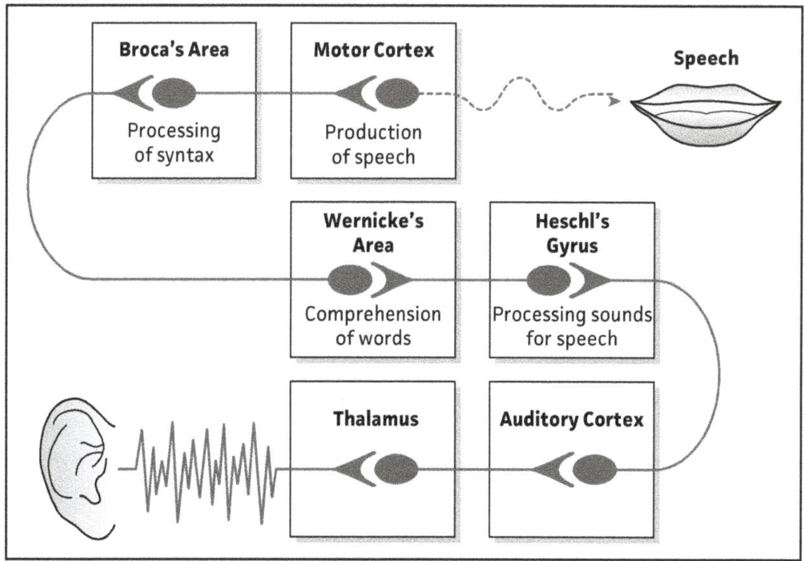


**Source:** Reprinted from Nevills & Wolfe (2009).

to comprehend the complexity of the process that happens in the child's brain to listen, understand, and speak.

- **Thalamus**—The thalamus serves as a relay station in the central, inner area of the brain for incoming signals from all the senses, except the sense of smell, and an output mechanism for sensory stimuli sent to areas of the cerebral cortex for interpretation.

- **Auditory cortex**—Located in the temporal lobe, the auditory cortex provides the ability to listen to sounds or words, hold them in working memory, and pull sounds together to make a word.

- **Heschl's gyrus (or area)**—A small left-temporal region where auditory input is rapidly processed as speech or language, rather than sounds not relating to words, is known as Heschl's gyrus.

- **Wernicke's area**—The language center responsible for comprehension of speech is known as Wernicke's area and typically located in the left hemisphere.

- **Broca's area**—The central region for the production of speech and processing of syntax, also most likely located in the left hemisphere, is known as Broca's area.

- **Motor cortex**—The lateral part of the frontal lobes, known as the motor cortex, extends from ear to ear across the roof of the brain. It governs coordination of movement and some cognitive processes. In the oral language pathway, it directs the mechanical process for speaking. The motor cortex may also be referred to as the motor strip.

Reading to children produces distinct benefits for several reasons. First, it increases their vocabulary and helps them become familiar with language patterns. Next, repetition increases the strength of neural connections. Finally, reading the same book to children repeatedly—which they love—serves to reinforce familiar words. Children often become so familiar with the vocabulary of a favorite story that they can "read" it with an adult, pretend to read it to a sibling, or recite it to one of their stuffed animals.

What is happening neurologically for a 3-year-old while an adult or older child reads out loud and talks to the child? Refer to Figure 2.3b. The primary **auditory cortex**, the interpretation center for hearing, becomes activated. Children respond to the sounds they hear every day. **Wernicke's area** is alerted as a youngster hears new and familiar words and makes connections to pathways to vocabulary already stored in memory. The networks for vocabulary become stimulated, fortified, and consequently more accessible. Also activated are the **motor cortex** and **Broca's area** to speak, repeat, and reinforce new sounds, words, and ideas. Knowing the complex process of oral language development helps parents and educators to appreciate the hard work that is involved for youngsters. They seem to engage with this tough work with continued curiosity.

The oral language pathway develops naturally. The human brain is designed to enable children to learn to listen, comprehend, and speak. In succeeding chapters as reading is introduced, the difference between the language pathway and the reading pathway will be stressed. Oral language develops spontaneously, without teaching, in a language-rich family environment. Reading does not just happen naturally for most children. The human brain does not "take to" reading without explicit instruction. To form the reading pathway, the language pathway must be redesigned and coerced to form a new route. The reading pathway is developed through explicit instruction and repetitive practice. The building process for reading is found in Chapters 5 and 6.

##  ACTIVITIES TO SUPPORT DEVELOPING READERS

In this section, the reader will consider how the activities of the oral language pathway are activated as a child listens to someone read. Other resources that teachers and parents can use to encourage the advancement of language skills include nursery **rhymes** and initial writing activities. With the advanced age of technology, it might seem that nursery rhymes are obsolete. Quite to the contrary, they remain engaging and critical to encourage careful listening to the sounds of language. Writing, also, comes front and center as children develop the motor skills to hold a writing tool and desire to express what they are thinking.

## LISTENING TO SOMEONE READ OUT LOUD

Reading to children encourages familiarity with the reading process. A 2- or 3-year-old child has much to learn about print—how the book is turned when it is "right side up"; that the print, not a picture, is read; and that you start at the beginning of a page and, after finishing that page, turn to the next. Children learn about reading by observing others read to them. The benefit of reading to a child is further enhanced when the reader involves the child. The adult may pause and let the child supply the next word. "The dog and her puppies were under the tree. I counted them, one, two, _________." Showing the pictures and asking a child to point to, name, or count persons or objects is another form of involvement. Child connection to the book is more important than "completing the story." Yet another way to involve the youngster includes encouraging the child to retell the story. "How did the story begin?" "What happened next?" And, "How did it end?" Asking youngsters how they felt when the story was read, or what their favorite part was, might also be appropriate conversation for some children. Discovery and rehearsal activities stimulate the child's memory and draw on background knowledge to reinforce learning.

## THE NURSERY RHYME EFFECT

### Cluck, Cluck, Cluck

| | |
|---|---|
| Cluck, cluck, cluck, cluck, cluck, | Four of them are yellow, |
| Good morning, Mrs. Hen. | And four of them are brown, |
| How many chickens have you got? | And two of them are speckled red |
| Madam, I've got ten. | The nicest in the town. |

Why is a nursery rhyme in a book on reading? The response is that when similar or repetitious sounds are voiced, they excite parallel brain cells and their connections. As these sounds are heard repeatedly, the neuron connections become stronger, and the sounds become more easily recognized as familiar. The young child's brain begins to distinguish between sounds that are alike and those that are different. This process is essential for phonemic awareness and, as such, will be explored in Chapters 5 and 6. The progression, beginning with phonemic awareness, moves into the realm of phonological processing for rapid word identification. Researchers have discovered that nursery rhymes are useful not just to soothe babies. Rhythm and language patterns from nursery rhymes and poetry encourage young children to develop a discerning ear for oral language (Reading Rockets, 2007). Readers of this book will most likely agree that nursery rhymes have not lost their effectiveness. Nursery rhymes are so well loved that Claire Bennett (2019) from the Professional Association for Childcare and Early Years (PACEY) featured them on the association's blog during World Nursery Rhyme Week. Reasons cited included development in the areas of language, cognition, social–emotional development, memory, comprehension of new words, listening, phonology, movement, and so on. There is no denying the importance of age-old rhythms and rhymes, and their new age additions as well.

## PRECURSORS TO WRITING IN THE FIRST THREE YEARS

Reading and writing skills develop together. While children generally do not start writing letters and words until around age 4, there are many opportunities for parents and caregivers to encourage writing behaviors earlier (Rogers, 2021). Between 12 and 15 months, little ones can be provided with resources for drawing or coloring and be encouraged to experiment with making marks. Children can be offered a wide range of media as they express interest in drawing, and develop what is called the pincer grasp (holding objects between the thumb and pointing finger). A fat crayon is a good beginning tool. The crayon may be used to make marks like large random arcs, blobs, and unintentional scribbling. As more interest is shown, adults may include finger paints, clay, and play dough, which are all good materials to use indoors, and step it up to "painting" with water or drawing with chalk on sidewalks for older children to experiment outdoors. Parents and caregivers also have opportunities to model or demonstrate the uses of writing by signing the child's name to a birthday card, writing an item the child wants

**TABLE 2.3** ● Early Writing Stages From Scribbling to Letter Forming

| Early Scribbling | Makes random marks |
| --- | --- |
| Controlled Scribbling | Draws a straight line or circle |
| Pictorial Stage | Makes distinguishable marks |
| Letter Stage | Uses letters to represent words |

on a grocery list, writing the date a book is due at the library on a calendar, or writing a letter to a grandparent as the child dictates.

Children pass through several stages as they develop their skills in writing (see Table 2.3). The first stage could be called *early scribbling*, where the child makes random marks on paper. Children at this stage are probably more interested in the physical experience than in what is being marked on the paper. As children's motor skills develop, the marks become more controlled, with efforts to draw a straight line or a circle. This stage could be labeled *controlled scribbling*. At this time, some children begin to distinguish between drawing and writing. With vertical lines under a picture, the child may ask, "What did I write?" or "How do you write 'Daddy'?" The third stage might be called the *pictorial stage*, where the marks and forms begin to be distinguishable. This stage is when the child understands that pictures and words are different symbols. In the final stage, which could be labeled the *letter stage*, young children begin to write letters to represent words and syllables and may be able to write their own names.

 COGNITIVE DEVELOPMENT

Chapter 1 identified that what is happening in the brain as a child learns is difficult to assess. A child's cognition progresses from abilities for paying attention to development of simple concepts. The fields of cognitive psychology and cognitive neuroscience come together in useful ways to help educators and parents understand skills that are more difficult to observe. Skills for early language are not as outwardly apparent as the developmental benchmarks given earlier. **Cognitive psychology** explains **mindfulness**. To be mindful is to hold concepts and ideas in mind for consideration. Educators can determine abilities of mindfulness by observation, but it is a more difficult task than to determine developmental milestones. Mindfulness deals with brain activities, including attention, concentration, memory, recall, and concept development. **Cognitive**

**neuroscience** explains what is actually happening in the brain while children perform a task, such as speaking or reading.

The summary of developmental benchmarks, provided earlier in this chapter, is now augmented with the cognitive brain development skills for 3-year-olds. The reader is directed to notice the importance of attention and focus, mentioned earlier in a study summary. The cognitive areas addressed for these very young children are sustained and selective attention for visual and auditory input, visual processing and discrimination, and auditory processing for phonological awareness. Cognitive actions incurring in the brain require close observance to how children process information. Information from the following chart of cognitive learning skills can be shared with parents as they search for ways to support their child's progress.

Some developmental areas cover a two-year period. This list is the author's summation from many sources, and is an indication or guide to development over the period of time from 2 to 4 years of age. A complete list of cognitive skills in children from 1 to 9 years of age is located in Appendix B.

## COGNITIVE SKILLS FOR LEARNING: AGES 1 TO 3

Attention

| 1–2 Years | **Visual and Auditory Sustained Attention**—Sustains interest without adult intervention for an elongated period of time. Watches the lips of a speaker and attempts to reproduce the same sound. Tracks and follows the actions of another person. Engages in play alone or with another child for a sustained time. Explores toys and moves around. Tries switches, knobs, and buttons on a toy. Holds something in one hand while using the other hand for a task. |
|---|---|
| 3 Years | **Visual and Auditory Selective Attention**—Screens out distractions for focused attention. Attends to a task in a place where visual and/or auditory interferences are happening. (For example, Mommy and Daddy are having a conversation and may be moving, but the interesting thing at hand is more important to the child. In a preschool classroom many other children are talking and moving around, but the drawing the child is doing is more important for the child's focus.) Calms down within 10 minutes. Joins other children to play. Asks *who*, *what*, *where*, and *why* questions. Can identify actions in a picture book. Knows to say own name. Talks well enough to be understood. Draws a circle. Avoids dangerous things. Can mostly dress self. Uses a fork. Can string beads. |

Visual Processing

| 3 Years | **Visual Discrimination**—Distinguishes differences among items, including objects, shapes, and colors. More advanced, *but not necessary* at this age, identifies some letters, numbers, sight words, and larger numbers beyond 1 and 2. |
| --- | --- |

Auditory Processing for Phonological Awareness

| 3 Years | **Discrimination**—Distinguishes differences among sounds. Listens and attends to simple nursery rhymes. Listens to words to identify if they start or end with the same sound—for example, *man, monkey, milk* or *funny, sunny, bunny*. Can say individual sounds for two- and three-letter words, such as *c-a-t, d-o-g*, and *s-a-t*. Notice this cognitive activity is about sounds from spoken words, and about sounds, *not letters*. |
| --- | --- |

Parents and caregivers are encouraged to use this chart for suggestions of brain-type activities that identify and encourage the child's journey to develop a thinking, prereading brain. Notice how the world of language reveals the many ways children can be enjoyed and also encouraged.

# 🧠 CONCLUDING THOUGHTS ABOUT 2- AND 3-YEAR-OLDS

Learning to talk is probably one of the greatest accomplishments of an individual's life. Structures for language are hardwired in the brain. Nearly all children learn to speak, but humans are obviously not born speaking. In this chapter, we have seen that the first three to four years of life are a cognitively critical period for developing children's language capacity, vocabulary, and beginning writing skills. The environmental aspects of children's lives—(1) their experiences, (2) whether they are read and talked to, (3) the opportunities they have to experiment with writing, and (4) new discoveries—provide an important role to build their brains with a strong foundation of neuron connections. It is this network of neural connections that proves critical for later reading success. The following chapter takes a look at the next year or two to see how the brain continues its rapid development for learning and language. At the onset of universal kindergarten, the beginning of formalized education for 4-year-olds becomes a reality, and studying the neurological aspects of language development allows for understanding how children at age 4 may or may not be ready for the rigors of a classroom learning environment.

## RESOURCE

Backpack Books. (2003). *A treasury for three year olds: A collection of stories, fairy tales, and nursery rhymes.* Backpack Books.

# Reflective Questions

1. How might you use the developmental benchmarks for 2- and 3-year-olds for yourself or to share with parents?

2. The cerebellum, or "little brain," at the back of the brain is curious yet very prominent and important for all parts of human development. How would you explain the cerebellum?

3. How would you define the cerebral cortex?

4. What is so different about learning to speak and learning to read?

5. Identify the stages of development children follow as they begin to write. Give some activities that support youngsters as they develop writing skills.

6. This chapter is full of how neuroscience explains the parts of the brain. Ultimately, these brain areas will be used to identify the reading pathway featured in following chapters. What do you want to remember from this chapter that will be practical "brain" information for reading this book, as well as for understanding and selecting teaching practices?

# CHAPTER 3

# Preparing for This World at Age 4

It is amazing to realize that during the preschool years the child's brain is constructing itself into a thinking, problem-solving, information-receiving instrument. Neuroplasticity, the ability of the human brain to respond to environmental input, allows the brain to grow connections, develop and formulate skills and procedures, and learn new concepts. Neuroscientists have aided our understanding of how and why children learn so rapidly. Since very young children have no other obligations, they spend all their waking hours trying to figure out their world. They observe and imitate by using a powerful system of **mirror neurons** (Taylor, 2016). This remarkable system allows children to activate a neural set of connections as if the child's own brain connections are actually doing what is being watched. Researchers feel this discovery can explain learning that begins literally at birth.

This knowledge does not support academic teaching prior to kindergarten. However, adults, who are aware of the marvelous manipulations the brain is undergoing, are able to provide activities in natural ways to encourage, support, and reinforce language learning. Guidelines presented in this chapter include natural, child-initiated, or child-focused conversation; adult attention; gentle grammar corrections through modeling, rephrasing, and extending thoughts and ideas; providing creative language; asking for descriptive language; and posing curiosity questions.

Learning the alphabet is more than singing the letters in one large, linguistic chunk to the tune of "Twinkle, Twinkle, Little Star." It also means being able to identify and say the names of the letters in the variety of forms they are represented. For reasons that will be clear in succeeding chapters, the sounds of the letters are not taught at this time—a child is simply asked to recognize and provide a name for some or all of the letters. Sounds for individual and combined letters can be learned later through an efficient, structured phonological processing program that includes phoneme identification.

## LANGUAGE AND SOCIAL DEVELOPMENT FOR 4-YEAR-OLDS

Whether at home or at school, a 4-year-old is preparing for some heavy-time brain activity. Story reading has expanded purposes as children gain skills for comprehension. They form mental images of stories, increase general knowledge and background information, and listen for inferences or interpretations during story time. At this age, children begin to pretend to read and become aware that print actually relates to spoken words. When the environment is filled with print, children quickly learn to identify common words. They want to reproduce words they know and enjoy opportunities to write or copy, for example, a grocery list, a birthday card, or a label for a toy or book shelf.

Phonemic awareness begins at this stage of brain development because the child is more acutely aware of the intricacy of sounds from spoken language and beyond, which may include musical instruments, birds singing, a lawn mower, or a dishwasher. Early childhood educators know that identifying phonemes as the smallest sounds in words is a critical precursor for reading decoding. During children's preschool years, astute adults provide children with activities that include rhyming, alliteration (e.g., *happy hippo*), words with sound patterns (e.g., *him, slim, Jim*), oddity tasks (e.g., Which does not belong? *fun, run, sing, sun*), and engaging phoneme sounds through music. Children begin to experiment with writing symbols, some of which are recognized and common. The structure at the back of the brain, the cerebellum, begins to be trained for writing and other learning tasks that the structure will do at the automatic level. All this reinforcement to the child's brain of how oral sounds, particularly the vocalization of words, can be used, mixed, or combined to represent print is done in a playful, often spontaneous manner.

### ORAL LANGUAGE AND VOCABULARY

Between the ages of 3 and 5, children make tremendous strides in their mastery of language. Researchers are intent on finding the most effective preschool settings for vocabulary development.

Authors Julie Dwyer of Boston University and Allen Harbaugh of Longwood University conducted a study to observe children in eight public preschools in different settings: centers, free play, transition periods, teacher-led large and small groups, read-alouds, and snack/meal times (see Dwyer & Harbaugh, 2021). The densest support for vocabulary development was observed during read-aloud of both fiction and nonfiction and teacher-led whole-group activities. However, there was a great variation among teachers for how effectively the time was spent. The researchers further concluded that none of the teachers in the study were leveraging other settings, like free play or meal times, to develop children's language skills. This study and others revealed a majority of teachers did not provide intentional language development support in any of the contexts studied (Dickinson et al., 2013; Dwyer & Harbaugh, 2021; National Early Literacy Panel, 2009). Intentionality for vocabulary and other language development can be increased with more understanding of what is happening in a 4-year-old's brain.

Consider the activity of a picture or book walk. Teachers can do this activity as a book is read to the class, or students may have individual copies of the book. The book is examined beginning with the cover by identifying the illustration, the name of the book, and the author(s). The walk continues as each page is observed with conversation about the pictures. The visual images may include identification of specific vocabulary or draw upon prior knowledge. At the end of the pages, children speculate about what they will hear as the story is read. In older grades, a book walk may precede individual reading.

Regardless of the setting—home or preschool—children are beginning to speak in more complex and complicated sentences, and are using language to meet their personal and social needs. They enjoy listening to and talking about the stories that are read to them, are beginning to identify familiar signs and labels, participate in rhyming games, are exposed to and engaged with digital media, and probably understand that print carries a message. Preschool children also show growth in the speech fluency they need to express ideas. Most children are now ready to explore what it means to be a reader and a writer. Whether their daytime is spent in a preschool or at home with parents or caregivers, these young children have reached a milestone in their literacy development.

## WHAT ABOUT SCREEN TIME?

Noticeably, young children are drawn to interact with media texts and other practices. Within the context of family, school, community, and culture, educators and parents alike are paying attention to digital media for young children, with personalized toys and books but also with smartphones, tablets, and computers. Through these devices young children are able to connect directly with distant family and friends. Along with the advantages come the highly unregulated availability of unknown others. Researchers have denied advantages of technology for very young children, even citing cognitive, behavioral, and health risks for children who spend time with technology rather than interactive social engagement (Hutton et al., 2020).

Watching television, using a computer, and engaging with applications on a cell phone have been lumped into the topic of screen time. The controversy over the use of electronic devices by young children existed even before the COVID-19 pandemic forced children to stay at home. If 4-year-olds are allowed access to screen time, what is proper for them to view, is there accountability for what they watch, and how long should they be engaged? Victoria Saylor of Common Sense Media and Jennifer Ehehalt of Common Sense Education were concerned enough about the mystique of screen time for children from infancy to age 8 that their organizations developed a tool kit with six videos in English and Spanish (see Common Sense Education, 2022). The product can be used by educators as intermediaries who work with families, including community leaders, promoters, family educators, family engagement coordinators, and school-based family liaisons. The videos are designed to facilitate meaningful conversations with families and caregivers to support youngsters in development of essential cognitive and life skills with, and also without, the use of screen time. The six topics include the following:

1. Raising Healthy Kids in a Digital World
2. Finding Balance With Media and Tech Use at Home
3. Choosing High-Quality Media for Your Kids
4. How to Make Meaningful Family Connections Using Media and Tech
5. Introducing Online Safety to Young Kids
6. How to Use Media and Tech to Build Life Skills in Young Kids (Common Sense Education, 2022)

Another recommended resource is Arizona's First Things First (2023). See especially the *Baby Brain* video (First Things First, 2017), which explains young children's growth and brain development with easy-to-follow language.

# PLAY THROUGH EXPLORATION AND PEER INTERACTION

To a certain extent, children are able to educate themselves when they are allowed to play through exploring, risk-taking, creativity, and peer interaction. What is meant by play? Begin with what is *not* play. Adult versions of play include activities of team sports or adult-directed games; this is not play for youngsters. A definition of play has been developed by Peter Gray and explained by a recent podcast (Reid, 2022). Using a review of descriptions from the combined efforts of many specialists, Gray identifies the results with five characteristics of "pure" play:

1. **The play is self-chosen and self-directed**—not led by a teacher or a coach. It may be an activity with peers of an equal status. It is social, involving compromise, expression of feelings, negotiations, and the ability to quit.

   *Observation*: Children at play moved freely from group to group and to independent play.

2. **There is a goal**—the goal is not winning. Rather, the purpose is intrinsically motivated. The reward is the play itself. There is no punishment or praise. Children are allowed to try something new, even if they are not good at it. Play-based time increases confidence and individual character.

   *Observation*: A 4-year old collected a combination of objects found around the playground and placed them on a lunch table. He was obviously well liked by other children, and four of them came to see what he was doing. They wanted to join his play. He placated them by handing them items he did not want or could pick up nearby, but clearly was into a game of his own liking. After a while an adult interacted with the group and made suggestions. The child was directed to return some of the items to their appropriate place, which he did. At that time recess ended. Although it was expected that the boy would go to his items before returning to the classroom, he did not. That play/game was over, and he was finished.

3. **All play has an element of imagination**—a type of stepping outside the real world. This play is a narrative to be acted out. In this way children learn to accept other people in their world. "If I am . . . then you are . . ." This is exploration into roles other people play. How many times do little girls want to play "teacher" or "mother"? Boys may prefer more active imagination: "I am . . . and I am going to catch you. You are . . ."

   *Observation*: A rather controlling young girl spotted two brothers about her age in the community swimming pool. She approached them and said, "I am the mother." Then, pointing to the older boy, "You are the father," she continued, before looking at the youngest child, "and you are the child." The boys were stunned and simply looked at her while she went on to say that the father needed to go to work. They never responded to her; rather, they swam off to another part of the pool.

4. **True play has structured rules**—they are never random. The child must behave like the character assigned: Daddy, Wonder Woman, and popular Disney characters are some examples. It must be decided how this person would act within or react to the situations that develop. The rules of true play differ from the rules of the real world.

    *Observation:* When other children are not available, an adult may be invited to enter into imaginary roles with the child. It is necessary for the adult to let go of authority and follow the lead of the child, even if it means being corrected by the child. Notice the adult does not participate in "setup." A child will figure out something—even out of nothing. It is all fair in play.

5. **Play is a nonstressful, highly conscious, mentally active activity**—no adult influence. This characteristic of play allows the child to "mess around." There is no penalty if the child fails. This type of play allows for creative responses to challenging instances in the real world.

    *Observations:* Play under these conditions may involve problem solving: Who should peddle the passenger trike, and who should be the rider? One pair decided the smaller boy should be the passenger. Play may require politeness, such as stopping to say, "I'm sorry." Creativity was viewed as children selected trays, normally used for clay play, to use as sleds on a small hill with artificial grass. A group at the sandbox showed tolerance as the "bossy" girl stood over them and barked directions. Some of the boys followed an ever-changing leader and simply ran from one area to another for an entire recess.

## SOCIAL ABILITY

Play activities can lead to sociability. Analyzing carefree play allows adults to be more present with the mindset of the child. Play is essential for the development of the social characteristics of a 4-year-old. And, it is ubiquitous. As presented, play is a means for social interaction and for learning about the feelings of others. Play allows children to try out different scenarios and to observe the reactions of others *without adult intervention.*

In the real life of a 4-year-old, socialization is also learned in situations that have structure.

There are *The Rules*—those in many aspects of a child's life, such as family norms, ways of behaving with siblings, behavior for the car, and how one acts at church, the library, or the grocery store—and then there are school and playground rules, which will be examined in the next chapter. Along the years, a young child learns to accept society's norms, or not. How is it that some children conform while others continue to ignore and rebel against standards? Peter Gray, introduced in the section on play, has a theory based on his observations (see Reid, 2022). While most children learn to inhibit their impulses, others do not. Gray speculates that attention deficit hyperactivity disorder (ADHD), which seemingly is becoming more prevalent, could be a result of lack of playtime for young children. Freedom in play is freedom to quit. If one child makes another unhappy, the unhappy one can quit and leave the play activity. A larger child must learn body awareness, and learn restraint during play that involves "roughhousing." All too often adults interfere and rob children of their ability to work situations out with understanding. With young children, the group will manage how much they will put up with from another child.

# CONTINUUM OF DEVELOPMENTAL BENCHMARKS: AGE 4

Rapid expansion of skills is happening for a 4-year-old in the areas of language, attention, concentration, and sense of sociability. Developmental benchmarks continue to advance in skills, some of which help a preschool child to interact with sociability in play relationships.

Developmental Benchmarks: Age 4

| 4 Years | Copies simple shapes. Follows instructions with two or three steps. Knows the concepts of same and different. Has some understanding of time. Can count and may be able to identify numbers 1 to 10. Knows body parts, and possibly where the brain is. Draws a person with four body parts or more. Uses blunt scissors. Copies letters and can identify some. Listens intently to a story read aloud and can predict what will happen next. Pays attention some of the time when other children talk. Can visualize and answer questions about a person or a thing from memory without seeing a picture first. Can write own name. Can recite days of the week and possibly the months of the year. Active with conversation at home, at school, and during play activities. Makes early writing and reading attempts. Has a sense of before, now, and after. Can sequence up to four pictures in order of occurrence. |
| --- | --- |

# WHAT IS KNOWN FROM NEUROSCIENCE?

Children from infancy to age 5 are experiencing tremendous neurological growth. At birth, the newborn's brain is about one-fourth the size of the average adult brain. It doubles during the first year and keeps its rapid development until it reaches 90% of its adult size at age 3. The 4-year-old is working toward full brain size at age 5. Do not be misled by size of the brain at age 5, however. Learning does not stop. Connections among neuron networks keep expanding, and the brain and spinal cord become more dense and heavy with connections as the years continue.

Children's brains are undergoing massive reorganization, building millions of new connections and at the same time pruning away previous ones that are unused. Which neural connections are kept and which ones are pruned depends largely on whether they are reinforced by experience. In a sense, the preschooler has a supercharged brain. Measurements made by Harry Chugani (1998) at Children's Hospital in Detroit show that 3- and 4-year-olds' brain cells are burning glucose at twice the rate of adult brain cells. This is not to say children are learning twice as much as an adult; rather, the youngsters are recording massive amounts of information by making connections in some helpful and also ineffective ways. Adults, at their stage of brain development, have a brain organized for learning. Adults are unconsciously more cautious about what information they are willing to hold in working memory, and purposeful in what they commit to conscious memory. Toddlers attempt to learn and connect meaning to almost everything they experience. Children at 4 generally do not lack curiosity, but are slightly more selective in their focus.

## ENERGY DEMANDS AND MATURATION OF BRAIN CELLS: NEUROPLASTICITY AND MYELINATION

Why do children's young brains demand so much energy? What is the brain doing during this period of rapid growth? The brain is continuously building itself. One of the human brain's most amazing capacities is its ability to sculpt itself based on what the child experiences. This process is called **neuroplasticity**. Almost nowhere is this explosive neural activity as evident as in the young child's brain's ability to learn and store the language or languages heard repeatedly. Brain wave measurements called electroencephalograms (EEGs) show a dramatic upsurge of activity in Broca's and Wernicke's areas (both introduced in

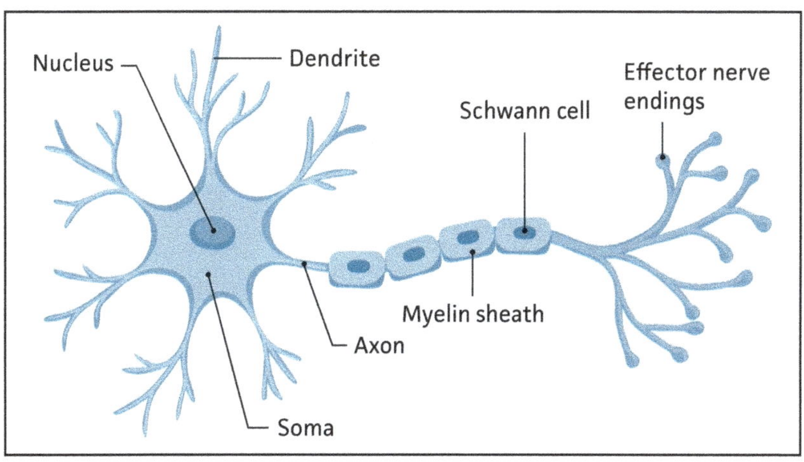

**FIGURE 3.1** ● Neuron with myelinated axons. Notice the new term *Schwann cell*, which produces the myelin for coating the axon.

**Image source:** iStock.com/Bulgakova Kristina

Chapter 2), which is reflected in the preschooler's snowballing vocabulary (Diamond & Hopson, 1998). The developing child's brain has reached a level of maturation to allow it to make great strides in language acquisition. Until around age 4, the language pathway of the brain is not fully functional. However, with maturation, which is identified through the process of **myelination** of the neurons' axons, Broca's and Wernicke's areas are fully accessible and ready to speed language learning to a new level. Going back to the microstructures of the brain, the neuron's speed and intensity of connections is expanded by the myelination process (see Figure 3.1).

Myelination is a maturation process in areas of the human brain where one type of **glial cell**, a **Schwann cell**, wraps itself around axons and allows for speedy transmission of the neural connections. In less elaborate words, the neurons' axons become coated with a fatty substance that increases the speed with which neurons connect. Even more directly stated, the child's brain thinks more quickly and with more complexity.

## THE FIVE SENSES AND MEMORY

The neurons of the brain continue to connect and fire with increasing speed and efficiency. This maturation process allows a child at age 4 to access memory, even though it requires a lot of practice and self-consciousness. What happens for a child to remember a name, concept, or event is not only astonishing; it simply happens. The continuum of developmental benchmarks for 4-year-olds provided earlier in this chapter gives explicit

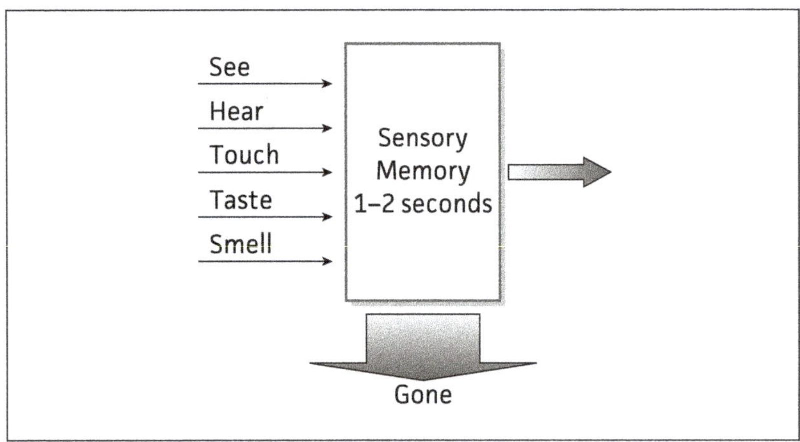


**Source:** Reprinted from Nevills (2011).

examples. To understand the complex memory systems that have been forming at this age, realize there are not easily identifiable brain structures for memory. Rather, many parts of the brain cooperate and work in unison.

The senses are always collecting information, but many 4-year-olds are able to unconsciously use their **sensory memory** system to sort out input that is not important. As demonstrated in Figure 3.2, the unneeded sensation is ignored and dropped instantly. For example, the air conditioner has a low hum in the classroom. Although the sound is received, the child's limbic center (described in the next chapter) determines it is not important, and the sound is not acknowledged. The instance of hearing the lawn mower outside is not only dropped; it is as if it never happened. Conversely, if what is heard, like attending to a book that is being read, is relevant to the child, that input is sent to and held in working memory for further consideration. Activities parents have been doing through the preschool years benefit the development of working memory where the child practices, reinforces, and rehearses meaningful sensory input. Working memory will be added to this figure in the next chapter.

## WHAT CAN TEACHERS, PARENTS, AND CAREGIVERS DO?

While the preschool years are a prime time for developing the emergent reader's preliteracy skills, it is emphasized there is no promotion by this author of "pushing down" the kindergarten or first-grade curriculum to younger children. The idea that "earlier is better" is based on a lack of understanding of the reading process, of children's brain development, and of the types of activities that are best suited for children of older cognitive ages. The California Department of Education (2008) in the extensive document titled *Preschool Learning Foundations*, volume 1, details the wide-ranging prereading skills appropriate for preschool children. A few preschool children have literacy and writing interest, motivation, and responses that are heightened when compared to their age-alike peers. Skipping some of the steps of thorough phoneme, phonological, and phonics programs may result in difficulties for students in later grades when presented with complex words. While some may be ready to read at age 4, reading should not be an expectation for preK children.

## DEVELOPMENTALLY APPROPRIATE ORAL LANGUAGE ACTIVITIES

It is important to emphasize that while the information and activities in this chapter are designed for the 4-year-old child, there is tremendous variance in children's background experiences, their rates of maturation, and their readiness to engage in prereading activities. Some of the guidelines and suggested activities in this chapter will be appropriate for 4-year-olds. Other children's brains will be a bit slower to develop, and they may not be ready for the activities until perhaps age 5. *Four years old*, as used in this chapter, refers to an age range (3½–5) rather than to every child at the age of 4.

Linguistic awareness is best developed within the context of the child's world through playing with words. The environment, whether at home or in preschool, can provide many opportunities to hear and play with language. The preschool child's environment has potential to be rich with opportunities to develop language and **emergent literacy** skills. Exploring objects for sameness, sorting or organizing play kitchen items, shopping for groceries, visiting a park, going to the library, sorting clothes for washing, and preparing a treat all offer opportunities to build vocabulary and increase the child's understanding of concepts. Reading poems and stories, engaging in dramatic play, seeing classroom charts and other print in use, and singing rhymes are additional activities that are appropriate at this stage of development. Given the caveat that earlier is not necessarily better, what are some of the appropriate oral linguistic awareness activities that best prepare the young child for more formal literacy instruction?

## ACTIVITIES FOR BUILDING ORAL LANGUAGE SKILLS

Preschool teachers and assistants can identify morning meeting as the first activity that occurs in preschool settings. Morning greetings and meetings include classroom news, the schedule for the day, calendar or day-of-the-week activities, observations or charting of the weather, discussion of the season, and counting the days of school. This dedicated time might include a morning message, which is a written note from the teacher to the students that is read or chanted. This time of the day includes a very brief focus on many different content areas. It is a ubiquitous practice that many preschoolers experience and expect.

Many of the activities that nurture literacy and language development suggested in the previous chapter for younger children continue to be appropriate for 4-year-olds, but at a somewhat more advanced level. As was noted at the beginning of this chapter, children at 4 have experienced a relatively large jump in brain development during the previous year. Their brains are now approximately 90% of their final adult size and weight. The 4-year-old has not, of course, reached the same level of cognitive functioning as an adult. These young, yet sophisticated, learners continue to enjoy many of the language activities they engaged in at 2 and 3, but with their newly developed language and cognitive skills, they can now be expected to be more active participants.

The quality of adult–child discourse and the amount of time allotted to these interactions appear to be critical factors. Conversations need to be cognitively challenging and vocabulary rich for literacy learning to occur. Every parent is more than familiar with the ubiquitous "Why?" of 3- and 4-year-olds. Sometimes, adults spend time carefully answering their children's questions and miss an opportunity to *engage children in a discussion* of what they think the answer might be. This mindful practice would lead to conversing about a child-initiated or child-focused question. Although it is a natural adult tendency to "absent-mindedly" respond to the barrage of questions, a well-intentioned adult can make the most of this language-enhancing opportunity by paying attention. Asking the child to rephrase a question or a statement encourages extensions of thoughts and ideas. Ask additional questions that provoke the child's curiosity, such as "Why do you think . . . ?" or "How do you suppose . . . ?" and "Do you wonder where . . . ?"

Responding in this way allows the adult to discover and correct misconceptions prior to them being reinforced in the memory's recall system. An example of a misconception could be a child learning that a moving vehicle is called "a car." The brain sets up a memory system to identify moving vehicles as cars. The child sees a truck and identifies it as a car. Hence the opportunity arises to explore many different types of moving vehicles. Remember, these are conversations, not lessons. They are effective when they are *natural, unobtrusive, and not dominated by the adult* (adapted from Hall & Moats, 1999).

During this natural interplay of conversation, teachers or parents are cautioned to be gentle on corrections to sentence structure and grammar. Modeling or rephrasing can continue the flow of the child's language in a safe manner. Children need to know they can experiment with words and ideas without being criticized.

## COMPREHENSION AND VOCABULARY BUILDING THROUGH STORY TIME

Earlier it was emphasized that story reading was observed to be an effective practice for vocabulary building. One of the many advantages of reading out loud to children is that it develops a sense of story—beginning, middle, and end—a key skill for future reading and comprehension of text. Being read to from many different kinds of books develops children's background knowledge about a variety of topics, especially those that are not a part of their present experience. One successful technique to help children understand what they are hearing is to ask them to "make a picture in your mind" (Bell, 1991). Further explore understanding by asking clarifying and descriptive questions. Encourage the young learner to imagine beyond what they see in the illustration on the page, which is a practice to keep information and words in working memory for rehearsal. An advanced form of questioning provides a story for children to practice listening without pictures. Comprehension of the story requires children to picture the characters, actions, and objects in working memory. What an enlightening experience it is when children reveal what they "saw" and realize their visions can be correct, just as differing responses from their peers can also be right. One child may picture the child in the story with short blond hair, while another may be envisioning the girl to have two long braids. In most instances it does not matter, but what is important is the action in working memory. This mental activity is the beginning of how the child's brain is trained to comprehend text.

Reading aloud to children means enjoying the book together, reflecting on the story, asking open-ended questions, inviting discussions of the meanings of words, and supporting children's curiosity about print. It creates opportunities to introduce children to new words that represent concepts with which they are unfamiliar. Talking together about new words allows children to begin to store an inventory of mental images so that the words have meaning. Additionally, questions of "if–then" and "What else do you think . . . ?" or "How could it be . . . ?" help the child make inferences, a demand to recall and accumulate information from different places in the brain. Extended questioning and the resulting responses are the beginning of what teachers know all too well as higher-level thinking skills. As a reward, research studies tell us that when parents or teachers engage in these activities as they read to children, the children are more likely to be prepared to comprehend what they hear. Whitehurst (2002) calls this practice **dialogic reading**. He argues that you do not learn to play the piano by watching someone play. Why would we think children would learn to read from passively listening to someone else read? A variety of activities have focused on conversation: listening, talking, questioning, responding, and exploring. Beyond knowing what adults can do, the focus turns to the developing list of motor and cognitive activities for children at or about age 4.

#  COGNITIVE DEVELOPMENT

Simple skills for cognitive-sensory imaging are beginning to develop at age 4 and are added to cognitive skill development. Here is an extensive list of the cognitive skills that are emerging for this age, which include attention, visual processing, auditory processing, sensory-cognitive processing, memory skills, and executive function. The cognitive skills have been gathered by the author from a variety of resources in the list of references at the back of the book. Order of development is the author's perception after extensive review of the literature. The listing, as such, is a reference tool for teachers who are working with 4-year-olds, and the developing skills may be provided for parents, as appropriate.

# COGNITIVE SKILLS FOR LEARNING: AGE 4

## Attention

| 4 Years | **Divided Attention**—Can attend to two activities alternatively at the same time (e.g., listening to music and drawing; riding a trike and paying attention to not ride into another child; listening to the teacher's directions and cleaning up from the last task). Can take on another character when playing. Asks to join in play. Comforts others if sad or hurt. Likes to be a helper. Changes behavior based on environment (e.g., library, classroom, playground, church, or grocery store). Says sentences with four or more words. Answers simple questions. Names a few colors. Tells what happens next in a known story. Can follow an auditory story (no pictures) and respond to questions. Maintains attention to the task at hand. |
| --- | --- |

## Visual Processing

| 4–5 Years | **Visual Figure Ground**—Puts attention on the focus item and disengages from disruptors or the visual distractions in the background. Finds specific items in a picture. Finds shapes within the images in a picture. Picks the one that is different from a group of similar items. |
| --- | --- |
| | **Visual Recognition**—Identifies an object regardless of its size or orientation. Can identify one letter, either lower or upper case, in various sizes and angles among other letters. |
| | **Visual Span**—Names objects from memory, such as the number of letters in a word. Learns a phone number or an address by singing or repeating a rhyme. Recites the letters in own name. |
| | **Visual Sequencing**—Recognizes a string of three or four letters in a certain order to name a sight word. Picks out the target word among others. Can put 5 to 10 numbers in sequence. |

## Auditory Processing for Phonological Awareness

| 3–4 Years | **Recites** simple nursery rhymes. |
| --- | --- |
| | **Produces** a rhyming word. When given *bat*, can produce *hat* or *mat*. |
| | **Recognizes** alliteration (e.g., understands beginning sounds for *sun* and *smile* are the same, but *sun* and *man* are different). |

(Continued)

(Continued)

<table>
<tr><td>4–5 Years</td><td>

**Sequencing**—Retains verbal sounds or words in a sequence. Can hold and repeat three to five different words in a sentence. For example: Repeat "I am full" or "The car has four wheels."

**Processing**—Processes verbal directions and follows with action. For example: "Put one hand on your tummy and pat your head with the other" or "Open your book to page 5."

**Identification**—Segments a word into syllables (e.g., *moun-tain, air-plane, eat-ing, hap-py, hap-pi-ness*). Segmentation may be accompanied with clapping.

</td></tr>
</table>

## Sensory-Cognitive Processing

<table>
<tr><td>3–4 Years</td><td>

**Imaging**—Forms a picture in the mind from hearing a word. For example: "See the cat." The child is able to identify what a cat looks like by pointing to a cat in a book. "Where is Daddy?" The child finds Daddy in a picture with other people.

**Predicting**—Determines what will happen next. For example: "The boy let go of the string tied to the balloon." The child responds that the balloon will go up or away to the sky. "Mommy set out a plate of cookies." The child responds that everyone will eat a cookie.

</td></tr>
</table>

## Memory Systems (Sensory, Working, and Long Term)

<table>
<tr><td>3–4 Years</td><td>

**Sensory Input**—Can determine what information received from the senses is important or worthy of attention. (Notice this is an observed ability.)

**Short-Term Memory**—Moves interesting information from sensory memory that is deemed important for further thinking. Note: it is available for recall for about 24 hours and is then dropped unless reviewed or practiced again. Can follow two or more directions.

**Long-Term Memory**—Moves input that has been practiced, rehearsed, and associated with other familiar items to long-term memory and can recall this input at will. For example: "Who are people you see at school?" The child's responses include friends, teacher, teacher's helper, and so on. "What toys do you like at school?" The child's responses include the play kitchen, the trucks, the trikes, the sandbox, and so on. Has memory for songs, rhythm, and body movements. May share "what I like to do at the park" or "at Grandma's house."

</td></tr>
</table>

Executive Function

| 4 Years | **Working Memory**—Has the ability to draw thoughts and combine information from long-term memory into working memory for a purpose. Can recall a parent's phone number and then identify instances when it would be important to know the parent's phone number. Recalls names of siblings with their birth order and tells something special about each person named. Engages in organization of manipulatives, simple organization or charting of tangible objects, and making associations. Answers questions or makes inferences from hearing a story. |
| --- | --- |

Notice memory systems are included in the chart of cognitive learning skills for 4-year-olds. A complete look at children's memory systems is given in the next chapter. Accelerated cognitive skills are converging to support the complex learning for school-aged children.

# CONCLUDING THOUGHTS ABOUT 4-YEAR-OLDS

From the complexity of this chapter, the reader is challenged to comprehend the rapid building of the brain, and the depth of response through behavior and language that can be expected from the average developing 4-year-old. Highlight the word *average*. Notice the warning that at age 4 most children are not prepared to become readers any more than they are ready for complex number concepts. Looking for *same* and *different*, for example, with all the other characteristics listed in the charts of developmental benchmarks and cognitive learning skills, may cause some concern, but parents and teachers can relax. These descriptors are suggestions of what *might* be happening—or what *will* happen—for children. Patience and enjoyment can be experienced as young children increasingly capture skills that advance them to become readers. The next chapter stays with 4-year-olds as they are exposed to classrooms and school routines.

# Reflective Questions

1. What is amazing to you from what you know about 4-year-old children? How can the home environment and school experience encourage their oral language and vocabulary development?

2. What are sensory and working memory systems? How does understanding these systems help to determine activities teachers can plan for learning?

3. What suggestions do you have about screen time for 4-year-olds? How could information be shared from your school to parents to give healthy guidelines for screen time?

4. Play still has an important influence on children's waking hours. What is new to you about play, exploration, and development of peer interactions?

5. Neuroscience provides information about every aspect of the 4- and 5-year-old brain as it becomes ready for reading. The microstructures of the brain comprise the neurons and their networks. What happens to neurons when they become myelinated? What happens to entire systems, like working memory, when all the neurons are myelinated?

6. If you are studying for a university course or in a school group, prepare a presentation or written product that could be shared with parents. How could you use this presentation/product to introduce them to activities and responses from 4-year-olds that represent human brain development?

# CHAPTER 4

# School Routines and Rapid Learning for 4- and 5-Year-Olds

The previous chapter ended with 4-year-olds. This one continues with brain development of both 4- and 5-year-olds. As U.S. states increasingly move toward and initiate universal prekindergarten (UPK) programs, it is important for educators of these young children to understand the cognitive development for a child at this age. Children possess unimaginable possibilities for the maturation of their thinking brains, which impacts how they learn in school and how they conduct social interactions with peers and adults. This chapter contains some of the multitude of research studies that have focused on preschool children and that relate to reading development. While teachers possess professional skills for developing language, providing appropriate environments, and building a fitting amount of play into the schedule, there are some additional areas that can be explored to maximize this unique time in childhood. Realize that the focus is on understanding when children are cognitively ready and able to academically advance.

The continuum of developmental benchmarks, which has progressively grown more complex over the preceding chapters, is complete in this chapter with specifics that can be expected from a 5-year-old. Art as a part of an overall curriculum for preK and UPK is now explored, as are social abilities. How children behave toward one another is another brain thing—one that rests in the limbic system, the innermost part of the human brain. Again, the cognitive attribute of attention, which allows children to learn, remember, and recall, comes to the forefront. The preschool environment for learning initial cognitive skills is a supportive precursor to the hard work of beginning to read.

## LANGUAGE AND SOCIAL DEVELOPMENT FOR 4- AND 5-YEAR-OLDS

People in decision-making positions at school districts, county offices of education, state legislative bodies, and the federal government are advocating for all children to become successful readers. An unknown number of foundations, universities, and other for- and not-for-profit agencies are providing research, articles, websites, podcasts, webinars, seminars, and newsletters for people seeking current best practices for teaching reading. It appears that almost everyone has something to say about the current state of reading for students in the United States and worldwide. Some advocate that children need to be in a school setting earlier than kindergarten, to start learning the complex process of becoming a good reader.

Los Angeles Unified School District, for example, has added close to 5,000 additional children to the already existing transitional kindergarten classes, as 4-year-olds are included in the district's enrollment. The school board unanimously approved this expansion in 2021 in an attempt to narrow the achievement gap for students who have families with limited resources. This action came in advance of the California Department of Education's decision to include 4-year-olds in public school classrooms in the 2025–2026 school year. Teachers request instructional support and materials for these programs, which are not watered-down kindergarten curriculum or slightly enhanced preschool plans. From previous experience, teachers know the decision is not only about including 4-year-olds. Decisions must also be made for a curriculum that builds continuity into the education of children beginning at the early ages of 4 and 5 and shows strong consistency through the elementary years.

Before the train of thought that promotes "earlier is better" is even considered, there is information to the contrary. Some in the current culture essentially are asking for children to be in an academic setting from early morning until middle afternoon, or possibly even later to accommodate working parents.

An academic school setting may compromise young children's need for socialization, play, physical activity, quality individual time with an adult, daydreaming, and many creative pursuits, according to Rae Pica (2015) and a series by Cambridge Neuroscience (2016) called *The Educated Brain*. Due to the high regard for academic pursuits, people in decision-making positions, including parents, are intruding further and further into the time children once had for the "other stuff." The big push is to use preschoolers' time well by engaging them in learning-type activities. The focus for this book, based on current research outcomes *and* a knowledge base of young children's needs while they rapidly develop cognitive learning skills, supports a different perspective.

## NEEDS OF PREK AND KINDERGARTEN CHILDREN

Keep in mind the direction preschool and kindergarten educators were headed prior to the COVID-19 pandemic, as they reacted to and implemented the Common Core State Standards. At that time, some programs treated young children as passive receivers of knowledge. They may have had limited opportunities to investigate, discover, or pose questions, as they were at times prompted to sit and listen. Their success or failure in school may have been determined by their ability to identify and memorize lists of letters, numbers, or colors. Correct answers in many cases were reinforced by external rewards, such as stickers, point charts, or kind words to a parent. Wait—there are fun and engaging ways to teach children, even when they are learning through academic standards, with prereading material. If 4- and 5-year-olds like to play *and* they can learn in playful ways, how can play *not* be one of the ways teachers teach (Strauss, 2014)?

As children returned to school following the COVID-19 pandemic, teachers realized that children needed much more than a "catch-me-up" assessment and a scaled-down curriculum. Everyone had become more sensitized to the emotional aspects resulting from the unprecedented long absence of face-to-face schooling. Likewise, it was acknowledged that some home environments were not the most conducive place to learn for young or older children. Children returned to school with different needs than when they left, and they were up to two years older when they returned. How could school be different, as well?

## PRESCHOOL AND PLAY

There is reason to establish the importance of the term *scientifically based reading instruction* as an application of rigorous, systematic, and objective-based procedures. The purpose of this thrust, according to the science of reading, is to yield usable direction and knowledge for the teaching of reading according to a strong background of research. According to the *Teaching Reading Sourcebook*, third edition (Honig et al., 2018), effective research can be recognized when it adheres to stringent rules. First, it must have peer review, which is evidenced by publication of an independent source for examination and/or criticism. Replication by other researchers/scientists with the same outcome is the second rule. And, finally, there must be consensus among the scientific community that the research conclusions are well founded. Sound scientific observation becomes a reliable source to tell the education world what works and how it works for teaching reading (Honig et al., 2018).

## THE NEED FOR PLAY TIME

Cathryn O'Sullivan (2022), a researcher and teacher trainer, through a webinar by edWeb provided her concerns for preK programs, which include too much large-group instruction, rigid behavioral controls, and too much teacher talking. O'Sullivan encourages "purposeful play" among children, while adults are in the background. When adults provide too much direction, children lose motivation, curiosity, and ability to independently resolve problems. Another support for this viewpoint is provided by Kathy Hirsh-Pasek (2017) as she defines play with four descriptors: (1) Child-directed play is *free play*, which turns into (2) play that becomes *co-opted play* when an adult intervenes. (3) Adult-initiated play that involves children is *guided play*, while anything that is (4) adult initiated and adult directed is *direct instruction*, even if it is dressed up in "play" clothes.

In conclusion, teachers themselves are encouraged to have fun with children by keeping a sense of curiosity and being playful with language. However, they are also encouraged to "back off" and allow time for children to have free range for pure free play. This promotion for playful adult responses does not indicate that play is a free-for-all; there is structure to the environment, there are commonsense expectations, and rules are in place to ensure safety for all children.

Play is definitely a theme to be developed. While the previous play descriptors are reasonable, direct instruction and play have been used with a purpose when children with multiple first languages are placed in a single classroom. The following section gives teachers' responses to this approach, which turned the cycle related earlier from what is generally best for children into teaching language through play activities.

The current increase in numbers of children who are entering early childhood education programs and speaking a language other than English has alerted educators to a critical need. Programs must respond to the best ways to serve the children and their families. A multiple-case study (Baker, 2019) investigated dual-language learners, also referred to in this book as English language learners, for their teaching practices in six communities. The communities were selected for their exemplary teaching. The languages represented by the children were not predominantly English or Spanish. Other languages represented were Mandarin Chinese, Hebrew, Korean, and Armenian.

The findings suggest that superior teachers hold asset-oriented beliefs about bilingualism and diversity. These teachers profess the wealth of resources and richness the young children and their families bring to the community, and to the classroom, through their varied cultures and languages. Teachers in the study welcomed all children with a sense of belonging. Rather than free play described earlier or self-chosen and self-directed play described in the previous chapter, teachers used *guided play* to foster relationships with children of diverse backgrounds. Initially, through guided play, children learned to communicate with each other. Then they were ready to experience independent play. The teachers were observed to scaffold and teach the English language as it was meaningful and supportive of each child's uniquely developing language pathway. Other educational supports included predictable daily routines, incorporating the children's home language whenever possible, and providing picture cues to aid understanding (Baker, 2019).

## INTEGRATE ART

The overarching push for "reading, writing, and arithmetic" in previous years had to be approached with sensitivity. One robust consideration honors childhood benchmark and cognitive development while incorporating the arts (Lynch, 2012). Art education is more than an add-on; rather, it provides simple creative activities that are building blocks for childhood development. Art activities when integrated with a robust curriculum can be a way to playfully achieve many important aspects of learning for preK and kindergarten children. Engaging arts, according to Mary Dell'Erba (2020), senior project manager for Arts Education Partnership, is one of education policy's top priorities, even though it is not identified among trending educational topics. She states:

From funding to literacy development and program quality, we are seeing policymakers' attention shift to early learners. Research demonstrates that arts integration improves literacy and school readiness skills for preschoolers in underserved communities, and exposure to the arts at an early age impacts the development of students' attitudes toward the arts. The arts are also strongly linked to the development of social skills and emotional regulation for early learners. (Dell'Erba, 2020)

A quasi-experimental study conducted in 2010 with three community-based early education settings produced some supportive results. Artists and teachers conducted an arts and literacy program for over 13 months. Four standardized tests were used for pre- and post-assessment. Improvements in alphabet, reading readiness, language and literacy, and overall reading scores were reported (Phillips et al., 2010). A note of caution is that this is one study and may not be cause for general purposes. Teachers and curriculum designers are encouraged to incorporate the arts into a preK or kindergarten program design with the following list of implied improvements.

**Academic Skills:** There is a correlation between art and school achievement. Here is an example for 4- or 5-year-olds. Choose an object from the curriculum, such as an owl. Children can learn a simple way to draw an owl by using and identifying different shapes or by cutting and pasting shapes. The simple owl figure can be drawn a number of times and be used for counting with one-to-one correspondence. The owl can be named and the name written. A sentence can be dictated or written by the child. A story can be read about owls, and children can answer simple questions about owls.

**Language Skills:** Talking about art and making an art object gives children an opportunity to learn colors and shapes, incorporates hand coordination, and even draws attention to sounds. For example, by using multidimensional reclaimed objects (cup, box, egg carton, oatmeal container, straw, string, etc.), children can construct a recognizable or new creation. A follow-up activity may include storytelling among children.

**Motor Skills:** Many of the motions involved in making art, such as holding a paintbrush, cutting with scissors, and scribbling with a crayon, are essential to the growth of fine motor skills in young children. According to developmental milestones defined for this book, 3- to 4-year-olds are ready for and capable of copying simple shapes, drawing a person with three or four body parts, using blunt scissors, and copying some shapes and even letters.

**Cognition:** The experience of making decisions and choices in the course of artistic expression carries over into other parts of life. Inside the child's brain, electrical and chemical connections are activated when children explore, experiment, and try new ideas with available materials.

**Visual Learning:** Sculpting with clay and threading beads on a string develop visual-spatial skills. Drawing of any kind allows children to experiment with shapes and colors as they develop a sensitivity to their creative selves. Imagine the brain work involved for a child to visualize a mother, and then to make lines and shapes on a flat paper that can be labeled a mother. In this case, the child is portraying a three-dimensional person in a flat image on paper.

Creativity for solving problems, seeing beyond something that already exists, is a cognitive skill set required of future scientists, engineers, doctors, architects, and teachers. Experimentation through art activities starting at this early age will encourage skills necessary not only for good readers, but also for readers who can give expanded responses, use their imagination, and be individually confident with their self-expression.

## SOCIAL ABILITIES

Right along with self-expression, the awareness of others is blossoming at ages 4 and 5. Not only are they experiencing more interactions with other children, but at this age children become aware of how other children—and, yes, even adults—feel. A child at this stage of development is able to converse about feelings. *Big conversations with little people* is a favorite topic for Lauren Starnes (2021), an author and chief academic officer of Goddard Schools. She promotes the idea that adults have a tendency to silence or ignore children's questions about unrelated or difficult topics. A difficult topic for conversation may be to talk about breaking school rules. It is easy for a teacher to tell, and equally important to take the time to listen. For instance, when a child consistently disobeys rules, the child can be asked what is known about the rules and what is understood. Talk can be about feelings—the child's and those of others who follow rules. Teachers can identify what new requirements are imposed upon this child when at school, enter into imaginary or true stories about similar situations, or explore role play, always remembering this is a 4-year-old—young and malleable.

Teachers encourage family partnership by sensitively communicating with families through general and caring conversation even without a school situation. Parents are engaged through the use of open-ended questions that elicit an expanded response, other than a simple response, such as "Good." For example, you might ask, "What is new for your family?" or "Has anything changed at home that I would need to know?" and "What does [child's name] talk about after school?" When you have conversations with a child or the child's family, expect the unexpected. Caring conversation leads to understanding a child at school and at home. Caring conversation through role play at school may even satisfy the "following school rules" situation introduced earlier, particularly at this young age.

This discussion continues to acknowledge how preschool systems are different and will continue to differ in the years to come. The following chart presents developmental benchmarks for children as they approach and reach their fifth birthdays and beyond.

## CONTINUUM OF DEVELOPMENTAL BENCHMARKS: AGES 4 AND 5

This section focuses on what can be expected of a child at or near 5 years of age. It concludes the continuum of developmental benchmarks spanning previous chapters. The complete continuum for infancy through age 5 is available in Appendix A.

Developmental Benchmarks: Ages 4 and 5

| 5 Years | Demonstrates one-to-one correspondence of items up to or exceeding 5. Identifies everyday items. Reads words from cards taped to items in the environment: *chair*, *bed*, *orange*, *truck*, *door*, and so on. Begins printing. Draws a picture of a person with at least six parts of the body. Follows three or more steps or directions. May be able to read books with repetitive words. Begins to establish a sight vocabulary of words. Works extensively with sounds of the language and can identify same beginning sounds, middle sounds, and endings. Changes beginning, middle, or ending sounds to make new or nonsense words. Identifies number of phonemes in long or complex words. Begins writing with simple vocabulary and "made-up" spelling. Remembers phone number, address, and birthday by month and day. Plays simple board and card games. Acknowledges and plays with other children. |
| --- | --- |

## WHAT IS KNOWN FROM NEUROSCIENCE?

Have you ever reacted to a situation, maybe a quarrelsome conversation, with a hurtful comment you wish you'd never spoken? Or, have you overreacted to a dangerous situation, like perceiving while you are driving that another car is about to run into you? You may respond by veering off the road before you realize the other car is not going to hit you. Sometimes children react in harmful or hurtful ways if they feel in danger. It may be a perceived danger, and even if a response is not necessary, one child may have already responded with a swing at another child. Let's investigate why these incidents happen, and then look at an adult's suitable response.

## SENSITIVITY TO SELF AND OTHERS RESTS IN THE LIMBIC SYSTEM

The **thalamus**, introduced briefly in Chapter 2, is a receiving station located deep inside the brain. The thalamus is actually in the very center of the **limbic system**. The purpose of this structure is to filter information from the five senses and to consistently search for indications of a dangerous situation. If the input received is not a threat to a person's well-being, the signal is sent forward to an association area in the cerebral cortex for interpretation. However, if a threat to the human body is perceived, an automatic defensive response is activated. One child thinks another child bumped into them to hurt them. Before the thinking part of the brain has a chance to "mull it over," a hard hit back is launched. These responses sometimes occur and are not intended to be spiteful. What might happen at school following this type of incident: quick anger, accusations, miscommunication, confusion, and possibly punishment?

The situation may be the result of the child's protection system sending a signal to the sensitive **amygdala** to activate a response. The amygdala does respond by employing the motor cortex and the body's muscular system. After the amygdala's split-second response, the thinking part of the brain (the frontal lobes) reviews the situation and, most likely in this instance, regrets what happened. It is too late. The problem created must be resolved, whether it is an adult asking for forgiveness for harsh words or a child promptly saying, "I'm sorry."

What is the amygdala that it can create a problem or respond to real danger? It is the "flight or fight" emotional center that overrides the thinking parts of the brain and responds when a threat is perceived. The human brain is designed to protect the body with a rush or surge of energy to increase muscle strength and blood flow from the heart and to activate other chemical-producing structures. Notice the location of the amygdala in

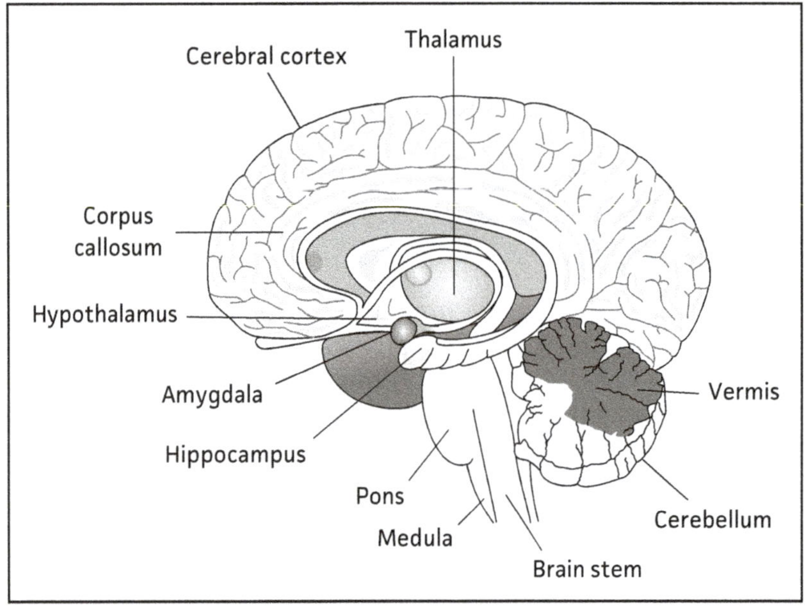


Source: Created by Herb Higashi. Reprinted from Nevills (2011).

Figure 4.1. It is in a prime place to send messages to all parts of the body through the brain stem.

Given this information, how can parents and teachers respond to a physical dispute between young children to avoid argumentative and defensive responses? Teachers generally respond by taking a deep breath, surveying the situation, and asking questions. When children have a chance to think through what happened, they may be able to realize the cause of the problem, along with a solution, even at age 4 or 5. However, if the adults around them, at home or at school, constantly take the lead to analyze the situation, children may become discouraged and lose or give up their willingness to respond sensibly.

## INNER BRAIN HAPPINESS

In normal circumstances, the thalamus is a pass-through station as it sends information to the appropriate areas of the brain for interpretation. It is also the pleasure center of the brain. Dopamine, a neurotransmitter, is produced during pleasurable experiences. The neurotransmitters invade the thalamus, and a person has a sense of pleasure and a desire to maintain the happy feeling.

What school situations give a 4- or 5-year-old pleasure—
those situations that cause them to experience a "dopamine
rush"? There are many. School is the place "where good things
happen." Children want to feel good, safe, and happy. Most
likely, there are many times when a child feels exceedingly
happy to be at school.

## MEMORY SYSTEMS

In Chapter 3, the system for sensory memory was explored.
Important information is passed from sensory memory to
**working memory** for practice and rehearsal. For a 4-year-old,
long-term memory, which is defined in Chapter 7, has also
developed to be useful for learning tasks at school. Children
begin to remember events and possess the ability to talk
about a past event. At very young ages, years 1 to about 3, all
three memory systems, sensory memory, working memory,
and long-term memory are in place. A very young child, 2 and
under, can feel and record in long-term memory loving, caring
actions of parents and others. Hurtful or scary times are also
input into memory. However, since language at this age is
underdeveloped, the youngster does not have a way to record
and later be able to recall these feelings with language. Most
children start to retell or recall important events between ages
4 and 6.

### WHAT IS WORTHY OF ATTENTION?

The memory systems of a 4- to 6-year-old have developed a
filtering process powered by **inhibitory neurons**. The human
brain has both unconscious and conscious ways to delete
sensory input that is unimportant or unwanted. A child in an
intensive play activity may not hear the bell indicating that
recess is over, or may even choose to ignore the sound of a
parent calling to come for lunch. Unconscious filtering happens
through specially assigned neurons, inhibitory neurons, in the
thalamus that are designed to mask and stop the signals from
being recognized. Sensations are blocked, and the thalamus
does not respond. Remember, much information received in
sensory memory is lost as if it never happened: a cough, the
sound of the heating system running, a slight discomfort of
being hungry, or the feel of one's shoes. Conscious filtering
happens if something is important enough to receive full attention: a phone ringing, a growling stomach, or feeling cold and
uncomfortable, for example, any one of which might be recognized. In this instance, the child has advanced to give a slight
response to unimportant stimuli, but does not change focus
from the situation that demands attention. The child then

decides if the annoying sensation is worthy enough to interrupt interest for the task at hand.

## WORKING MEMORY

The ability to stay engaged with an activity is an indication that a child in the age range of 4 to 6 years is ready for more advanced learning. Teachers working with these children can expect to hold the attention of their students for time periods of up to 10 minutes. Age-appropriate activities motivate children to attend. Sometimes the child may consciously want to think about the activity or information and choose to concentrate long enough to remember and manipulate it in working memory, or even move the learning or concept into memory for the long term. Concentration involves practice and rehearsal of the word, thought, or concept.

Think about the difference between children who eagerly respond to a question with several sentences and children who respond, "I don't know." The eager response indicates a child

**FIGURE 4.2** ● During activities of rehearsal and practice in the working memory, information may stay for 10 to 30 seconds, or as long as 24 hours, if it is reinforced with connection to the frontal lobes.

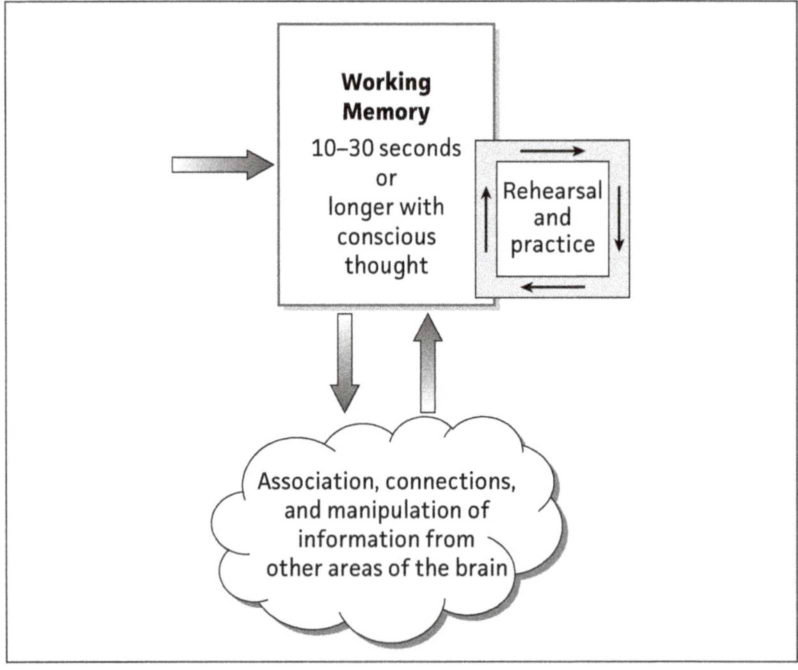


**Source:** Created by Herb Higashi. Reprinted from Nevills (2011).

has begun to store information in long-term memory, and is able to retrieve the information appropriate to the question. The "don't know" response may be an indication that the child is still in the developmental stages of moving information from the working memory system, or may be experiencing difficulty in understanding the question.

Notice the term **hippocampus** in Figure 4.1. The hippocampus is a pair of structures located under the surface of the temporal lobe and at the underside of the limbic system. It is designed to temporarily hold information. If the information is interesting and thought about or discussed, it may be retained in working memory for recall (see Figure 4.2, which further develops the presentation of sensory memory in Figure 3.2). If enough rehearsal, remembering, and recall takes place, the information or concepts may be sent by neuron signals to store the information in other parts of the brain, particularly in the frontal lobes, for long-term memory. Teachers who consider the amount of practice that is needed for most children to move ideas, concepts, and information out of working memory into long-term memory can plan instructional practices to meet the needs of the human brain to accomplish this feat.

Teachers who understand memory systems use reinforcement through association and manipulations to help children hold information in working memory for up to 24 hours. The more repetitions there are, the more likely words, ideas, and concepts will be remembered for an even longer time. Teachers help children remember important parts of the school day when they review the day's events prior to dismissal.

## WHAT HAPPENED TODAY AT SCHOOL?

- What do you remember from our calendar time?
- What letters did we learn today? Or, what are some words we talked about?
- What can you tell me about the book we read?
- What is a "must do" and a "may do" activity that you did in class?
- Who did you play with today, and what did you play?
- What would you like to tell your family about school today?

An end-of-the-school-day *planned discussion time* helps children retain important learning. First thing the next school day, *recall and memory time* can reinforce yesterday's activities and learning tasks while supporting children to access memory systems. Conversation may sound like this:



## REMEMBERING YESTERDAY

1.  What new words do you remember from yesterday? (It is always appropriate to give a hint or prompt.) What does the word mean? Everyone repeat the word and tell your partner what it means.

2.  We read a story together. What was it about? Tell one or two things you liked (or learned) from the story to your group of three.

3.  What and with whom did you play at recess yesterday? What did you like about the play time?

4.  What was the weather like yesterday? What is it like today? Is it different or the same? When weather is like it is today, what do you like to do after school?

Connections activated in the brain are reinforced for concepts or items that are important to remember and recall, and also for those things that give working memory an opportunity to practice. On the other side of remembering everything, unconsciously or consciously, the young child's brain filters information to protect itself from overload. Consciously, the child may be thinking, "I don't care about the weather; it doesn't matter to me." In this case, the conversation about weather may not receive much attention. Or, unconsciously, the brain may not have neural systems for contemplation about the weather. The weather information may be unconsciously dropped as if the conversation never happened. Filtering systems protect children from overloading their brains with what appears to them to be minutia at this stage of memory development. Adults can intentionally help children know what is important to remember by review, reinforcement, repetition, and recall of preschool curriculum.

## WHAT CAN TEACHERS, PARENTS, AND CAREGIVERS DO?

Some call the new programs for 4-year-olds "universal preschool." Others look at this change as simply providing preschool for all 4-year-olds. Whatever a state or district names their program, it is different from what we have previously called preschool, and it most likely is not intended to be an academic prekindergarten. Certainly, the power behind the extensive research that the science of reading represents is impudence enough for universal preK. One study pointed to improvements in behavior and attendance for children who participated in preschool programs. Moderate gains in academics were not substantial enough to warrant the programs, however (Nold et al., 2021).

This book so far has provided an extensive look at brain development and its complexities during the first five years of a child's life. No amount of teaching or exposure to academics can hurry the process of brain development. A child will learn as a child is ready to learn. Simply stated, children need to be cognitively ready emotionally and developmentally for explicit reading instruction. For preK programs, beginning reading skills—phonemes, phonology, high-frequency or sight words, and alphabet letter names—are appropriate. Next is a consideration of classrooms or places to house the new emerging universal preK. What type of space is needed? And, how can brain development for a child of this age be reinforced?

## CLASSROOM ENVIRONMENT: PRESCHOOL

Assuming there is an empty classroom that needs to be set up for 4-year-olds, what could it look like? How can it be inclusive by recognizing each young learner's unique needs? What must it contain to acknowledge the state standards that define learning for children at this age? How can the room accommodate the number of children in attendance and provide space to move around, choose from a variety of options and activities, and provide accommodations for the whole group, as needed? Are bathroom and washing facilities available? Is there a place or cubby for each child to call their own? These are some of the questions educators can answer to prepare for 4-year-olds in a private or public school setting.

Four-year-olds need to feel safe away from their home, whether they are monolingual English speaking or bringing the rich experience of learning from other cultures and languages. They are learning how to get along with others. School-type rules are new and might be challenged. Youngsters need an environment that is stimulating, but not too much. It is suggested to add to a rather simple environment at the opening of the school year, rather than to overwhelm a child with an overly stimulating classroom all at once.

Children are developing connections in memory systems designed to remember, and remembering takes repetitions and practice from focused areas. Objects on the precious wall space need to be purposeful. When the children arrive, they find comfort as they are introduced to areas of the room, one by one, explaining and inviting the children to explore, enjoy, and appreciate. Some use the terms *must do* for activities children must complete during a day and *may do* for activities that are optional or free choice. It's okay to announce, for example, the puzzle area is closed today as the area is made over with new and different puzzles. A 4-year-old's brain learns slowly with repetitions and lots of active engagement.

## DEVELOPING HABITS OF MINDFULNESS

Developing systems for remembering is a pretty tall order for a young child. In addition to working with academic-type activities, the next area of focus is the child's ability to attend and pay attention through what are identified as priming skills. Development of these mind-training, habits-of-mind skills greatly enhances the possibility that cognitive skills can progress as expected.

### PRIMING SKILLS FOR LEARNING TO LEARN

Priming skills—*attention, concentration, memory,* and *organization*—are often assumed to be "ready for action" in school-age children. Although these skills were introduced with a discussion of mindfulness in Chapter 1, here is a deeper look at their cognitive development. For many children in the early grades, and some in later grades, these skills are not fully developed.

### PRIMING SKILL: ATTENTION

Since children's brains are designed to automatically filter incoming stimuli, they may need prompts to attend specifically to a prereading task. The brain is challenged to perceive visual symbols, interpret them, and determine if they are identifiable with letters or sight words that are already known. The complexities of maintaining attention to identify and learn sounds don't automatically happen for most children without practice. Teachers are familiar with children's behavior of dropping their pencil, poking another child, or making a noise to distract others when they lose ability to attend. Children are most successful when they learn in an environment that invites curiosity for the tasks at hand.

### Attending to Tasks

It is accepted that children receive a multitude of sensory input from the classroom environment, and some 5- and 6-year-olds need help to develop the kind of selective attention that school demands. There are external noises—children moving, papers shuffling, a cough, a truck driving by outside—and there are internal signals from the child's own body indicating hunger, thirst, or a feeling of being too hot or cold. Learning to read demands that attention be paid to specific sensory input, such as a teacher's signal or a written prompt, while ignoring irrelevant sensory information. Teachers can provide various prompts for young learners to develop the habit of focusing on relevant instructional stimuli.

## Sustained Focus

Sustained focus in a lesson on sound–symbol relationships might last a tightly directed 10 to 15 minutes. Highly motivating, hands-on activities such as writing letters in a tray of sand or using colored markers on wipe-off boards may sustain children's focus longer. In addition to varying the length of instructional periods, kindergarten and first-grade teachers often schedule "brain breaks" with quiet time, large motor activities, songs, or games to rejuvenate mental energy.

Teachers know that giving breaks during instructional times results in increased learning. But why does it happen? During times when children pay intense attention and concentrate, the neural systems employed work hard and demand brain fuel (oxygen and glucose) in huge quantities. Eventually, increased blood flow and the neuron-firing systems get fatigued. Children will disengage when the work gets too tough.

Indeed, mind wandering is so commonly acknowledged among young children, and even among adults, that a number of researchers decided to study it. Numerous reports on the wandering attributes of the adult brain indicate wandering thoughts occur 30% to 40% of the time and focus on life's problems or things that need to be done (Ritter, 2007). While this information is not available for children, an instructional plan to regularly change activities is a smart plan. Not only do student behaviors indicate a readiness to refocus, but the added benefit is that neural connections quiet down and learning can be consolidated.

## Getting Set to Listen

Teachers use varying attention-focusing strategies for classroom management to help children develop a habit for following directions and switching tasks. Prompts may be specific directions, such as "Stop what you are doing," "Put down whatever is in your hands," "Look at me," or "Return to your desks." In each case, a finite amount of time is allowed for children to transition from an active task and to be ready to listen. A signal, such as the teacher raising fingers one at a time with the expectation that children will give full attention by the time all fingers and the thumb are visible, reinforces required behaviors.

In the same way, teachers can prepare students to pay attention to their peers with attending and listening behavior. In the classroom, the key points for active listening can be identified, posted, and practiced. The rules might read like this and be accompanied with a picture:

1. One person talks.
2. Look at the person.
3. Listen to and imagine what is said.
4. Wait to raise your hand.

Most teachers automatically use prompts that demand attention from their class. Teachers who prepare children for transition activities—to get ready to work, to listen, to go outside, or to clean up—model expectations and help the children to disengage from one activity and prepare for the next.

## PRIMING SKILL: CONCENTRATION

A child focusing on and engaging with incoming stimuli for an extended period characterizes concentration. The child enters a state of consideration, understanding, or remembering. The invitation for students to engage in learning can be staged with nontraditional strategies, such as strengthening sensory stimuli with vivid pictures, colorful labels, soft or loud verbal input, missing words to be filled in, or "through" rhythm or rhyme.

What about a child who cannot hold objects, letters, or words in working memory at the level of classroom peers? A helpful response is to work independently with the child to identify and picture attributes of the items to be remembered. Start with two words. Talk about the first word—*watermelon*. Ask questions: "What does a watermelon look like? What colors do you see when you cut it open? Do you like to eat watermelon? What is the word you will remember?" The adult may have the child repeat each question and then give the answer. Then follow with the second word that needs to be remembered. Continue this and other practice processes to extend the number of words that are expected to be remembered.

A skill deficit for concentration is closely related to the next topic, memory.

## PRIMING SKILL: MEMORY

Concentration-extending activities occur within normal classroom routines; for instance, the teacher gives directions and then pauses, forcing children to practice and rehearse in working memory how they will execute the command. One example is for the teacher to say, "When I say 'ready,' you can number your paper from 1 to 5." Or the teacher might say, "Pass your paper to the front of the room when I hold up both hands." A more difficult example is to prompt, "Hold these words in your mind until I say go; then tell them to your partner" or, for older children, "Write the words on your paper in the same order." This direction in its simplest form provides word clusters, such as four hamburger toppings (*ketchup, relish, mustard, tomatoes*), types of zoo animals (*tiger, elephant, giraffe, anteater*), or weather patterns (*rainy, sunny, cold, warm*). The strategy increases in intensity when the words do not cluster or chunk together around a common theme, such as *recess, bananas, shoes,* and *dog.* And as would be anticipated, increasing the number of words, items, directions, or numbers will increase the level of practice and rehearsal needed to hold the items in working conscious memory.

Purposeful simulations of distracting conditions provide powerful cognitive preparation for classroom environments during the early school years and beyond. Classroom environments with large- and small-group activities, learning centers, and individual work areas help children learn to concentrate on tasks assigned to them as individuals.

Parents who wish to help children develop memory skills can apply these examples at home by giving two directions that need to be done in sequence. For example, "Put on your shoes and then get in the car" or "Finish your cereal, put your dish in the sink, and then get dressed for school." Modification of holding a series of words could be "Listen carefully and remember these words [name related words or a sentence] and go tell them to your father."

## PRIMING SKILL: ORGANIZATION

Often, children need prompts to organize their thinking. The priming skill of organization prepares emergent readers to structure thinking into big ideas, categorizes information into meaningful networks, and provides connections to previously stored information.

## At School

At school, teachers can use mind-mapping strategies that reflect the way the brain sorts information into categories (represented by neural networks) and ultimately helps students manipulate and recall the information. Try KWL (Know, Want to know, and Learned) if students are studying arachnids, for example. They might start with spiders as one type of arachnid. To use a mind-mapping strategy, the teacher writes *spider* in the middle of the whiteboard. Students provide information from previous experience with spiders. If the teacher perceives student experience with the topic is limited, actual spiders or pictures of spiders can be introduced to establish an initial knowledge base. This information is organized under the heading "What We *Know*." Then children are asked what questions they have about spiders. The teacher records their responses under the heading of "What We *Want* to Know." This technique strengthens existing neural networks and develops new connections to be used for storage of new information about spiders. Teachers check for students' previous knowledge and experience, and correct misconceptions (e.g., that spiders are insects). It also provides direction for the continued study of spiders and other arachnids. The final step to this sequence is to chart "What We *Learned*." An added benefit to KWL happens when teachers prompt children to decide how they will remember what they learned. Sample or prompted responses could be to draw a picture, tell someone else, or dictate what they want to remember. The "What We Learned" chart is posted for viewing, reviewing, remembering, and sharing. The last chart may be available for review for several months or more.

## At School and Home

Through experiences such as mind mapping, children put conscious effort toward ordered thinking and develop self-confidence for the next reading tasks. In addition to needing structured prompts to help organize their thinking, children often need help to organize their materials and physical workspace. At home, parents can encourage students to take an initial look *through an entire school homework assignment* before they begin to work. This practice allows them to collect the materials they need and to ask questions before they begin their work. Children find it easier to be organized when they have a special place to work. Families who provide a work area for young children with good light, tools for writing, and space to complete school assignments encourage good habits for more difficult tasks in following years.

Children need to know before they start their work at school or at home how they will know that they are finished, and what to do when the task is done. Self-prompted questions might be "What will my work look like when I am finished?" "Where do I put the completed work?" "What happens for cleanup?" or "Where are school materials kept when they are not being used?" Students can learn internal dialogue when they are young as a way to organize their task, assess what materials are necessary, direct their thinking toward a work strategy, and be clear about what to do when they complete the assignment.

## CONCLUDING THOUGHTS ABOUT ROUTINES AND SCHOOL FOR 4- AND 5-YEAR-OLDS

Preschool at age 4 and kindergarten possibly at age 5 mark the beginning of a core transition in the life of young learners. Children arrive at school with tremendous variation in their maturity and prereading foundations. Despite a significant range of experiences, including exposure to print, variation in vocabulary, primary language, understanding of story structure, and other foundational prereading skills, all children are expected to transition from prereaders to beginning readers during their first two years in a formal classroom.

What happens in the brains of these 4-, 5-, and 6-year-old children during the years they are learning to read? Neuroscientists have shown that different structures of the brain are activated as children learn and practice new skills they will need in a literate world. Massive amounts of brain development occur in the preschool years, as neurons (nerve cells) in the brain continue the process of making connections and forming huge networks to store and assimilate the information and concepts the child is learning.

Priming skills (attention, concentration, memory, and organization) are important for cognitive development, aided by teacher direction and parent activities. Children who lag behind in these skills need to be identified and supported. Although the chart of cognitive learning skills was not advanced in this chapter, it will continue.

Four language pathways are identified in the next chapter. Understanding the language abilities of 4- and 5-year-olds validates the oral language pathways for listening and speaking. The reading pathway has two variations: one for *reading out loud* and a second for *reading silently with comprehension*. Although it has been stated that some children appear to learn to read through exposure—and they probably do—most other children learn to read through explicit, direct instruction. Decoding (phonemic awareness, phonological processing, phonics, word attack skills, and spelling), reading comprehension (vocabulary, reading with understanding, literary responses, and analysis), and reading fluency (silent and oral reading with prosody), discussed in Chapters 6, 7, and 8, respectively, are yet to be developed.

The transition from the relatively fun and playful preschool environment will take a serious turn as children are prepared in kindergarten for the thoughtful work that must be undertaken to become readers.

# Reflective Questions

1. What are your ideas about play activities that can be incorporated into the school day?

2. Attention and concentration are identified as skills students need to become readers. Describe some brain-compatible classroom prompts and activities to strengthen attending and concentration abilities. Consider and explain how parents can be encouraged with home activities to develop paying attention.

3. If you are reading this book for a university course or as part of a study group, make a practical list of strategies teachers or parents can use to help children organize information and concepts into memory networks. Share and expand your ideas with other group members.

4. How can art be validated for teaching 4-year-olds? Give examples that are in addition to those in this chapter.

5. What can you say about caring conversations with children and families? Why are questions so important for a child's sociability?

6. Explain the advantages and disadvantages of the prompt responses from the amygdala, located in the limbic system, to any emotional situation in a child's life. How can understanding this system be helpful to anyone engaged with children in a school, playground, or home setting?

**7.** How do you describe practice and rehearsal strategies according to the way the brain wires itself to learn?

**8.** How are classroom and learning practices for 4-year-olds different from classrooms designed specifically for 3- or 5-year-olds?

# CHAPTER 5

# Preparing for Reading at Ages 4–6

Educators and researchers have been grappling over how to teach children to become proficient readers for decades. Publishers have raced to develop new materials each time there is a general shift to a new set of standards. The task to review research and select instructional programs that are research-based according to the science of reading can be prodigious. Current availability of resources pursues a national and international audience. There is no lack of worthy information. To determine where to expend energy and resources is of certain importance for teachers, school districts, and counties, as well as state education departments. Each search for one item of importance to reading education is exponentially expanded as other sources appear due to the advancement of computer searches.

Vast amounts of the information about materials and methods for teaching reading are available through podcasts, webinars, and seminars, and also from websites sponsored by universities, organizations, publishers, networks, and governmental agencies. All the sources are specifically aimed at the teaching public. Then comes the question: How can educators and district decision makers wade through the vast information available as they decide what materials will be effective and direct how to teach reading?

*Building the Young Reader's Brain* provides significant information that may be missing to appropriately respond to the dilemma that surrounds the teaching of reading. There is not a simple answer. Children learn through functions of the brain. All people involved with education benefit when answers to the following questions are understood. How does learning result from neurons connecting? How are systems for learning and memory developed so children can recognize, remember, recall, and write words and phrases? How do connections happen among the brain's structures for specific tasks including reading? And, what understanding does neuroscience bring to support instructional methods and practices for teaching young children to read? Answers to these questions and others from Chapter 1, along with reflective questions at the end of each chapter, provide the missing pieces for how to teach reading. The pieces of information that come from understanding how the brain develops, organizes, learns, and remembers provide what is needed.

This chapter leads the reader to complete the visual view through words and figures of what is emerging in the brain to prepare for reading. The heavy work going on in the child's brain is explained. The brain pathway for oral language (an auditory function) is changed to become also a pathway for reading (a visual process) both silently and out loud.

Previous chapters have had sections specifically for *What Is Known From Neuroscience?* and *What Can Teachers, Parents, and Caregivers Do?* This chapter deviates from that format. *The main thrust of this chapter is to delve into teaching practices that coerce the pathway the brain uses for oral language to become a pathway for reading.* It is laden with ways for teaching beginning reading that are specifically designed to prepare students' brains to connect and establish a strong foundation to begin reading. Readers of this book will find teaching activities for phonological processing, print awareness, and writing development. Powerful information about pathways in the brain using the cognitive processes for visual, auditory, and sensory input are provided in the chart of cognitive skills. This is a must-read—and potentially a must-*reread*—chapter.

## READING COMPETENCY: AN EXPECTANCY

One particularly good find for those who seek information about effective teaching programs is from a partnership of the Institute of Education Sciences (IES) within the U.S. Department of Education, established in 2002. The website provided by this organization is titled What Works Clearinghouse (https://ies.ed.gov/ncee/wwc). A subtopic, *What Works in Literacy*, reviews reading curricula for scientific efficacy of the program and effectiveness ratings of literacy components (communication, comprehension, literacy achievement, phonological processing, reading fluency, and writing achievement). Each reading program is identified by grade level. Importantly, the ratings adhere to the Common Core State Standards (see Common Core State Standards Initiative, 2010) and the National Reading Panel's (2000) report, which identified five pillars for teaching reading. Another resource is EdReports (www.edreports.org). This organization strives to support educational curriculum, program, and material selection that demonstrates high-quality instructional materials. These are two of many resources that provide support for district personnel and educators as they seek curriculum materials for teaching reading to all the varied needs that are represented in a single classroom. *The pillars of reading and the curriculum selected with the science of reading in mind provide the "what" used to teach students to read.* This book can be differentiated from others written with a focus on explicit research-based reading, as it provides promising practices gathered from neurology. *With neurological reports and findings infused into the formula for teaching reading, an enhanced understanding of the human brain provides the "how" and "why" students learn to read.*

## ORAL LANGUAGE DEVELOPMENT

Somewhere near the age of 4, the oral language pathway is in place. As the reader may recall from Chapter 2, Broca's area, responsible for producing comprehensible speech, and Wernicke's area, the lexicon or dictionary of meaningful words, are functional for most children in this age group. These areas of the brain allow for a snowball expansion of vocabulary. Many sources address the number of words children know at different ages, and they all vary. Some report receptive vocabulary, and others state numbers that represent speaking vocabulary. Using broad terms, the numbers provided here are a cumulative "estimate" to give readers a general target. The average **receptive vocabulary** for 3-year-olds is about 900 words, 5-year-olds know between 3,000 and 8,000 words (notice the huge range), and one year later the number of words known, for the average 6-year-old, is around 13,000. Realize the number of words understood during listening is much larger than the expressive vocabulary a child uses when speaking. It is no small wonder how a child beyond toddler age can learn linguistically at such a geometric rate.

Children arrive at preschool and kindergarten with an ability to speak without any formal teaching. Why is reading different? The exclusive answer is—*there is no natural pathway among*

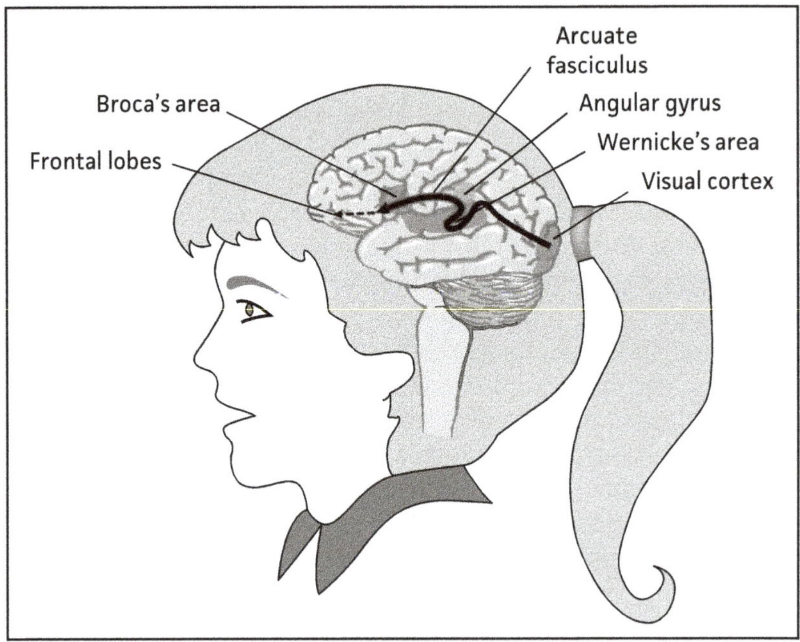


**Source:** Reprinted from Nevills & Wolfe (2009).

*the structures of the human brain designed to deal with language expressed with written symbols.* There is a predesigned pathway for children to hear speech sounds, distinguish the uniqueness of sounds, and slowly be able to replicate the sounds heard in their environment. Breaking the code for the language of listening and speaking requires manipulation of all forms of words and sentences, and includes the intricacies of intonation. To speak, the brain must follow a complex process to select words, choose their order, form a phrase or sentence, and activate sounds for words. Sound complex? Yes, it is. Once that code is "broken" or deciphered, children understand and engage in speaking. Figure 5.1 presents the pathway under development for reading, in which visual stimuli received from the eyes are swiftly escorted to the back of the brain. Most terms represented have been defined in Chapter 2. The glossary at the back of the book can be accessed, as needed. The new structures are the arcuate fasciculus and the angular gyrus, both defined as follows.

The **arcuate fasciculus** is a band of neural fibers that connects Wernicke's area with Broca's area. Located at the junction of the occipital, parietal, and temporal lobes, the **angular gyrus** is perfectly situated to be a bridge between the visual **word recognition** system and the rest of the language processing system.

It is near Heschl's gyrus, which is a part of the oral language pathway. The letters of written words appear to be translated in the angular gyrus into the sounds of spoken language, or phonemes, discussed later in this chapter. This function of hearing sounds without letters attached occurs naturally for oral language, but it is necessary for the angular gyrus to become a step in the reading pathway. Sounds must be practiced, repeated, reorganized, and literally "played with." These activities (recognized as phonemic awareness and phonological processing, included in the discussion on phonemes) stimulate the angular gyrus to become an accepted detour in the well-established oral language path.

Here is a missing link. The detour to the angular gyrus is an essential addition to the oral language pathway. That addition must be taken for fluent reading and eventually for reading with comprehension. *Neuroscience research and imaging techniques have proven what educational studies (the science of reading) have touted. Phonemes and phonological activities stimulate the angular gyrus to become a common part of the previously built automatic oral language pathway for reading to be successful.* While it can be argued that some children will make this detour without any special instruction, most children do not! Hence, the educational teaching practices include playing with phonemes and other phonological processes. Phonological processes, explained later in this chapter, include phoneme segmentation and substitutions, syllable counting, letter symbols and sounds, decoding, and spelling. *Missing any portion of these instructional processes puts many a young child at risk of reading failure.* Teachers approach this serious business of teaching reading, and all the while they are encouraged to maintain a playful, curious approach to their teaching. That requirement is a tall order.

A danger exists of overstating the significance of a given cortical area for a particular function, as it may be that each area is involved in many more than one language function (Kristanto et al., 2020). The brain's language areas are not neat components with clearly defined borders. The areas of the brain associated with language and reading—the reception, comprehension, processing, and production of language—continue to be studied. As stated, it is difficult to map the detailed functions of the language system directly onto the brain's complex anatomical structures. Scientists have, however, produced a tentative architecture of the brain's language pathways that has fairly accurate validity, and is useful in this quest to understand what goes on in the brain when used to process both oral language and reading.

## WHY A READING PATHWAY?

The practice needed to become a reader and build a reading pathway begins in the early years through listening and talking. As previously emphasized, storytelling, reading nursery rhymes, drawing out and elongating words, and singing all prepare the child's brain for what needs to happen to read. The practices must be intensified and expanded through conversation for most readers in prekindergarten, transitional kindergarten, or kindergarten with the added component of playing with words and their smallest utterances, phonemes. At this stage of language development, exposure to print, identifying letters by their names and different fonts (not associations with sounds), and recognition of simple sight words are an important part of the curriculum.

## BASICS: FROM SLOW TO GO READING

The silent reading pathway makes some dramatic requirements of a child's young brain. The auditory cortex, first defined in Chapter 2, is called upon to start the process for listening and speaking, but now the input is from the eyes—*a visual process*—as seen in Figure 5.2. Sensory input is directed to the thalamus

**FIGURE 5.2** ● Flow chart of the silent reading pathway.

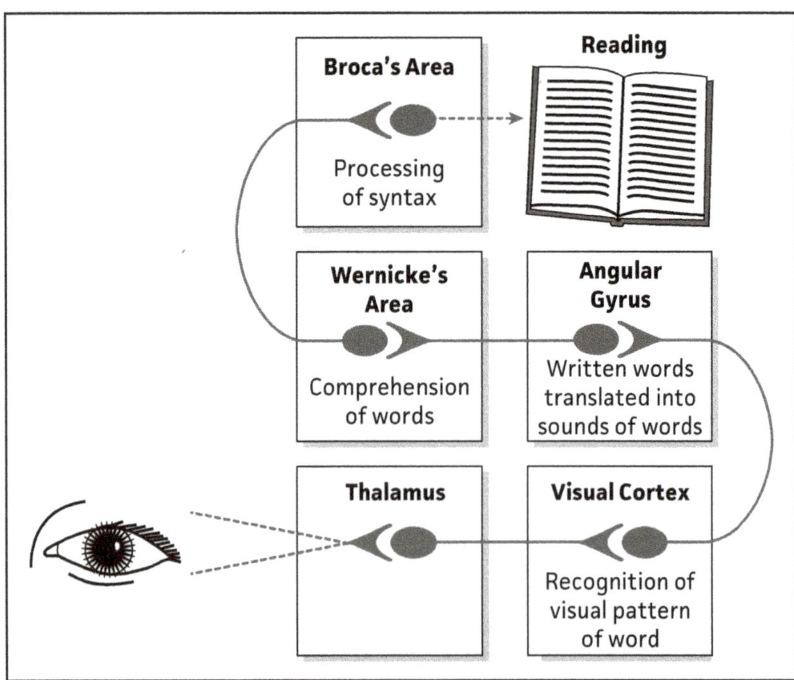


**Source:** Reprinted from Nevills & Wolfe (2009).

and is released when no threat or danger is perceived. The thalamus directs the input back to the visual cortex, specifically the visual association areas. This area of the brain was introduced in Chapter 2 as one of the lobes of the cerebral cortex. Now the lobe is specifically looked at for its association between a visual pattern and the word that is represented. The brain follows the sequence that happens first slowly, but later instantaneously as the reading pathway is complete.

The human visual system is one of the most studied and best understood areas of the brain. Visual information is contained in the light reflected from objects. As light rays enter the eyes, they are transduced, or changed into electrical impulses, and are sent from the eyes through the optic nerves to the thalamus to relay the information to the primary visual cortex located in the occipital lobes, defined in Chapter 2. The visual cortex recognizes the visual pattern of a word as an already existing visual feature. The brain has adapted the **visual memory** system to allow it to process letter strings, as well as other visual features. Even though the features of the word have been extracted, the string of letters has not yet been perceived as a word.

### THE ORAL READING PATHWAY: ONE MORE THING

It is easy to refer to Figure 5.2 and visually add the motor cortex for production of speech when a child is reading out loud. This very slight alteration to the figure makes a significant difference for a child to produce the sounds for words. It takes practice and more practice to read out loud. The pathway increases with intensity as reading out loud gains the expectation that the child will also be able to comprehend. More information on the comprehension aspect of reading is provided in Chapter 8.

## TEACHING PRACTICES TO DEVELOP THE READING PATHWAY

Research before 2000 validates over and over the importance of phonemic awareness for future reading success. Consensus is that speech is composed of individual sounds, or **phonemes**, which are essential for learning to read. There are 26 letters in the alphabet of the English language and 44 phonemes, the smallest unit of sound in spoken language. Included are consonant sounds, digraphs, short and long vowel sounds, diphthongs, and *r*-controlled vowels. Recent studies validate that students with reading disabilities often lack the ability to hear and manipulate phonemes, and this applies even to children who have average or above-average intelligence. Adequate research included in the 2000 report from the National Reading

Panel, and now considered to direct the science of reading, confirms that preschool children benefit from age-appropriate, explicit instruction in areas of phonemic and phonological processing. This instructional practice remediates and overcomes reading difficulties *before they materialize.* It is known that playing with sounds actually forces the brain to access all the brain structures needed, including the angular gyrus, for the brain's reading pathway.

## PHONEMIC AWARENESS AS A PART OF PHONOLOGICAL PROCESSING

A distinction exists between the terms *phonemic awareness* and *phonological processing.* As stated, **phonemic awareness** is the understanding that spoken language is made up of identifiable units or sounds and the ability to break words into their tiniest parts. **Phonological processing** is a broader umbrella term that includes phoneme activities, such as counting the number of phonemes in a word, blending phonemes, or distinguishing phonemes for onsets and rimes. An integral part of learning to read through **orthographic mapping**—a process the child's brain uses to permanently store words in long-term declarative memory, available for rote recall—phonological activities include perception, recall, and production of language at all levels of the speech–sound system. While phonological activities focus solely on sound, when letters for sounds are introduced, the activity is identified as *phonics.* **Phonics** explores the connection between spoken sounds and words and the letters that identify them.

### PHONEMIC AWARENESS EXAMPLE: TEACHING ALLITERATION AND RHYMING

The simplest or most basic level of phonemic awareness, beginnings and endings, which may be referred to as **onsets** and **rimes,** involves not much more than being able to hear and recognize the smallest sounds of words. For the onset, **alliteration** means to identify similar beginning sounds, and alliteration activities can begin simply. Playing with their friends' names—*Happy Henry* or *Marvelous Megan*—or tongue twisters—*Peter Piper picked a peck of pickled peppers*—are fun ways to introduce 4-year-olds to alliteration and increase their ability to distinguish between similar beginning phonemes.

For the rime, or the ending sound of a word, you may recall from Chapter 2 that teaching nursery rhymes is one of the easiest and most effective ways to increase a child's ability to hear the similar sounds—in this case the similar *ending* sounds—of rhyming words. Recall also that the pattern of words in a rhyme or song appear to be stored in implicit or unconscious memory, and are easily brought to conscious memory as a whole thought or chunk. Think about the endings to the phrases "'Hey diddle diddle the cat and the _________" or "Jack and Jill went up the ___________." The unconscious part of the brain remembers the rest of the phrases without conscious processing.

One natural and spontaneous way to work with children on alliteration and rhymes is to find literature that deals playfully with speech sounds such as the forever-loved Dr. Seuss books—for example, *There's a Wocket in My Pocket!* (Dr. Seuss, 1974)—or Jane Yolen and Mark Teague's (2000) *How Do Dinosaurs Say Good Night?* Classics, well known by teachers, include *There Was an Old Lady Who Swallowed a Fly* (Nursery Rhymes, 2022); *Brown Bear, Brown Bear, What Do You See?* (Martin & Carle, 1967); and the *Five Little Monkeys* series of books by Eileen Cristelow (2010). Teaching strategies to use these books with children include the following:

## STRATEGIES FOR READING OUT LOUD TO CHILDREN

1. Read and reread the stories.

2. Comment on how the language uses beginning sounds or rhymes or repetitions.

3. Stop when reading and encourage children to predict what word or words would fit next.

4. Elicit responses to questions about sound patterns, such as asking about the sound heard at the beginning of the words for alliteration.

5. Expand language patterns by creatively inventing new versions of how words could be put together to express the same thought or concept.

The effectiveness of alliteration and rhyming can be strengthened by adding music. Young children have an amazing capacity to remember not only the musical tunes but also the words of songs and nursery rhymes they've learned.

### PHONEMIC AWARENESS EXAMPLE: ODDITY TASKS

A second level of phonemic awareness, **oddity tasks**, requires young children to compare sounds to determine if they are the same or different. In a fun and informal way, children hear two or three words that rhyme and one that doesn't (e.g., *cat,* *mouse, rat*); the adult asks them to tell which one doesn't belong. Or, the children may be given two or three words that begin the same and one that begins with a different sound (e.g., *pig, hat, pie*). Other more difficult oddity tasks ask children to make their decision based on the ending sound (e.g., *dog, hill, pill*) or the middle sound (e.g., *man, fun, bat*) in a word. These oddity tasks are especially usable with prereaders by forcing the child's brain to stray from the typical oral language pathway and begin a route that can be designed for decoding words (a process described in the next chapter).

### PHONOLOGICAL PROCESSING EXAMPLE: WORD AND SYLLABLE COUNTING

Activities beyond those for phonemic awareness connect whole words with their phonemic or sound parts. Syllables can be thought of as the bridge between words and phonemes, with words being easiest to hear and phonemes being more difficult than syllables. For preschool children, counting syllables in words is game-like as children are asked to clap hands or march in place for each syllable in their classmates' names (e.g., *John-ny* or *A-lex-an-dra*), objects in the environment (e.g., *win-dow* or *play-ground*), or feelings (e.g., *un-hap-py* or *cheer-ful*). When the children are successful with these, they are ready to advance to more difficult multisyllabic words (e.g., *prin-ci-pal, but-ter-fly*, or *ev-er-y-one*).

## PRINT AWARENESS AND WRITING PRINCIPLES

Print is everywhere. From cereal boxes to fast-food and road signs, children are surrounded by letters combined in a myriad of ways to form thousands of words. At some point, it is essential for children to understand print as a code translation process through which meaning is understood. One transitional principle is pairing an object or picture with a word. A simple matching game can introduce or reinforce the association between the actual item, a picture of the item, and the printed word.

## DEVELOPMENTALLY APPROPRIATE PRINCIPLES OF PRINT

Metalinguistically, we can put what children need to learn about print into developmental milestones (see Figure 5.3). **Print interest** is attained when the child shows that print is stimulating and worthy of attention. Next, the child develops

**FIGURE 5.3** • Print described in developmental stages.

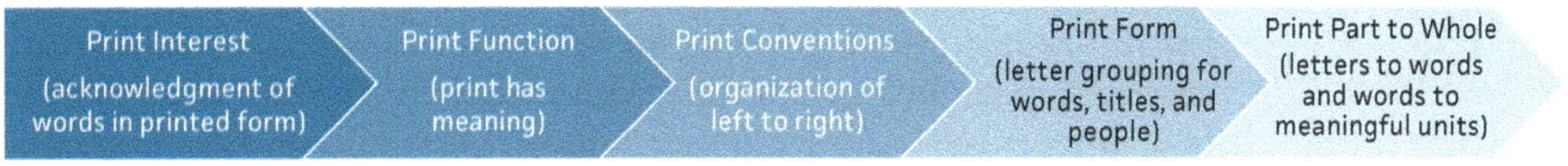

recognition that print provides meaning, which becomes **print function**. The organization of print, **print conventions**, functions to recognize that there is an organizational scheme of left to right, and ways unique to a variety of genres or categories. There are letter groupings for words, story titles, and even names of people they know. Closely associated with conventions of print is **print form**. Here, the child realizes that print units, letters, and words have names and are organized in specific ways. The last stage is **print part-to-whole relationships**. At this stage, a child sees that letters can be combined to make words and words are grouped together to create larger meaningful units (Pence & Justice, 2008).

This hierarchy develops naturally in a print-rich environment. Although the advancing young students may be at different levels of understanding, a planned sequence of activities can support development of this essential progression. Teachers can emphasize these steps when working with older children, or with English learners, who have not been exposed to written language. The sequence for developmentally appropriate **principles of print** is expanded with attention to each area: print interest, print function, print conventions, print form, and print part-to-whole relationships.

### PRINT INTEREST ACTIVITIES

What children need to know about print and its relevance to reading can be summed up in four basic principles:

## FOUR BASIC PRINCIPLES FOR PRINT

1. Words are read, while pictures are viewed.

2. Words appear and are read in English from left to right across the page.

3. Letters placed next to each other form words, and words have a space before and after them.

4. Letters each have a large and small version and can be printed in various forms (fonts).

Parents and others direct children's brains to automatically respond to these principles by pointing to words as they read, making signs and labels for items in the children's world, and pointing to different letter forms from the children's world. **Print knowledge** is addressed when children realize a letter may appear with different fonts within their environment (e.g., letters on the cereal box that differ from the way they are represented in the book just read).

## PRINT INTEREST AND EARLY WRITING

Scribbling is one of the earliest forms of writing engagement. In homes or schools where children observe adults writing for different purposes, children will mimic adults by making marks on a paper and then asking adults what their "writing" says. Adults should not expect a representational product. These attempts at writing are an exploration of print, which occur more readily when children have tools for writing and various opportunities to write. Many preschool classrooms have a writing center, a post office, a restaurant with order pads, or a doctor's office with prescription pads where children can engage in pretend writing. Providing scribes to help children preserve their ideas or describe their artwork is another common practice.

## PRINT FUNCTION AND TEACHING THE ALPHABET

The letters of the alphabet are taught for recognition of the shapes, sizes, and names of the letters, but not their sounds. As previously noted, there are 26 letters of the alphabet but over 40 phonemes. Students are taught the alphabet for recall. It is a rote memory skill. The caution here is to stay with teaching the alphabet with letter names, not sounds. Associate the letter with a picture of an object that starts with the letter name. Logically, an association for the letter *b* would be a picture of a bear, but not the color blue. Another example is the letter *g* can be connected with *goat*, but not with *ghost*.

Some teachers have changed the sequence of teaching the alphabet from a letter a week to a letter a day. This teaching methodology is based on the work of Hal Pashler and colleagues (2007). The best pacing of instruction from a study guide, *Organizing Instruction and Study to Improve Student Learning*, includes five basic teaching recommendations that can be applied to teaching the alphabet:

1. Space learning over time with frequent repetitions.

2. Interweave work example solutions with problem solving.

3. Combine and enhance graphics with verbal descriptions.

4. Connect and integrate abstract and concrete examples of concepts.

5. Use quizzes and timing exercises to promote learning.
   (Pashler et al., 2007)

Researcher and author Ray Reutzel (2015) promotes these practices for teaching the alphabet. His suggestions are in alignment with how children use their brains for learning and remembering. How do writing lessons look for teaching a letter a day? Lessons are a tight 10–15 minutes. A letter a day is taught for 26 days. When the first cycle of all the letters of the alphabet is finished, the teaching cycle is repeated. By the fourth repetition of introducing the 26 letters, most children will know and be able to identify alphabet letters from long-term nondeclarative rote memory. Those who do not will receive additional instruction.

Lessons include alphabetic knowledge and beginning principles of print (capital and small letters or differently sized and shaped fonts). Teachers decide the sequence and may choose to begin the series of the 26 letters in sequence or base the order on shapes or familiarity with the letters. Sequence of the letters is almost universally taught with the alphabet song to the tune of "Twinkle, Twinkle Little Star." This repetition, embedded in almost every child's procedural memory, supplies the correct alphabet order.

For more frequently used letters, two letters a day may be appropriate. Lessons teach capital and lowercase letters concurrently. Teachers may change up the teaching routine by using highlighters, colored pencils, or wipe-off boards. The letter writing exercises are talked through by identifying and modeling shapes, forms, and sizes of the letters. Speed of writing letters can be timed with a stopwatch, individually or in groups, as students begin to process and write with automaticity. Parents and caregivers can help when the letters that are taught are sent home on a weekly basis, or even more often, during the first cycle of teaching. This practice of multiple cycling for the letters of the alphabet is consistent with research, and with the way the brain learns best with spaced repetitions.

## PRINT FUNCTION AND INVENTIVE SPELLING

As preschool children begin to write, they often use their implied knowledge of word sounds, called invented spelling (or phonic spelling). Beginning writers may use the symbols they associate with the sounds of the letters they want to write (e.g., "lk" for *like* or "bkz" for *because*). Some educators and parents have worried that invented spelling promotes poor spelling habits. Research indicates quite the contrary. Studies find that inventive spelling is an engaging and cognitively strenuous activity that leads to stronger literacy skills in the following years (Loewus, 2017). Great Schools (2022), a nonprofit providing information to parents and teachers, encourages invented spelling, as it allows children to communicate in writing long before they are ready to spell words correctly. Eventually, they will move through five stages of writing: *precommunicative* (blocks of letters with no understanding of the letters), *semiphonetic* (letters stand for some particular sound), *phonetic* (use of common spelling patterns), *transitional* (use of common patterns and word structures), and *correct* (use of basic rules from the English spelling system). Teachers are urged to pay attention to the words students use as they move through these stages to support them with appropriate phonics instruction, and possibly to choose words children use in their writing as additional spelling words (Great Schools, 2022).

Catherine McBride-Chang, a researcher, conducted a study with 93 children by assessing them four times in almost two years. The outcome ascertained that invented spelling was stable, highly associated with phonological tasks, and predictive of standardized decoding tests over time. She went so far as to state that invented spelling, assessed in early kindergarten, could be used as a predictor of decoding skills in place of traditional phonological awareness tasks (McBride-Chang, 2010).

## PRINT CONVENTIONS

Children learn that words are written from left to right, and then they move down a space and continue from left to right. Teachers specifically demonstrate how the conventions of print work when they model on a board, point to words as they read, and expose children to beginning decodable text. The structure of writing quickly advances to the next stage, which is how print is formed.

## PRINT FORM

All teaching areas for beginning reading come together as children realize that letters join to form words. Words have a space before and after them. Children are alerted to different types of words: people, places, and things (moving or still). As children learn alphabetic knowledge; it is combined with their expanded awareness of phoneme, phonological, and phonics aspects of words. They are able to group letters and letter patterns, the **graphemes**, to form words.

## PRINT PART-TO-WHOLE RELATIONSHIPS

The miraculous part of beginning reading and writing is that it is happening simultaneously. At this end of the spectrum, when letter shapes are connected with letter sounds and groups of letters are collected together to form words, the child is poised to connect visual, auditory, motor, and cognitive areas of the brain. The result is being able to put words into meaningful units and sentences for reading and writing.

## DEVELOPING WRITING SKILLS IN BRAIN TERMS

The progression of print development calls upon brain structures to be used in new and interesting ways as fine motor control increases. Developments occur in the motor cortex, the frontal lobes, and the cerebellum (refer to Figure 5.4). Planning, timing, and execution of hand movements are involved through activation of the motor cortex. The frontal lobe is accessed to coordinate and orchestrate the movements

**FIGURE 5.4** ● Location of areas in the cerebral cortex identified for writing.

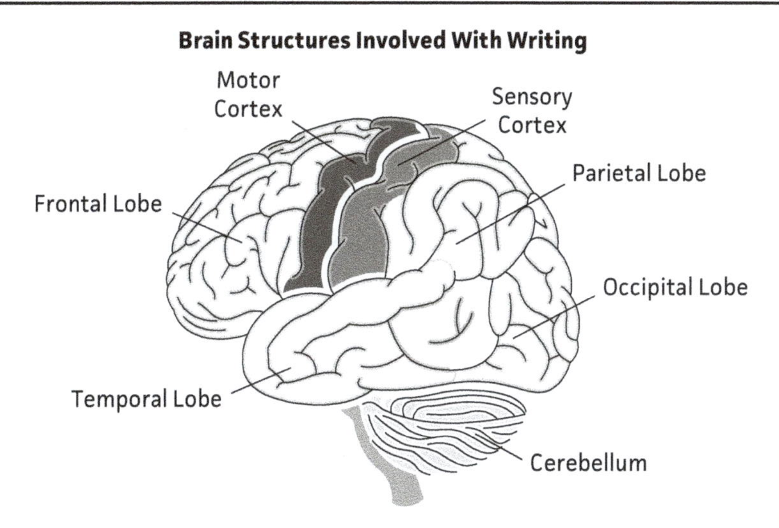


1. Planning, timing, and execution of hand and finger movements are initiated by the motor cortex.
2. Orchestration is controlled by the frontal cortex.
3. The cerebellum coordinates unconscious, precise hand movements for marks on the paper (Berninger & Richards, 2002).
4. With practice, neural circuits wire, and writing actions become automatic.
5. Writing engages additional parts of the brain and expands the potential for learning during reading.
6. Writing provides practice to increase the ability of a student to store information about words in neural networks for retrieval.

**Source:** Reprinted from Nevills & Wolfe (2009).

(Berninger & Richards, 2002). As the youngster continues to experiment with various writing forms and different writing instruments for a variety of reasons, the cerebellum becomes stimulated. The reader most likely remembers from Chapter 2 that the cerebellum is the relatively small, but cognitively powerful, structure located in the lower back of the cerebral cortex. This two-hemisphere mass is connected to the rest of the brain as a super support system for automatic movement, balance, and various other cognitive functions (Cherry, 2022). It is as if the cerebellum needs to be trained through practice, practice, and more practice. *At some stage of practice, which is different for each, the child's concentrated effort is reduced, and the cerebellum takes over many tasks with seemingly effortless fluidity.*

Although the cerebellum's role in writing is examined here, its involvement in reading activities and all aspects of human learning are important. The cerebellum is active to take care of things unconsciously (e.g., brushing teeth, tying shoes, reading words while thinking about meaning, or writing an email message by thinking about what to write, not how to type or how to use the thumbs for cell phone messages). To train the cerebellum for expanded tasks of reading decoding and writing encoding, teachers can provide activities to increase the rate of brain processing through naming activities.

## NAMING FOR PROCESSING SPEED

Why are the brain's **processing speed** and accuracy for naming such critical factors? The earlier discussions regarding automaticity make it clear. Children who do not visually process quickly may not automatically see letters grouped into words as wholes, and they will have to invest a great deal of conscious effort to decipher each letter. This cumbersome process leaves little "space" in working memory for remembering. The ability to name most of the letters automatically will make it easier for the child to recognize patterns of letters—a key to reading words. Note also that speed of processing can be checked when learning the alphabet by verbalizing or writing the letters.

An early indicator of reading speed can be predicted by an informal assessment for *rapid naming of objects*. The objects to be named include colors, symbols, letters, numbers, or pictures. One simple test involves naming 5 different objects that are randomly assigned on a page of 30 to 50 objects. There are up to 10 rows of objects with 5 objects in each row. The child is asked to say an object and then to move as quickly as possible to identify the next object, and so on. The amount of time, in seconds, it takes to name all objects is recorded. Or, in one-minute timings, the number of items named is recorded. These activities are repeated with the same chart or similar charts. Progress with rapid naming is recorded.

The writing option of this naming process is to have the letters or numbers voiced or dictated. Children write their response. The speed of naming is continually increased as students are able to respond and produce a written response with accuracy and rapidity.

Because of the importance attached to early identification, rapid automatized naming (RAN) is suggested as a part of kindergarten screening. Although teacher observation generally provides identification of children who exhibit slow processes for naming and ultimately for slow reading fluency, an informal naming assessment is useful for identification of children who, at the very onset of reading instruction, show early signs of slow processing. RAN is identified in Chapter 8 as a skill for reading fluency. This naming process can be determined by normed formal assessments, but informal naming sheets can be developed and used to encourage rapid identification of objects at this early time of learning.

#  COGNITIVE DEVELOPMENT

The attributes of priming skills are summarized from the previous chapter. They are critical to the brainwork required to develop readers. **Attention** to a prereading task requires most incoming sensory signals unrelated to the reading task to be consciously or unconsciously dropped or ignored. **Concentration** on reading activities means children must maintain sustained, directed, thoughtful focus on specific visual or verbal cues. Teachers encourage students through oral thinking modeling to rehearse, practice, or subvocalize instructional materials. These mindful practices do not happen automatically.

Of similar difficulty is the series of consciously stimulated activities needed for a child's brain to unconsciously move information from working to long-term **memory** for prompt recall. This complex memory task described previously requires directed rehearsal and practice, which young children are not self-motivated to do. The final priming skill, **organization**, happens with a unique design in each child's brain. Teachers and parents who are aware of the important role organization plays in the developing brain for memory and for school success provide many opportunities to structure thinking. Some examples are grouping similar items, identifying same and different, and charting pictures and writing names of things that go together. Even drying and sorting silverware as a home task is productive brain work. More examples of priming skills are exhibited in the following chart of cognitive learning skills, under increasingly specific, technical headings.

## COGNITIVE LEARNING SKILLS CHART

A sampling of skills provides expectations as children stretch their nervous systems to prepare for the important, desired task of becoming readers. The areas covered include attention flexibility, visualization, auditory processing for identification and substitution, and sensory-cognitive skills for imaging and predicting. The skills identified in this chart have been developed by the author following extensive review of the literature. They are another support that can be shared with parents to fortify skill development at home.

## COGNITIVE SKILLS FOR LEARNING: AGES 5 AND 6

### Attention

| 5–6 Years | **Attention Flexibility for Visual or Auditory Input—** Can focus and refocus with rapidity. Follows Random Automatized Naming (one-minute timed identification) to focus, say the name of the item, detach, refocus, name, and detach over and over again. Begins with shapes and advances to letters, numbers, simple sight words, beginning number facts. Follows rules, and takes turns. Sings, dances, or acts for others. Tells a story with at least two events. Counts to 100. Understands words about time (e.g., *yesterday, tomorrow, last week, morning, evening*). Pays attention for more than 10 minutes while blocking out unimportant sensory stimulation (screen time not included in the time limit). Writes complete name. Can identify by name all the letters of the alphabet in first grade. |
|---|---|

### Visual Processing

| 5–6 Years | **Visualization**—Has the ability to look at words or listen to words, sentences, or a complete story and form a unique vision in the mind from what is heard or read. Responds to questions without individual picture prompts. (Note this is an extremely important skill for comprehension.) Recognizes and accepts different responses as the teacher questions other children.) The child may draw a picture to demonstrate understanding. Upon seeing the beginning of a high-frequency word, the child is able to complete the word by adding the missing letters. |
|---|---|

## Auditory Processing for Phonological Awareness

| 5–6 Years | **Identification**—Recognizes phonemes in words with four or more phonemes (e.g., *d-o-g-h-ou-se, k-i-ch-en, p-u-m-k-i-n*). Identifies words when phonemes are given (e.g., *an-i-mal* for *animal*).<br><br>**Substitution**—Uses a different beginning, middle, or ending sound to form a new word or a nonsense word. This response is for sounds of words only, no letter association (e.g., "Say *mother* without the *m* sound"; "Change the *b* sound in *boat* to a *g* sound"; "What word is different—*turtle, money, toys,* or *tumble*?"). |
| --- | --- |

## Sensory-Cognitive Processing

| 5–6 Years | **Imaging**—A simple story is read without pictures. The child imagines the story and is able to answer simple questions not given in the story about objects or people. For example, in a story about a leprechaun, the leprechaun is not described. The child is able to answer questions about the size of the leprechaun, his clothes, whether he is wearing a hat, and whether he would be a good friend.<br><br>**Predicting**—A new story is read, but stopped before it ends. The child is able to tell what could happen next, or how the story might end. For added value, other children express their endings—acknowledgment that each child processes thinking uniquely. |
| --- | --- |

## Memory Systems (Sensory, Working, and Long-Term

| 5 Years | **Memory Manipulation**—Moves words, items, and concepts from long-term memory into working memory to create something new. Makes a sound and attaches a letter, beginning with consonants. Uses a category, such as colors, food, or animals, and names items that would go into that category. |
| --- | --- |

## Executive Function

| 5 Years | **Cognitive Flexibility**—Takes action to change an idea or plan when the input from other sources changes. Realizes that furry animals with four legs can be many types of mammals. Names different types of transportation. Knows the difference between food that is grown on a tree and food that grows in the ground. Has print awareness, holds a book correctly, and knows the cover, title page, and story pages. |
| --- | --- |

Cognitive skills expand and become more complex. Cognitive learning skills charts continue to be available at the end of the following chapters, and a comprehensive version, through age 9, is available in Appendix B.

## CONCLUDING THOUGHTS ABOUT BEGINNING READERS

Being a good reader or, even more desirable, a competent, proficient reader is every parent's desire for their child. This is a tough chapter. The topics provided a stark difference from previous ones that were playful and relied on what naturally happens—children learn to speak and have conversation with real words and real sentences. The listening and speaking pathways develop spontaneously. Teachers, who are aware of this complex development in the brain, use instructional practices to support these language developments for both reading and writing. Chapter 5 emphasizes precursors for learning to read and building both the oral and silent reading pathways. This building process is the very foundation for reading, and it is tough work for most children, requiring purposeful teaching.

Between the ages of 4 and 6 years, young children transition into full-fledged students. Along with this change the serious work of phonological processing, conceptual formations, access to memory systems, and development of initial skills for writing. Cognitive skill development needs are considered. During all this serious change teachers stop and regroup when student behavior indicates the work is too hard. Teachers then turn learning into something fun, like a game, remembering the nature of children at this age: play music, dance, sing, stretch, and exercise. Children and their teachers can still enjoy the precious activities students at this young age desire, and upon which they thrive.

# Reflective Questions

1. What thoughts do you have as you look at Figure 5.2, the flow chart for the silent reading pathway? Notice, particularly,

the description of the angular gyrus. Why is this structure so important to the work teachers do when they teach reading?

2. Phonemic awareness and phonological processing are often used interchangeably. How would you explain each with an example?

3. Explain the development of print awareness and give a real-life example of each step.

4. Why do teachers teach names of letters—not their sounds—at this stage of cognitive development? What difference does speed of naming make?

5. Talk about "invented spelling" and how to work with children at this stage of writing.

6. This book defines priming skills as abilities that children need to become successful learners. These "habits of work" may be missing for some children and, if so, need to be taught. Give an example of each and how teachers or parents could help children who are unaware of these processes.

7. **Bonus questions:** Is there a relationship between priming skills and cognitive skill development? What is the purpose of providing cognitive skill development? How can teachers use this information? *These questions will be answered in Chapter 11.*

# CHAPTER 6

# Teaching for Reading in First Grade

Up to first grade, teaching mixes a certain amount of playfulness with some serious learning. Now, as 6- and 7-year-olds, children have realized they are learners as school becomes a full-time, big-kid job. Their life has changed as they wake up to alarm clocks or a parent's insistent calling, have less play time, are expected to work, and are required at designated times to sit and listen. With all this change, children need to feel secure and safe in their classrooms. Children also want to feel important, as well as to learn routines and boundaries, and they can be encouraged to become responsible learners.

First graders may state that they are going to learn to read in first grade. First-grade teachers can foster and keep the excitement children bring with them the very first day of school. Reading requires the young person to become curious by thinking about and focusing on something, learning print, and drawing upon what is already known about words. During the course of the first-grade year, a child unconsciously, yet steadily, builds a neatly organized pathway to become a reader. Teacher-led explicitly sequenced instruction with oral practice and rehearsal activities helps a primary school child's brain to build a reading superhighway that will lead to accurate reading with understanding in following grades. Although this process is touted as ideal, the present situation for reading instruction and ultimately achievement across the United States may not reflect this ideal.

This chapter, like the previous one, deviates in design, as a dive is taken into the serious process of teaching beginning reading according to the five pillars of the science of reading identified in the National Reading Panel's (2000) report (phonemic awareness, phonics, fluency, vocabulary, and comprehension). The science of reading, linked with the neurology of reading, fosters interplay between the two. Specifically, the science of reading provides information for selection of teaching materials, what to teach and assess, and methodologies for teaching. As stated throughout this book, *neurology helps educators to understand why the science of reading works.* Most importantly, as teachers understand the complex cognitive work that accompanies the lessons that are taught, they are able to discern variations for teaching. These variations may include activities to encourage children to pay attention, concentrate, and organize their thinking. To know how children's brains develop for memory allows teachers to make instructional decisions, such as "How long should this lesson be?" "How many times do students need to review this concept?" "Do my students have vocabulary words stored in long-term memory so they can comprehend this science lesson?" or "What is the best way to review this information and get the students engaged?"

In the chapters of this book, readers are given what is expected to be taught from the science of reading along with the Common Core State Standards for individual grade levels (Common Core State Standards Initiative, 2010). The sections featuring what teachers can do to achieve high levels of learning for their students to read proficiently are based on what is known from the science of neurology.

##  CONSIDER A FIRST GRADER

It is the opening day of first grade. The children are anxious. They are excited to be going to "big school," and they want to learn to read. They bring with them some specific characteristics. They are strict judges, and most have a strong understanding of right and wrong. They want to be right, so they operate well in an environment with specific directions, rules, and boundaries. There is a serious side to 6- and 7-year-olds, but they also are used to being outside and active; it is difficult to be still. And, if they are talking or working on a task, they do not like to be interrupted or redirected. What is a teacher to do?

# STARTING SCHOOL RIGHT

In brain terms, children need to feel safe and secure in school. The limbic system, the primitive part of their brains, rules, and the thalamus stimulated by the amygdala can override their thinking parts, the frontal lobes and other cortices. So security comes first. Some teachers say they never smile until the end of the first week when they have control of the class. That may be good for seventh grade, but not for 6- and 7-year-olds. Some practices quell fears and invite young students to feel comfortable and ready to engage beginning on day one. While experienced teachers may have their first-day routine in good order, beginning teachers may find suggestions in this section helpful.

Here are some examples of activities to try on an opening day. To help students feel welcome when their teacher greets them at the door, the teacher might hand them a number that corresponds to a seating chart posted at the front of the room. Children would then help each other to match their number with one on the chart and find their desk. Certainly those numbers could be used in other ways, but the advantage of a seating chart is that children do not have "free choice" and the teacher can immediately call them by name. Teachers who additionally have children make their own name tent can learn immediately about their class's motor skills and writing abilities. Introductions are an important time for teachers to share short stories, especially why they became a teacher. Children, as they are ready or comfortable, can likewise introduce themselves by responding to one or two prompts.

At the same time, classroom rules may be introduced. For example: *Listen to others. Help other children. Use classroom voices. Promise to do your best.* All rules have a positive voice. A final example for providing a warm, welcoming environment is to have a note for parents at the end of the day to begin a family and teacher partnership. The note may include information about the first day of school and classroom expectations (rules). Other communication on subsequent days could include the first-grade teacher's ideals for learning, what students will be learning the first two weeks of school, a class schedule, school notices, and/or a school supply list. Information that could be forthcoming might be community resources, such as a handout from the library, or a running record that will accompany homework packets along with a reading log form. Right at the start, partnering with the family is established to support the point that this classroom is the best place for children and their teacher to spend their days learning together.

# CLASSROOM ENVIRONMENT FOR ENRICHED LEARNING

Places and comforts for children can be provided in addition to chairs and tables or desks, such as soft pillows, mats, a carpet area, and cushions of different shapes and textures. Remembering children are good at sitting and attending for about as many minutes as they are old, allow them at times to attend instruction, complete school assignments, or play games in positions other than sitting at a desk. When children get fidgety, take a break and let them mirror the teacher's physical exercise movements. As this activity becomes routine, a classmate may take the role of providing stretches and exercise. Large-movement exercises, like jumping jacks or marching or holding the body against gravity as with yoga poses, provide rejuvenating breaks and allow brain activity to slow down. During this slowing down from mental activity, learning begins to make needed connections and to consolidate.

First graders like to talk, and at times their need to talk exceeds their ability to talk about meaningful things. Since talking allows for oral language expression, teachers can provide talking time. Teachers use these times to know the children better. Conversations can be directed with starters, topics, or word games to use their need to talk, which in turn reinforces learning.

A cool-down area can be provided for children who are over-stimulated from recess, or who need to deal with behaviors or emotions that need to be regulated. The area might be filled with beanbag chairs, a weighted lap pad, a sealed glitter jar, a drawing pad and crayons, calming scents, squishy hand objects, and other sensory items. Let every child have access to this area at the onset to know what is available. Think also about having students list all the statements they like to hear when they have done a task well—for example, "Good job," "You nailed it," "Good for you," or "You are awesome." Write these statements on papers that can be folded and placed in a plastic container. When children need a boost, they can go to the container for affirmation and naturally learn to recognize and read some words.

A theme of playfulness was emphasized in earlier chapters. Although mastering decoding and encoding is serious business, it can also be fun when teachers "change up the environment" with game-type manipulatives and activities. Teachers can draw upon many sources to find these variations to teaching. One suggestion is to use Google to find supports, which might include fiddlesticks, a flip chute, a bead slide, mirror practice, phoneme segmentation, or a phonics phone.

Children like to have an environment that meets their age-level characteristics. Consider how they are welcomed and settled into school, how school routines are in place, how school expectations are known, *and* how the environment can include activities that have a fun or game-like appeal. The serious work of building and reinforcing the reading pathway for first graders to become readers is then in place.

## INSTRUCTIONAL ESSENTIALS: READING AND LANGUAGE ARTS GUIDELINES FOR KINDERGARTEN AND FIRST GRADE

In the early primary grades, reading instruction focuses on phonological processes, and includes phonemic manipulation, phonics, and print processing. The goal is to recognize words as a procedural, automatic process. Research from the National Reading Panel's (2000) report supports instructional activities for **encoding** (constructing words) as a precursor to **decoding** (reading words). Additionally, teaching high-frequency words through rote practice activities allows students to read decodable text independently. Rote practice for identifying high-frequency or sight words also builds a repertory of words that do not follow rules for phonics or spelling and need to be memorized. Other instructional activities such as storytelling, listening to stories, book or picture finger walks, play or puppet acting, answering questions, having conversations, writing simple sentences, and learning to spell words all augment teaching encoding and decoding. These primary steps prepare students for more complex reading skills in subsequent grades.

The road to building a reading brain for decoding words and achieving reading fluency is not a uniform, one-size-fits-all pathway. Every teacher knows that children in each first-grade classroom exhibit a wide range of reading potential. Some children have already developed skills that put them in the right place to learn. They are equipped with priming skills, which means they are motivated, attentive, able to concentrate, and relatively well organized. Many, but not all, of these children are on their way to becoming competent readers by the end of first grade. In the real-life classroom, however, this is not the norm, and teachers must prepare to meet the needs of all children regardless of their level of readiness. Even children who appear to be readers may have missed some important steps along their reading development pathway that can only be identified through assessment.

## COMMON CORE STATE STANDARDS

Education in the United States is centralized through the Common Core State Standards (CCSS), which were adopted in 2010 and implemented in either the 2013–2014 or 2014–2015 school year in most states. Since that time, states have had a variety of responses to the Common Core, adopting the standards, adapting them, or ceasing their use. Individual states may adjust the standards to apply to their population, and each state selects their own curriculum materials and determines instructional methodology and practices. Readers are encouraged to be familiar with the standards in the state where they teach or work. As the name reveals, the document identifies standards for English language arts and mathematics (Common Core State Standards Initiative, 2010). Other subject areas were adopted in subsequent years. The CCSS for English language arts (ELA) provides specific skills that children need to develop. A summary of the ELA standards for kindergarten, reviewed by the author in 2022, gives validation to the specificity with which they are written, and alerts first-grade teachers to skills expected from the kindergarten year. Here is the starting place for first grade.

### A SUMMARY OF THE COMMON CORE STATE STANDARDS FOR ENGLISH LANGUAGE ARTS IN KINDERGARTEN

**Kindergarten—Reading Literature**

Answer questions; retell familiar stories; identify characters, settings, and major events; answer questions about unknown words; recognize common types of text; identify name and role of author(s) and illustrator(s); compare adventures and experiences of characters in different stories; and actively engage in group reading activities.

**Kindergarten—Reading Informational Texts**

Answer key details in a text; identify main topic and key details; describe the connection between two individuals, events, ideas, or pieces of information; ask and answer questions about unknown words; name author and illustrator and define role of each; with support, describe the relationship between illustrations and the text; identify reasons the author gives to support the text; with support, identify similarities and differences between two texts on the same topic; and actively engage in group reading activities.

**Kindergarten—Foundational Skills**

Print concepts of organization and basic features of print: follow words from left to right, top to bottom, and page to page; recognize spoken words are written with a sequence of letters; understand words are separated by spaces; and recognize both upper- and lowercase letters.

Phonological awareness for understanding of spoken words, syllables, and sounds (phonemes): recognize and produce rhyming words; count; pronounce, blend, and segment syllables in spoken words; blend and segment onsets and rimes of single-syllable spoken words; isolate and pronounce initial, medial vowel, and final sounds (phonemes) in three-phoneme consonant-vowel-consonant (CVC) words (except those ending with /l/, /r/, or /x/); and add or substitute individual sounds in simple one-syllable words to make new words.

Phonics and word recognition to know and apply grade-level phonics and word analysis skills in decoding words: demonstrate basic knowledge of one-to-one letter–sound correspondences for most frequent sounds of each consonant, associate long and short sounds with common spellings (graphemes) for the five major vowels, read common high-frequency words by sight, and distinguish between similarly spelled words.

Fluency to read emergent-reader texts with purpose and understanding.

Kindergarten standards continue with equally specific skills for *writing, speaking, listening,* and *presentation of knowledge and ideas.* Even at this very young age the expectations are many. Kindergarten, rather than first-grade, standards are given here as expectations for beginning first-grade students.

## TEACHING DECODING: PHONOLOGICAL PROCESSES AND PRINT AWARENESS

A young child's brain is hardwired for speech, not reading. Building a reading brain does not happen with naturally designated neural mechanisms for reading; the reading system must be developed. Structured teaching of phonological processes, discussed in the previous chapter, systematically leads the emerging reader's brain to facilitate links between the areas of the brain that need to be connected for reading. This allows words stored in implicit long-term memory for speaking or listening to be reconsidered and manipulated when they appear as printed symbols. Children become aware of phonemes by working with sounds they already know. They blend sounds, segment words into sounds, replace sounds, add sounds, and delete sounds through structured phonemic play. Each time sounds and combinations of sounds are introduced in another way, the child is engaged with brainwork through practice and coarticulation. The automatic process for phoneme manipulation becomes a part of long-term memory as an initial skill fundamental to the entire reading process. With practice, children ultimately associate visual patterns with words that they hear and speak. Refer to Figure 5.1 from the previous chapter, and add the motor cortex to review the complex pathway required for a student to read and then to pronounce words to speak.

## MASTERING DECODING WITH PHONOLOGICAL PROCESSES

*Phonological processes* is an umbrella term to identify children's conscious mental operations, perception, interpretation, recall, and production around the sound structure of oral language when they learn to decode successfully. This information was provided first by Torgesen and colleagues in 1994 and then by Moats in 2000. It is now common knowledge among educators that phonological processing requires a child to be able to identify, segment, manipulate, and blend phonemes; pronounce words; and identify words and syllables. A child needs many concepts and skills to become comfortable with abstract symbols representing letters. Furthermore, the child must manipulate different letters for successful decoding of text.

This section provides a review of phonemic awareness and expands print awareness and **alphabetic principle** through phonics, while a discussion of vocabulary development, processing speed, spelling, and writing follows as these skills develop in tandem with the decoding processes.

### PHONEMIC AWARENESS FOR INDIVIDUAL SOUNDS

Phonemic awareness is a conscious understanding that words are made of individual sounds (phonemes) from speech, and the ultimate awareness that these sounds represent letters of the alphabet. Common research from the past 30 years reveals most children need focused teaching to become skilled in phonemic awareness. Reading experts through the years identify a lack of phonemic awareness as one major cause of reading difficulties in children and adults who are poor readers. The case for auditory sound production is taken a step further as the sight of a word sets off a signal to pronounce the word. It is the sounds for pronunciation that have been stored in memory. Speech through **auditory memory** is the brain's system for recall, *not* strings of letters seen visually. Certainly, this conclusion supports the understanding that the oral language system develops first. This oral language pathway is more likely to provide the massive storage system for remembering spoken language. It is then co-opted to articulate written language when it is presented.

For adults who already know how to read, it seems quite logical that sounds heard in speech are paired with the letters on the printed page. However, it is commonplace knowledge that without direct instructional support, phonemic awareness eludes approximately 25% of middle-class first graders and substantially even more of those who come from homes where they were not exposed to literacy-rich activities in their early years. To address serious reading problems children have when they cannot hear, identify, or understand the concept of phonemes, a supplemental classroom curriculum specifically for phonemic awareness can be taught with planned activities for rhyming, alliteration, oddity tasks, phoneme segmentation, phoneme blending, phoneme manipulation, and syllable splitting. Engaging in activities designed to develop specific skills for children identified with a reading disability is important work. Planned, sequenced, explicit phonemic awareness and phonological processing are not the same as the random, spontaneous activities that children engage in during their infancy and preschool years to develop oral language.

In Chapter 5, phonemic awareness was addressed through rhyming and oddity activities. Now, more advanced phonological processing skills are given for phoneme segmentation and phoneme manipulation.

*Phoneme segmentation* requires children to break words into the smallest possible sounds they can distinguish. In the case of *hand*, this would be *h-a-n-d*, with children providing sounds for each letter rather than identifying letter names. The opposite of phonemic segmentation is phoneme blending. To blend, the teacher pronounces sounds with an exaggerated, slow pronunciation, such as *h—a—n—d*, then asks the children to put the sounds together and to say them quickly as a meaningful word.

In *phoneme manipulation*, children are asked to change the sound they hear at the beginning or end of a word to another sound and, consequently, to another word. Note that the results may be a real or nonsense word. For example, children are given the word *fox*, and the teacher asks that the beginning sound be changed to the /b/ sound. The response is *box*. If children are then asked to change the middle sound to /i/, they may laugh as they realize that *bix* is not a real word. Phoneme manipulation places extended demands on oral language structures, as this sensory input is meant for deciphering individual sounds from words that are already familiar in their entirety.

For these tasks of phonemic awareness, the brain begins the tedious yet awesome task of unconsciously reshaping pathways that are a part of the oral language process. It is reiterated that neural pathways children use for reading begin with those used for oral language interpretation. These are then co-opted to connect and to make sense out of sound and letter relationships for reading.

## PRINT AWARENESS AND PHONOLOGICAL STRUCTURE

Awareness that print represents sounds and words provides a foundation for a child's brain that is under construction for reading. The awareness happens gradually, and when a child's brain has scored this point and stored it in long-term memory, it is a monumental building block in the reading process. Print awareness develops in most children through interaction with their environment prior to school attendance. During school, print awareness experiences are enhanced with pictures, colors, shapes, and symbols, which bring the concepts of print to the young student's attention.

Beginning in preschool, children may recognize the logo for Target or the title of a Dr. Seuss book. Gradually, they begin to recognize a word such as *zoo* for its unique appearance. This type of prealphabetic learning can also be described as *logographic reading*. It becomes a complex process of letter recognition, phoneme processing and maneuvering, learning sounds with attached letters or letter strings, and predicting relationships between letters and sounds.

Reading depends on an awareness of how alphabetic letters are represented through their phonological structure as words. During the transitional phase of putting letters to sounds, children must recognize that phonemes may overlap or run together in speech, but the phonemes as letters are represented distinctly in print. For example, *next door* becomes coarticulated in speech and may sound like *nexstore*, or *an animal* may appear to be *a nanimal*. Speaking sounds occurs rapidly. It may be difficult for some children to determine how a spoken word or letter string is spelled. As children become familiar with phonemes, their sounds, and their letter representations, they become adept at automatically reconciling inconsistencies between sounds and the letters that represent them.

## ALPHABETIC PRINCIPLE THROUGH PHONICS

Phonics, introduced briefly in Chapter 5, is a system to identify symbols used in alphabetic writing that represent sounds. It is a means to describe sound–symbol reading instruction, which may also be referred to as a phonics approach to reading instruction. Almost all beginning reading programs include phonics instruction, either **explicit** or **implicit**.

> ## PHONICS INSTRUCTION: EXPLICIT OR IMPLICIT
>
> **Explicit, Systematic Phonics Instruction**—Correspondence between sound and spelling is taught directly, overtly, and systematically.
>
> **Implicit, Incidental Phonics Instruction**—Correspondence between sound and spelling is incidental from reading whole words as they are encountered in text.

The National Reading Panel (2000) conducted a meta-analysis to review and analyze the two different practices. It is no surprise that children who received explicit, **systematic phonics instruction** were favored to become better readers. Explicit phonics instruction *can and should include implicit or incidental exposure to phonics* during normal reading of text.

## KEY UNDERSTANDINGS ABOUT LETTERS AND SOUNDS

An effective phonics program has instructional components that (1) give teachers support for systematic instruction for sound-to-letter understanding for words, sentences, text, and writing; (2) offer student assessments to know when instruction needs to be modified; and (3) integrate alphabetic knowledge, phonemic awareness, vocabulary development, and text reading.

## SOUNDS TO LETTERS, NOT LETTERS TO SOUNDS

Programs to introduce the 26 letters of the alphabet by attaching sounds to the letters not only appear to be ineffective; they also can cause confusion for students. A teaching program that presents print to sound teaches only part of the code. This approach, which previously was found in some conventional phonics programs, leaves gaps for sounds that have to be added on to the sound recognition system that the child has constructed. Of more than 40 phonemes, 12 remain unexpressed when phonics is taught according to the 26 letters of the alphabet. As noted in the previous chapter, the alphabet is taught specifically in short teaching time periods of 10 to 15 minutes for the identification of the 26 letters, not for their sounds.

Since the initial publication of this book, significant information about teaching reading has become available, and when applied to how the human brain functions, it makes perfect sense to to support the sound-to-letter instructional approach. Skilled readers look at thousands of words and instantly recognize their meanings. To do this from their visual appearance alone (pattern recognition) is not possible. It is the repetitive pronunciation with attention to the sounds of words that glues them to long-term memory and rote recall.

Common sense reveals that with a letter-to-sound approach, some letters have no uniquely defined job. For example, the letter *c* shares sounds with *k* and *s*. Some letter names bear little relationship to the sounds of the letter they represent. For example, the letter *x* is named *eks* but sounds like /ks/ or /z/. Children may confuse these sounds during spelling and attempt to spell a word such as *box* as *boks* or *boz*. Best teaching practices and the National Reading Panel (2000) report clearly support explicit teaching that first distinguishes each sound and then attaches a letter or letters to the sound. Children may be asked to identify the sounds in words such as *mat*, *sad*, *pan*, *pale*, or *made*. If children know the rules that govern short and long vowels, they can apply the rules to these predictable words.

Other than including these elements for systematic instruction, one particular approach to the explicit teaching of phonics is not recommended over another. Likewise, there is no specific recommendation for sequence of sound introduction or number of sounds, and there is no set of rules that identify the ideal phonics program. Strongly emphasized is that to read, children must understand the sound-to-letter relationships that are studied through the teaching of systematic phonics.

Phonics instruction using practices that are brain-compatible is the most ideal way to teach reading.

## PRIMARY WORD WALLS

Word walls used in some primary classrooms can be effective when they are designed to reinforce vocabulary development. Word walls for phonics, however, can be illogical, complex, and confusing if they are based on the alphabet. An illogical word wall list for *Aa* might include *and*, *away*, *all*, and *are*. A first-grade child who tries to make decoding sense out of this list containing irregular sounds for the letter *a* may become confused about **letter–sound relationships**. A list that is compatible with the way children learn would list a phonics sound, such as /ā/ for *wait*, /ă / for *hat*, and /aw/ for *bought*. Word walls may be better named sound walls. They can become highly effective when children interact with the word lists by adding new words that have been learned.

## ORTHOGRAPHIC RULES

Almost all words are completely regular by orthographic rule, but words use patterns that are somewhat obscure and do not exist peacefully with other decoding rules. One example is the rule that states all words ending with a *v* must have an *e* at the end. The words *shove*, *live*, and *leave* all have the required *e* after the *v*. But the final-*e* rule that says the preceding vowel should make a long sound is in conflict.

Teachers identify these inconsistencies through a systematic and explicit approach to teaching phonics with orthographic rules. Children, then, can make sense out of letters, sounds, and words and develop the cognitive capacity to deal with the inconsistencies of English.

## IDENTIFICATION OF COMMON LETTER BLENDS AND WORD FAMILIES

Children may be confused when they are asked to use a word attack strategy that requires them to sound out words letter by letter. Much of the predictability of English comes not from individual letters but from letter spelling units where two or more letters together make a sound. A better approach, one firmly based on phonics instruction, is to identify the following when approaching the traditional "sounding out" process for unknown words:

- Common consonant blends (e.g., /bl/, /br/, /pr/, /shr/, /thr/, /tw/)
- Vowel graphemes (e.g., /ai/, /eigh/, /ie/, /ough/, /ou/, /augh/)

- Word families (e.g., a base word, such as *care*, identified in *careful*, *caring*, and *uncaring*)

Practices that can lead to confusion for a child's brain include letter-to-sound strategy, primary word walls based on the alphabet, incomplete orthographic rules, or sounding out individual letters in words. The human brain seeks order and patterns that are meaningful. A child's brain with its pattern-seeking nature needs clear, logical word recognition strategies to use.

## WORD RECOGNITION GAINS SOPHISTICATION

As children move through the primary grades, they gain more sophisticated ways of learning new words. They progress, for example, from attempting to sound out all letters, to recognizing letter patterns and phonemes, then to decoding words by syllables and identifying morphological components. Using the word *uncomfortable*, first-grade instruction would sound out the phonemes, *u-n-c-o-m-f-o-r-t-a-b-le*. Second-grade students would look at syllables, *un-com-for-ta-ble*. This allows them to extend letter combinations, seek larger orthographic units, and look for predictable beginnings and endings. By the third grade, students' advanced abilities allow them to look at larger and more complex orthographic units. Third graders would approach this sample word as *un-comfort-able*.

Effective instruction follows a progression of word recognition strategies during the early elementary years. This instructional design allows children to build meaningful units of **morphemes**, words, word origins, and understanding through a core knowledge base when they are in fourth grade and beyond.

## TEACHING ENCODING: SPELLING AND WRITING

Learning to spell occurs simultaneously with learning to assign letters to sounds for decoding. Moreover, decoding (print to speech) must be taught with encoding (speech to print) for brain-efficient teaching. While decoding is reading words, encoding is constructing words. Writing becomes an effective road to early reading as it efficiently activates memory for sounds and left-hemisphere brain structures for word processing. Children learn the same new patterns of language across the domains of listening, spelling, reading, and ultimately writing, thus strengthening the networks of neural connections as the brain categorizes words. This categorization happens first for articulation, then for meaning, and finally for letter representation. Words are learned with efficiency and with greater likelihood for retention and retrieval when they are practiced at different times in different ways. This practice happens through phonological processing instruction designed to pair spelling and writing with learning to decode.

## SPELLING

Spelling instruction can be based on a number of premises, such as sound–symbol correspondences, syllable patterns, orthographic rules, word meanings, word derivation, or word origin. Instruction is most compatible with the reading structures of a child's brain when spelling words are meaningfully organized into groups with common word patterns and coherently sequenced grade by grade. Louisa Moats (2000) suggested a spelling program linked to phoneme awareness in kindergarten, consonant and vowel correspondence for first grade, more complex spelling patterns for second grade, and syllabication, compounds, and word endings for third grade. That recommendation remains consistent with a progression of learning and the complexity of words stored in long-term memory.

A spelling list of 10 to 12 words per week may additionally contain words children are using in their reading or writing that exemplify orthographic patterns from a sequenced word study program. Ideally, the study of **orthography**, the spelling of words, in the early school years is closely matched with words that occur in reading texts with high frequency. Spelling lists also contain some of the commonly misspelled words children use in writing.

Systematic instruction for phoneme-to-grapheme spelling is emphasized through the second grade and beyond. As children become more sophisticated with their ability to decipher new words, selection of words for spelling study takes a vocabulary-building emphasis. Intense spelling instruction for letter and word patterns in the early school years secures an understanding of words and their parts to allow older children to employ self-initiated analysis techniques with new vocabulary they encounter as their reading becomes more advanced.

# STORYTELLING AND WRITING

Children in kindergarten and first grade are capable of developing complex thoughts far in advance of their ability to express these thoughts in writing. When they are expected to write independently, such as for storytelling, the difference between what they know about words and what they are physically capable of recording on paper becomes apparent. Recognizing this disparity, teachers can take an active role during their students' early writing efforts by allowing students to dictate their ideas and stories. This intensive one-to-one interaction can be handled by parent volunteers or older student helpers who write for the children. Whole-class stories are developed as the teacher writes on an overhead projector, on a projector from their computer, or more traditionally on a large chart. Writing, as a developmental skill, is a natural and necessary companion to the process of learning to read.

**FIGURE 6.1** ● Order of thought as a child writes words.

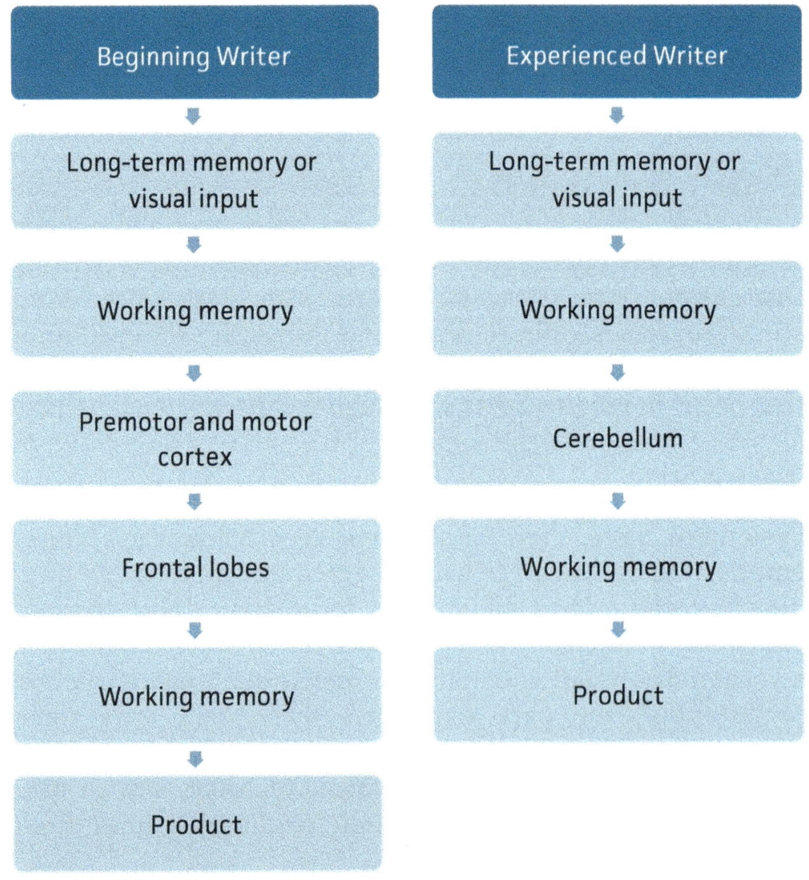

Although writing is a natural partner to a reading program, it does not happen easily in the child's brain. Writing places a new set of demands on the developing brain by calling on the motor cortex to respond in new ways. Picture a child who is beginning to experiment with writing. The youngster concentrates on holding a pencil between the thumb, pointer finger, and middle finger. At first, this feels and looks awkward, and the child must concentrate on gripping the pencil with the appropriate amount of tension and really think about touching the lead of the pencil to the paper. As the fingers press and move the pencil, the child consciously thinks about the shapes that are being made, staying within the lines, and manipulating the pencil.

While this physical struggle is visible, what is going on in the brain is not (refer to Figure 6.1). Planning, timing, and execution of finger, hand, and arm movements, initiated in the premotor and motor cortex, are ultimately orchestrated by the frontal lobes. As the writing process becomes automatic, the cerebellum, located at the lower back of the brain, unconsciously coordinates the precise hand movements when a child puts marks on the paper (Berninger & Richards, 2002).

With practice, the neural circuits used for writing function automatically, and the child no longer needs to be conscious of this very complex process going on with the hands and fingers. Teachers can provide other classroom activities, such as arts and crafts projects, including stenciling, tracing, coloring within small spaces, cutting, and pasting, to encourage the mechanics of writing. In a well-designed program, writing and spelling work in tandem with reading, and children have an outlet through writing to expand the complex thoughts and ideas that come into their minds.

## BEYOND DECODING AND ENCODING

Reading is a developmental process that involves being able to identify words in text, understand what the words mean, seek connections for word meanings, and do all this with speed and fluency. In first grade, reading instruction designed to build the reading (decoding and encoding) pathway moves on to include comprehension skills, speed of processing (fluency), and development of high-frequency and sight vocabulary. It is imperative to recognize reading skill development is not addressed in a sequence of skills. One skill does not have to be proficient before the next is taught. *The human brain develops in all areas at the same time.*

## BUILDING VOCABULARY FOR TEXT COMPREHENSION

Comprehension depends greatly on the words a child knows and can call on automatically. Educators are encouraged to provide a wide variety of listening and print exposure experiences during the first two years of school, including books based on the alphabet, informational stories, classic and contemporary literature, children's magazines and newspapers, dictionaries, and reference materials. Teachers can initiate questioning and discussion before, during, and after reading these materials to help students comprehend and draw meaning from them as well as develop new vocabulary.

Emphasis on vocabulary building must happen concurrently with phonological processing and decoding instruction during the early school years. Vocabulary development initially happens during dialogue. Teachers who discuss the meaning of words with children and provide opportunities for children to engage in conversations about words enhance their spoken language. The ways children store language and vocabulary in accessible long-term memory for retrieval are expanded. For example, share time in first grade helps children learn to express their ideas or experiences in complete, coherent, syntactically correct sentences.

When a teacher also provides opportunities for students to respond to the vocabulary used by their peers, the experience takes on an additional level of learning sophistication. A teacher may ask another student, "What did you hear Tony say?" or "Can you add to what Tony said?" Or, "What did Natalia just tell us about how she thought the story would end?" or "Did anyone have a different idea for the story ending?" Providing many experiences for children to listen and respond to each other can be a powerful learning tool for comprehension.

## TEACHING HIGH-FREQUENCY AND SIGHT WORDS

Teaching high-frequency words is not an either–or proposition. An emergent reader who is building strong decoding skills can simultaneously learn, and will automatically add, common sight words that are instantly recognized and learned without conscious effort. Words such as *and, from, the, of, to, that, for, was, are, with,* and *you* should be recognized by sight, as they are not included with sound-to-print instruction that prepares students to read decodable text. High-frequency words are words that are commonly heard and read in the English language. Some of these words are decodable with regular phonics instruction, but others are irregular, which means they are not phonetically identified but must be read as unique and be rapidly known. These words could be names of the children in the class, the name of their school, or the name of their city of residence. Additionally, they could be words common to a school subject, such as social studies, math, or science. Once learned at the automatic recall level, the words reside in long-term memory within neural networks of similar words and experiences. As children learn high-frequency vocabulary and sight words, more interesting stories are accessible for them to read.

## A PRACTICE EXAMPLE

Picture a first grader carrying a ring with hole-punched cards. Each card has a word, not just any word, but a word that needs to be memorized, possibly from the Dolch sight words, developed by Dr. E. W. Dolch in the 1930s, or words the student wants to use in writing. The student's task is to read or identify those words to an older child or adult and make a tally mark on the back of the card each time the word is pronounced correctly. When 10 (or another number based on the child's memory needs) tally marks are reached, the card is removed from the ring. A number of these word cards may be traded for a prize or recorded on a chart or in a journal. Words known by sight are taught using rote memory techniques, such as this one that operates through frequent, repetitive exposure.

## LIMITATIONS TO LEARNING WORDS BY ROTE MEMORY

There are cautions and limitations to teaching sight words and high-frequency vocabulary. Some children with excellent memory skills learn to easily store new words in long-term memory. Rather than going through the hard work of learning and applying the orthographic rules for encoding and decoding, these children rely on their innate ability to memorize new words in the early grades.

Remedial work with students who are identified as unsuccessful decoders indicates that many of these children have excellent memory skills for all words. Consequently, they unintentionally or unconsciously ignore decoding and phonics rules and memorize every word they need to read. They are generally successful readers until the middle or end of second grade, or as long as they are exposed to relatively short words. However, when they are faced with text that has longer multisyllabic words, words that look similar, and words with many letter sequence deviations, they begin to show signs of reading difficulties. Instruction that encourages students to learn too many sight words during the early years can give a false sense of reading success, when actually the children are taxing memory capabilities in place of developing decoding strategies. Remedial work with students who are identified as unsuccessful decoders indicates that some of these children have excellent memory skills for recognizing sight words.

#  COGNITIVE DEVELOPMENT

As with previous chapters, the chart of cognitive skills for 6- and 7-year-old students is provided as a guide. These skills may provide insights for students who are not progressing as expected. Early identification of children who are not maturing according to these milestones of cognitive skill development can alert educators to hone in on areas that indicate a need for additional teaching. Refer also to the cognitive skills chart in Chapter 5 for children who are experiencing reading difficulties.

## COGNITIVE SKILLS FOR LEARNING: AGES 6 AND 7

Memory Systems (Sensory, Working, and Long-Term)

| 6–7 Years | Takes a root word that is known and manipulates it with a prefix, suffix, or plural. Takes what is known about planting seeds and growing from long-term memory and expands it with new information, such as harvesting and eating. Takes what is known about their home neighborhood and expands that information to where their school is located. |
| --- | --- |
| | Draws on several or many items or concepts from long-term memory to contemplate and add new information or to change misconceptions. For example: What is the job of the school principal? What is the job of a cafeteria worker? How is the breakfast or lunch prepared? Why does our community have police officers? What activities are available for children in our community? |

Executive Function

| 6 Years | **Reasoning**—Logically works through complex or competing information (family relationships, for example: "My father and my uncles and aunts have the same parents, who are my grandparents"). Uses mathematics reasoning to talk through story problems. Provides an answer to a question, and talks to explain the solution. Talks about playground problems and develops a list of potential solutions. |
| --- | --- |

# CONCLUDING THOUGHTS ABOUT READING IN A FIRST-GRADE CLASSROOM

Some pretty incredible work, resilience, and adaptation resulted from educators and support staff during the COVID-19 pandemic, and also as students returned to school late in 2021. Rushing to support education at all levels were institutions, foundations, agencies, and publishers who stepped up with ways of doing online instruction. Teachers were reached electronically with supportive programs and advancements for the teaching of reading. The important aspects of teaching reading have been defined and validated by sophisticated research. School districts are providing enriched, revised, and replaced reading programs. Teaching practices supported by what is known from neurology's brain science provide the added support teachers can use as they make choices when they instruct children to become readers.

Children have brains designed for successful oral language that are modified for the complexities of reading. Educators have "what is going on in there" information to understand the miracles that are happening inside the human brain. Children progress from being ready to read, to decoding and encoding and from developing vocabulary and understanding, to reading with fluency and accuracy. In tandem, they begin to learn phonics for spelling patterns and to record their own stories and ideas in writing. Not all children develop these skills at the same rate. The next chapter continues the pathway to reading with an emphasis on the memory systems involved through the entire complex process.

# Reflective Questions

1. Describe a first-grade student. What can they expect from their first-grade experience?

2. In this chapter the Common Core State Standards for kindergarten are summarized as an indication of what is already expected when a first-grade student begins the new school year. Which expectations would a first-grade teacher want to assess at the start of the school year?

3. The brain has structures that are hardwired to attend to and produce speech. What is different about the demands that are placed on the brain to respond to input for reading?

4. If you are reading this book as part of a university course or study group, ask groups of three people to prepare and present a short lesson that plays with sounds using phoneme awareness activities. Have the group define concepts children are learning when they practice sounds through these exercises.

5. Prepare an outline or concept map to be used for a short faculty presentation to trace how pronunciation and articulation of sounds to letters, not letters to sounds, efficiently direct a child's brain to remember words. Consider a discussion about how phonics instruction is taught if you are at a school.

6. Writing is a natural accompaniment to a reading program. In what ways do teachers prime their students and their brains for the physical process of writing?

7. Comment on some of the many advantages and identify a disadvantage of teaching sight and high-frequency words.

8. How or when might the chart of cognitive skill development be useful to a second-grade teacher? If there is a first-grade educator in the group, describe a specific child who could benefit from being assessed for cognitive skill development. What other concepts would you add to the chart for children at this age?

9. What are some computer resources that would be useful in a first-grade classroom?

# CHAPTER 7

# Second-Grade Readers

A visitor to any second-grade classroom will see simi-larities to the first-grade classroom across the way. However, the urgency of learning to decode text has settled into more specific objectives, such as learning phonics and spelling patterns, decoding and encoding multiple-syllable words, learning and remembering the more irregular features of English, *and* the overriding push to learn to read fluently and accurately, with prosody and comprehension.

Teachers welcome their students to second grade. They are eager to know each individually, and curious to identify skills or deficiencies for reading that they bring with them. Most of the early days and weeks will be an adjustment period—both for children and for their teacher. Teachers may find the variety of reading skills among their students is vast. The Common Core State Standards (CCSS) for second grade are demanding and become progressively more challenging. Instructional materials based on these standards are available from the Common Core State Standards Initiative (2010). As teachers discover discrepancies in children's learning that are not covered by prepared instructional materials, they make modifications to teaching materials, make their own practice materials, or find lessons from other sources, often at their own expense.

Teachers respond to their students' unique needs by differentiating and extending student background knowledge to build the highly diverse perspectives required by the CCSS. In this chapter, educators will find many unique approaches based on what is known about a child's brain. Of particular importance is acquiring an understanding of the brain's unique built-in memory systems for expansion and creating diverse thinking. Students' brains use the oral language pathway designed for listening and speaking in new and expanded ways to become proficient as a reading pathway for all aspects of reading.

## READING AND LANGUAGE ARTS STANDARDS FOR SECOND GRADE

For second-grade students, the CCSS include six major categories (see Common Core State Standards Initiative, 2013). To summarize briefly does not do the standards justice, but for the purpose of grasping the importance of second-grade work, here is a glimpse at some of the unique expectations.

### COMMON CORE STATE STANDARDS FOR SECOND GRADE

**Reading: Literature**

Describe responses of characters in a story, poem, or song; explain story structure; acknowledge characters have different points of view; compare the same story told by different authors; read grade-level materials at or above proficiency.

**Reading: Informational Text**

Understand author's purpose; explain diagrams; compare and contrast two important points from two texts with the same topic; by year's end, experience different types of informational texts with proficiency at or above Grades 2 and 3.

**Reading: Foundational Skills of Knowing and Applying Grade-Level Phonics and Word Analysis in Decoding Words**

Identify words with inconsistent but common spelling–sound correspondences; recognize and read grade-level irregularly spelled words.

**Reading: Reading With Sufficient Accuracy and Fluency to Support Comprehension**

Read second-grade text with purpose and understanding, accuracy, appropriate rate, and expression; use context to confirm or self-correct word recognition.

## IS THERE AN ORDER TO TEACHING ENGLISH LANGUAGE ARTS STANDARDS?

What comes first in reading development: comprehension or fluency? Listening or speaking competency? Reading or writing skills? Some argue that children must be fluent readers to comprehend what they are reading. Fluency, discussed in more detail in Chapter 8, is the ability to read out loud with accuracy and at an appropriate rate. Fluent reading is also characterized by giving the appropriate prosody and expression. Fluent reading sounds much like speech with pauses and rise-and-fall patterns. A fluent reader's brain automatically processes the underlying connections among the reading structures for decoding, and is free to devote full attention to the meaning associated with words.

**Comprehension**, the other part of this equation, is tied explicitly to vocabulary and background knowledge. The answer to the question of what comes first—comprehension through vocabulary development or speed of processing text (fluency)—is neither. Both appear to be developed simultaneously as a child becomes a proficient reader; furthermore, different reading skills are dependent on one another. Teachers provide skill development simultaneously for all aspects of reading, not one after the other. The brain's memory systems are important to understand. All aspects of memory are needed to develop successful readers as they address and conquer the CCSS for reading and English language arts.

# WHAT IS KNOWN FROM NEUROSCIENCE?

Realize there are not memory boxes for storage in the human brain. While figures representing memory areas can be shown on a diagram, it takes many cortices and systems on both sides of the brain, even in the primitive limbic system, to conduct a process for memory beyond initial sensory input. The frontal lobes in a child's brain are called to coordinate progressively more expansive memory abilities as children advance toward adulthood. Think about the mind expansion as children seek to respond to complex classroom demands and build extensive life-reflecting and academic vocabularies, through more and more complex neural connections. The human brain responds with automatic processes, while children expand connections between thoughts and concepts in novel, exciting, and required ways, as early as second grade.

Learning to *pay attention* and extending attention to focused *concentration* are the first two cognitive attributes, called priming skills, given in Chapter 5. The third support, memory, is the development of permanent, automatically accessible storage for words, information, concepts, and skills necessary for competent readers. Functional memory accesses three systems: sensory memory, working memory, and long-term memory.

## SENSORY MEMORY

Sensory memory is constantly receiving information from the environment. Incoming signals from the five senses are for the most part discarded. However, sensory memory is important to the reading process. (Refer back to Figure 3.2 in Chapter 3.) If the human brain paid attention to all the stimuli that arrived from the senses, a second grader or an adult would never move beyond all that is received. So there are systems to protect humans as learned earlier. Most sensory information is dropped and never remembered: a cough, a bird outside, a hard chair, clothes that are too loose, and so on.

If, however, the input is of value, such as words or pictures on a page, a teacher giving instructions or telling a story, or a mother making chocolate chip cookies, sensory memory takes notice and passes the information on to working memory. There is a slight, but rapid, detour through the primitive part of the brain to ascertain there is no danger before the information is routed to an association area for working memory. For example, that recognized and acknowledged smell is chocolate chip cookies.

# WORKING MEMORY

An extremely small amount of the massive information being transmitted by all of the senses is selected as important for the task of reading. Pertinent input from sensory memory, which is most likely from the occipital (visual) lobe, is moved into working memory. Working memory in the human brain has been attributed to the hippocampus in the limbic system. It can also be gathered from scattered areas for association, rehearsal, and practice.

Once in working memory, the information will remain available for up to 18 seconds (McGee & Wilson, 1984) or, according to Woolfolk (2008), 5 to 20 seconds. To maintain information for a longer period, the brain uses an *articulatory loop* as it holds information in working memory for rehearsal. Rehearsal or practice of this type engages the brain in **subvocalization**, a conscious process of holding the string of words or other information to be repeated over and over.

This practice eventually develops in children, but in second grade, it is aided when teachers model what it sounds like to subvocalize. Spelling is an easy example.

"I'm thinking of the word *friend* from my spelling [or vocabulary] list. It begins with *fr* and finishes with *end*. The tricky part is the *i* in the middle. So, I have *fr-i-end*. It is spelled *f-r-i-e-n-d*, *f-r-i-e-n-d*, *f-r-i-e-n-d*."

More difficult to subvocalize is a list of items, steps, or rules. With subvocalizing practice, the 18-second limit can be extended for the targeted material. During this silent but active brain work, other information stored in long-term memory is enlisted as the memory system for new information expands. (Refer back to Figure 4.2 in Chapter 4.) An association loop extension is activated, as the child seeks background knowledge in visual or auditory centers. Consider the activity of association as elaborative rehearsal (Wolf, 2007; Woolfolk, 2008).

Thinking that involves the elaborative, associative loop would sound like this: "I already know about hurricanes. My family had to stop when we were traveling because of bad weather caused by a hurricane" (long-term memory). "Hurricanes, spelled *h-u-r-r-i-c-a-n-e-s*, are violent storms causing winds over 70 miles per hour" (new information being rehearsed through working memory). Making the association with previously stored information creates a "hook" and increases the possibility that new, associated information will be remembered in long-term memory. See Figure 7.1 as a guide for instructional

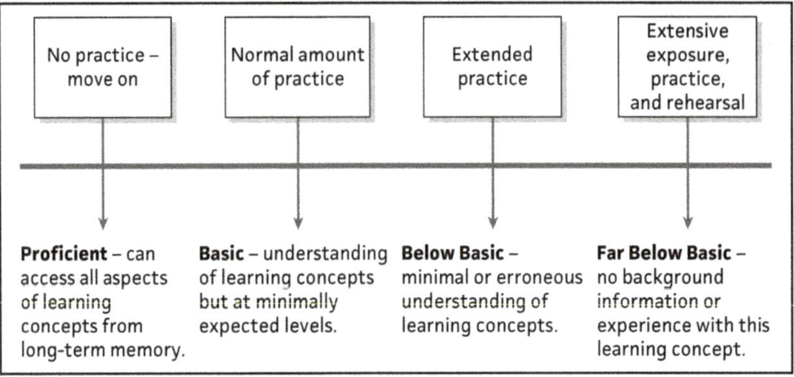


**Source:** Adapted from Nevills & Wolfe (2009).

planning to accommodate students who need more time with working memory practice.

## LONG-TERM MEMORY

With enough practice, the information, concept, or skill becomes available for recall or demonstration from **long-term memory**. Teachers plan to help students hold relevant sensory input in working memory through practice and association until the material can be recalled automatically from long-term memory. Varying amounts of practice are needed for children based on assessment of what they already know. The same amount of rehearsal and practice activities for the entire class frustrates both teachers and children, as they realize that they "already have it" or "still do not get it."

Teachers can find or design supplemental classroom activities to help children who lack proficiency in any aspect of building the reading pathway. Additional time is needed to consciously provide practice and instruction to reach competency of essential reading skills. For example, second-grade standards require that students identify words with inconsistent but common spelling–sound correspondences. Consider the words *book* and *moon*. The medial sound should be the same, but each is different. Some children hear the differences and understand these unique discrepancies. They read these words as if they are sight words without pausing. Other children need one or all of the following supplemental instruction activities to remember this inconsistency:

- Using rote memory to practice these words with many repetitions

- Reading, verbalizing, and relating to other words with the same inconsistent spelling

- Seeing the selected words on their spelling list and interacting with them multiple ways and times

Rehearsal is a function of working memory. When the material is remembered in long-term memory, it appears to reside in multiple areas of the brain, which depends on the task the reader is attempting. It may be a vocabulary word placed in a memory area with codes for its orthographic word form (the sequence of letters and their shapes). A word may also be stored in a memory area for phonological properties (the process used to identify, manipulate, produce, and remember speech sounds). Regardless of the storage location, neuroscientists using functional magnetic resonance imaging (fMRI) techniques have noted that as tasks become more complex, they are likely to be managed and finalized through activity in the frontal lobes. How does this look in terms of brain activation? Orthographic word forms may be initially stored in the visual association part of the brain. Phonological properties may be stored in the auditory processing area. To understand a sentence or paragraph, it is the frontal lobes that have the task of pulling it all together from different parts of the brain for meaning and comprehension.

## LONG-TERM MEMORY HAS TWO DISTINCT SYSTEMS

The ultimate goal of rehearsing and manipulating information in working memory is to move it into long-term memory so a child can recall and use it at will. Remember there is not a box in the brain for long-term memory as it is depicted in the figures provided. Rather, words, ideas, and concepts are stored and then accessed from many different parts of the brain. Think about file cabinets. To liken the functional brain to an image that makes sense, picture a huge number of file cabinets in each of the brain's lobes. Each file cabinet is prepared with files too numerous to imagine. When a child practices and rehearses something enough times for it to be stored for long-term memory, it is stored in an appropriate lobe's file cabinets with similar types of items learned. When developing a complex concept, the frontal lobes retrieve information from many different file cabinets. Then the CEO (frontal lobes) pulls everything together to vocalize or write a cumulative response.

To plan instruction that matches the complex storage systems that make up the brain's memory functions, readers of this

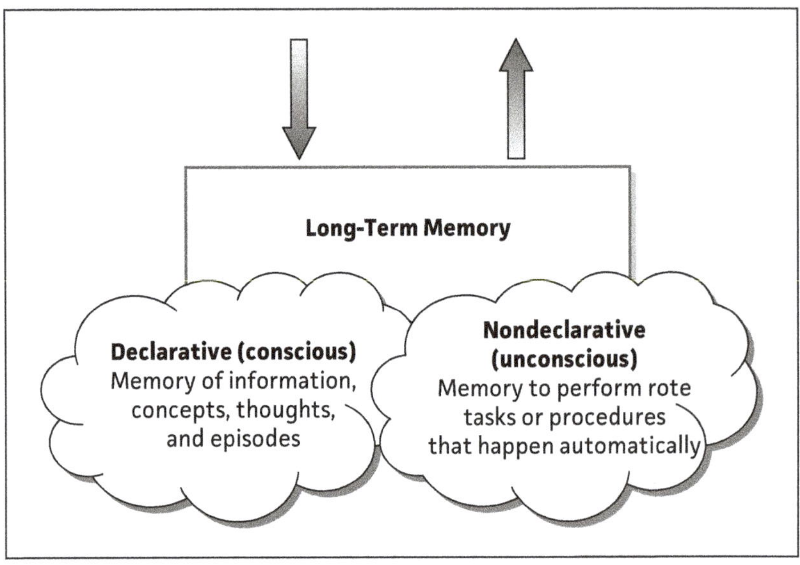


**Source:** Created by Herb Higashi. Adapted from Nevills (2014).

book can understand two different long-term memory systems the brain uses to store long-term recollection for reading development, illustrated in Figure 7.2: **declarative** (conscious) and **nondeclarative** (unconscious) memory.

## DECLARATIVE (CONSCIOUS) MEMORY: SEMANTIC AND EPISODIC

Declarative memory allows children to store information in an organized format to subsequently recall it by speaking or writing. To access declarative memory, most likely the child thinks consciously about the subject; has a quick, internal mental discussion about its attributes; and makes an overt response. Memories stored in the brain's declarative long-term system are *statements of fact, data, labeling, and events that require conscious effort to recall.* The brain calls on the hippocampus, which the reader may recall from Chapter 4 is a pair of structures under the temporal lobes in the limbic system to identify a category for the information to be stored. Other areas of the cortex, particularly the temporal lobes, provide the collection of stored sound information. Information stored in long-term declarative memory uses two very distinct memory processes: semantic and episodic.

## SEMANTIC MEMORY

Words, phrases, sentences, and other forms of text recalled and articulated through speech or writing reflect an individual's background information and experience. Student recall, articulation, or written response is identified as the **semantic memory** system. When children practice spelling words, they are working to get the information into semantic long-term memory. When they complete worksheets that match definitions with words, they are reinforcing learning for semantic memory. Likewise, using blocks or letters to represent sounds in words during phonemic manipulation provides practice for this type of memory. Some reading concepts that competent readers hold in semantic memory include phonological rules, **syntax** and **semantics** for language, spelling patterns, and word meanings. In each case, the child can declare or use written means to tell what is known from memory.

Classroom activities are designed so students can master information and concepts and store them in long-term semantic memory. Teachers may be surprised at the variety of ways they support their students to learn materials that ultimately will reside in semantic long-term memory (see Table 7.1). To identify those activities, think about reading tasks designed for students to practice, rehearse, prompt, organize, recall, write, and sequence. As children sort a list of words into categories with phoneme labels, for example, what is the memory goal? They are developing organizational patterns of sounds to be stored in declarative semantic memory.

## EPISODIC MEMORY

While lessons are strategically planned for children to practice and manipulate information for semantic memory, experiences recorded in episodic memory generally happen with careful planning at school or more commonly by chance in the real world. Long-term declarative memory, or **source memory**, of a happening or occurrence is accompanied by strongly felt emotions or active engagement. These experiences become a part of an **episodic memory** system.

An episodic experience is an active way to get information into long-term memory, but it is not always accurate. As an experience is retold, it is enhanced or fabricated with plot and detail additions or limited with omissions. The details become less clear and often become distorted with each recall. This phenomenon is experienced when adults retell a joke or silly story. Each time the humorous situation is repeated, the details become less like the original version. Likewise, children form their own individual long-term memories of an episodic

| PROCESS | TEACHER DIRECTIONS | STUDENT RESPONSE |
|---|---|---|
| Practice | Put your spelling words on flash cards to self-check the letter sequence for the word. | Writes, spells, sorts, and practices words. |
| Rehearse | Say the phonics rules and match three words for each. | Reviews rules and shows understanding by placing the words that match each. |
| Prompt | Find the words that begin like *bubble*. | Selects words from a list or page. Creates own list. |
| Organize | Put your words in groups that share beginning, middle, or ending sounds using this chart or one of your own. | Completes a chart that organizes words into groups with the same beginning, medial, or ending sounds. |
| Recite | Look at the words, decide what rule they follow, and recall what sound they make. Say the rule and the words with your partner. | Reviews the word list to identify the orthographic rules and vocalizes the words. |
| Write/Dictate | Write the words or sentences as the teacher says them. | Listens to sounds and attaches graphemes to write words or sentences. |
| Sequence | Put these words for the days of the week, or months of the year, in order. Put other words in order (e.g., *big, tiny, little, huge*). | Sorts and orders word cards. Or, writes the words in order. |

**Source:** Adapted from Nevills & Wolfe (2009).

experience. If they talk about the experience at home, chances are strong that they will each have a unique way of describing what they remember and what seemed most interesting to them.

Classroom episodic memory experiences take time and planning. The precise learning objectives must be known and discussed with students to focus their attention. Teachers decide that the activity—a field trip, an elaboration activity, acting out a story, or role play of an incident, for example (see Table 7.2)—is the best way for students to learn the idea, topic, or concept. What children remember from an episodic activity depends on each child's needs and interests. Learning outcomes are dependent on what the teacher emphasizes through discussion and activities prior to and following the experience to validate and accurately fortify the experience. Planning episodic activities takes advantage of the emotional aspects of the brain and a "fast route" to long-term memory.

**TABLE 7.2** ● Examples of Teaching to *Declarative* Episodic Memory

| STRATEGY | LEARNING EVENT | STUDENT INVOLVEMENT |
| --- | --- | --- |
| Experience | Taking a field trip. Having a guest speaker. | Firsthand sensory stimuli. Heightened activation from the limbic system. |
| Elaboration | Enhancing an incident from a story with words beyond what the author told. | Expanded conceptual understanding by speaking about pictures, expanding situations, and identifying new details. |
| Story play | Reading out loud and/or having actors act out the story. | Active engagement and acute attention to peers. |
| Role playing | Pretending to be the character or person named on a card, in a story, or in a particular incidence. | Active engagement while anticipating another person's perception. |
| Demonstration | Showing a story or details from informative text through a PowerPoint presentation, with props or regalia, on a story board, or through pictures. | Heightened attention due to novelty of presentation. |

**Source:** Adapted from Nevills & Wolfe (2009).

# NONDECLARATIVE (UNCONSCIOUS) MEMORY: ROTE AND PROCEDURAL

Semantic and episodic declarative memory stores the "what" part of memories. "How" something is done accesses nondeclarative or implicit memory. Nondeclarative memory consists of short responses, procedures, and skills that have been practiced to the point that they can be performed automatically without conscious thought.

## ROTE MEMORY

Children use rote memory to respond with automaticity to flash cards, to call someone by name, or to say "thank you." In automatized rapid reading, a timed reading of letters or words, rote memory is tested. As applied to reading, an example of *rote* nondeclarative memory is rapid identification of words without thinking about their attributes. Fluent readers decode words almost effortlessly below the level of conscious thought, allowing the reading brain to consciously focus on word meaning.

## PROCEDURAL MEMORY

While rote memory is generally for shorter responses, procedural memory provides for reading processes. An example of **procedural nondeclarative memory** is the ability of a reader's eyes to rapidly race across a line of print, seeing every letter but stopping for none. Other examples of automaticity include talking and writing in sentences that follow rules for grammar, using correct syntax, turning the pages of a book, typing on a computer keyboard, and using the phone keypad. Procedural memory responds to a situation or a prompt by setting off a sequence of skills that are needed to accomplish a task, *and* the student does not have to think about how it is done.

To culminate descriptions of the three memory systems, and specifically the attributes of long-term memory from this chapter, refer to Figure 7.3. A complete traditional model of the sensory, working, and long-term memory systems is seen with their interconnectiveness and dependence upon one another.

## REDUCING THE COGNITIVE WORKLOAD

Children do not begin reading complete sentences with automatic fluency and comprehension. There are a multitude of skills they must master, beginning with concepts of print and concluding with world or background knowledge. Classroom activities to turn the individual reading attributes of decoding, comprehending, and reading with fluency into an automatic procedure include rereading stories, practicing sight words, rapid identification of new or nonsense words, and other rehearsal-type strategies. Children use the articulatory loop in working memory to practice information and associate it with previous learning. Using the articulatory loop allows the information to eventually become an automatic response from procedural memory.

This process sounds confusing, but the activities normally happening in a second-grade classroom allow students to make the transfer with ease. When students are able to transfer information into long-term memory, their working memory is not overwhelmed; they feel more confident as learners. With this added self-assurance, they are able to attend to tasks that involve more and more difficult concepts and problem solving.

## FORGETTING

Second-grade teachers following the science of reading may no longer have a weekly list of spelling words, isolated from reading lessons. This practice proved to be ineffective. Children would learn the words in short-term memory for the test, and then unconsciously dump the words out of working

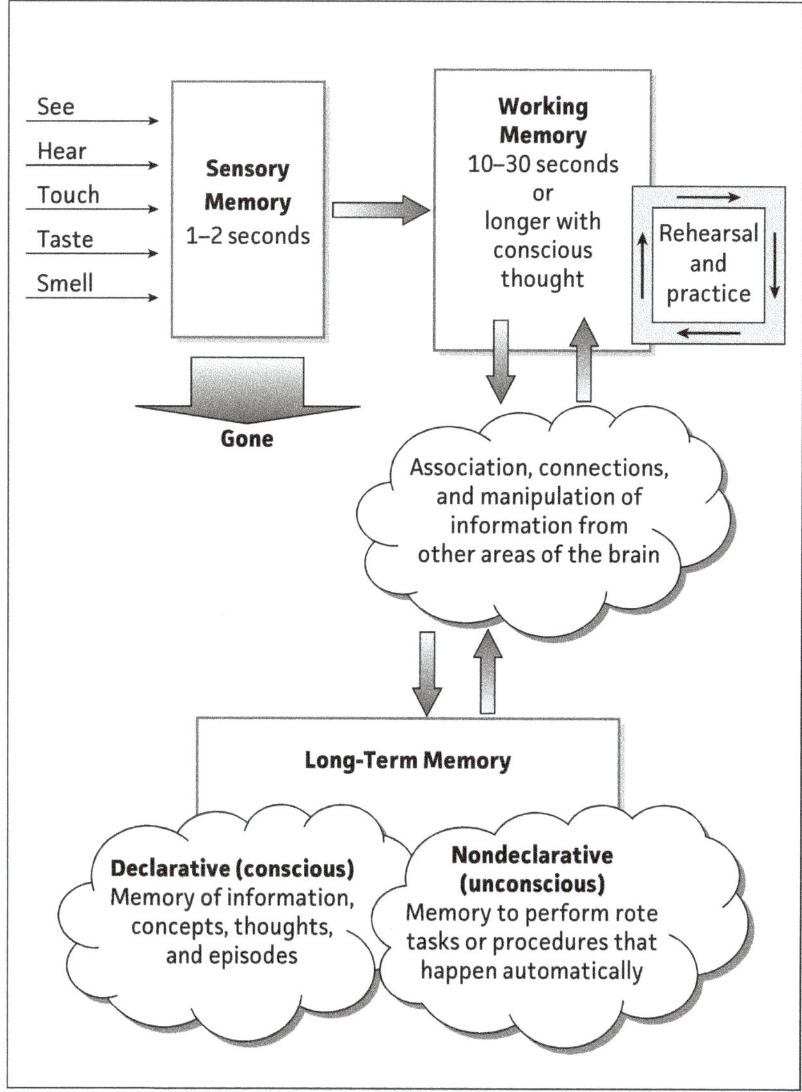


**FIGURE 7.3** ● A complete traditional model of the memory systems beginning with input from the sensory system with a small amount of important information transferring into working memory where information is manipulated until it moves to permanent storage through the conscious declarative system or the unconscious procedural system.

**Source:** Created by Herb Higashi. Adapted from Nevills (2014).

memory. The *Science of Reading Handbook* (Snowling & Hulme, 2005) recommends extending practice of the words, which in brain terms means rehearsal and practice in working memory. This practice does not happen in isolation; it is related to other language arts activities. Teaching practices for repetition and reinforcement may include sentence dictation or identifying word patterns or families. Children encounter the spelling words in their reading and writing experiences, both before and after the spelling test.

An interesting side note is that Ebbinghaus's Forgetting Curve from the 1880s was subsequently validated in a research study (Murre & Dros, 2015) and highlighted by MindTools (n.d.). A German psychologist, Hermann Ebbinghaus, wanted to understand why forgetting happens. In 1880, sophisticated imaging devices were not available, nor was it known what was happening in the human brain when learning occurred. Ebbinghaus's report was based on charting his own experiences. He found that (1) memories weaken over time; (2) the most memory loss happens soon after learning; (3) remembering is easier when meaning is attached; (4) it matters how something is learned; and (5) how the learner feels affects what will be remembered. The previous is a pretty good summation of all the memory information presented in the preceding pages. Classroom practices for transferring important skills and concepts into long-term memory are covered in the next sections, but here is a short list: allow time between practice activities, overlearn items and concepts, attach meaning (a hook) to new learning, and insert a challenge or goal that students are able to attain.

## WHAT CAN TEACHERS DO TO TEACH THE WAY THE BRAIN LEARNS?

Teachers have a large repertoire of information about how to teach phonics, word decoding and encoding, and vocabulary to develop student comprehension and reading fluency. From the vast array of strategies and instructional considerations already available to them, the ones listed in this chapter are specific to the way a child's brain is coaxed to maximize instructional time and learning efforts. Specific parts of the CCSS summarized earlier are addressed: (1) reading literature, (2) reading informational text, (3) developing vocabulary, (4) communicating through writing, and (5) language.

### 1. READING LITERATURE

The CCSS require that students be able to describe character responses and different points of view, compare stories with different authors, and read grade-level materials at or above proficiency. All these expectations rely on extensive exposure to literature and dependency on memory systems to describe, acknowledge, compare, and read proficiently. The following two examples look at second-grade expectations and brain-friendly teaching.

## AN ILLUSTRATION EXAMPLE

Why would second-grade teachers be encouraged to *occasionally* use reading material that is void of colorful, descriptive pictures that accompany most reading materials? In prereading and early reading experiences, illustrations can lure and invite children into the world of text. However, as children become readers, the likelihood is that illustrations will be more attractive than the accompanying text. A child's brain responds to the sensory stimuli that are easiest to understand. Vivid and inviting illustrations cause children to tend to ignore the linguistic content of the story and rely on pictures to provide responses to comprehension questions. Text with pictures may inhibit the way children access background information from their own memory systems. Accessing stored information is essential for children to create their own internal, meaningful understanding to describe, acknowledge, and compare. Teachers promote self-reflection and visualization by intermittently withholding pictures until children have read the text and responded to questions. Insightful comparisons result when the illustrations are finally provided.

## ROBUST VOCABULARY INSTRUCTION

Researcher Isabel Beck and her colleagues (2013) developed a process for bringing words to life for teaching vocabulary from literature and the following CCSS area of informational text. They use a program to incorporate a "read, reread, and discuss" strategy. New words are taught after the children hear the story for the first time. Vocabulary instruction follows this sequence: conceptualization, repetition, definition, other contexts, children's examples, and finally continuing repetition. A vocabulary chart allows children to revisit new and former vocabulary frequently and continually during subsequent stories. For example, the teacher may say, "Remember the word *trouble?* How could you use that word to tell about something that happened in this story?" Children learn vocabulary development for listening and speaking concurrently with vocabulary development for reading and writing. Oral language development will advance quickly through activities such as read-alouds, but *eventually, children's reading vocabularies will catch up with and advance beyond what they are able to understand through oral language activities.*

# 2. READING INFORMATIONAL TEXT

Informational text, aside from being nonfiction, includes biographies, reports, essays, online articles, event flyers, and even teacher's manuals. Young readers are not so far removed from early childhood when the whole world was new. They are still eager learners about animals, airplanes, and stormy weather, to name a few of the broad range of topics that interest them. In addition, children, even in the early grades, may be expected to follow signs, read instructions, heed warnings, and use newspapers, magazines, and books that are available to the public in general. Exposure to informational texts beginning in first or second grade can pique children's interests and curiosities. Of equal importance, text based on information about the natural or social world prepares students with background needed for later-grade expectations.

## LEARNING ABOUT THE WORLD

*Informational* texts are generally those that intend to communicate information about the world, presumably from someone more knowledgeable than the reader, which contain factual content and technical vocabulary and have consistent repetitions of a topical theme. Indexes and diagrams or other graphical elements are frequently included in text that is informational in nature. *Narrative informational* writing, or **narrative text**, provides information about the natural or social world, yet is written with narrative features, such as books in the popular *Magic School Bus* series (Cole & Degen, 1986–2020). When information about the natural or social world is conveyed through verse, it is *informational-poetic*.

Informational text expands background information and builds background knowledge networks needed for comprehension. The rationale for using texts with information moves beyond the notion that children are interested and likely to pay attention. For vocabulary evolution and linguistic enhancement, teachers can explore factual information with their classes. Using factual, concrete vocabulary, children are able to classify, categorize, and define new vocabulary. For problem solving, contrasting, and making comparisons, children can draw on facts, ideas, and concepts from non-narrative text.

## ACADEMIC VOCABULARY NEEDS OF ALL CHILDREN

One of the buzzwords among reading and language arts educators is **academic vocabulary**, which by its name suggests it is beyond words used in everyday interactions. Rather, it is language used for cognitive academic interactions. Often utilized for teaching English language learners (ELLs), this specific vocabulary is identified as both general and content-specific vocabulary. For second grade, academic vocabulary identifies the terms that may be confusing to students and provides a definition and example of the new terms or phrases. Some examples of academic vocabulary include *define, sort, main idea, recall, facts, details, observtion,* and *conclusion.* Further expansion of this type of vocabulary might include *image, imagine, curious, details, different,* and *similar.* To learn academic vocabulary, students are engaged with a term by stating a description, giving an example in their own words, or responding with an oral or written response. Using another memory output strategy, students construct a graphic representation of how to respond to the term or phrase. Students may need to rehearse the term at a variety of times through discussion, games, and other activities requiring oral language involvement. This type of activity matches with best practices for brain-friendly learning of these important direction words that may otherwise be illusive.

## HARD READING MATERIALS

Reading can be hard or easy depending on the relationship between the capabilities the child has to read the words. Additional considerations include the knowledge or experience base required for the text to be understood, the level of commitment the child has to read the selection, and the complexity of the writing style. An example is a child who has a strong desire to know more about prehistoric beasts. The child is well versed in the topic of dinosaurs from conversations with parents, television or screen viewing, and previous book experiences. Also, this child is considered to be a strong reader by the classroom teacher. However, the selected book or selection may have a vocabulary load with too many new terms, a linguistic structure that is more common to scientific text, or organization of ideas that appear in a different discourse or style. The text can become too difficult, even to the child who is seemingly ready for more in-depth information.

Accelerated Reader and Lexile Framework are two standard school programs that use research-based methods to determine the readability levels for a large variety of children's books. Both use computer-assisted management systems. Accelerated Reader gives a zone of proximal development for children to ensure that readers feel challenged without being frustrated with their reading selections. Lexile Framework characterizes each reader with a measure, called a Lexile, and forecasts the level of comprehension that the reader will be able to attain with a selected text. In each case, the programs are designed to align with state standards and often with basal readers. Books for leisure reading are also given a reading level. Equipped with this detailed information, teachers and parents can help children select books to match their individual reading skills and their interests, or know when to support the child who insists on a book that is too advanced.

## 3. DEVELOPING VOCABULARY

Text has far too many words to teach each word that is unfamiliar to all or part of the class, and vocabulary instruction can take up a lot of class time. Teachers carefully make their own choice of new words each week or use words selected by the textbook publisher. This number is insignificant compared to the number of words students are learning and need to learn to meet grade-level expectations.

Vocabulary development, then, must take on other, more efficient strategies. Children learn to strategically analyze unknown words on their own. The CCSS and the science of reading support foundational skills of knowing and applying phonics and word analysis for decoding words.

For example, teachers explicitly teach the **morphology** of new words through identification of prefixes, suffixes, and roots that help students to identify words' meanings. Understanding morphology also supports pronunciations and to determine their parts of speech. Children learn to identify prefixes (the most common are *un-*, *re-*, *in-*, and *dis-*) and suffixes (some with heavy use are *-s*, *-ing*, *-ed*, and *-ly*). Words are then broken into parts—beginning, middle, and ending. Frequently, the middle part of the word is from a word family that children already know. The word *unfriendly*, although lengthy, becomes identifiable when it is viewed as *un-friend-ly*. Word families have the same base formation as seen with *time*, *timed*, *timetable*, and *untimely*. Children can expand vocabulary by chunking letters in long words into morphemes that hold meaning through self-applied analysis strategies, without needing explicit instruction for each new word that they encounter.

Vocabulary grows through interactions with people, activities, and books that introduce new words, ideas, and concepts. Advancement of vocabulary does not take place from students' own reading during the initial school years. Their reading content is not as advanced as their oral language levels. Reading vocabulary may not catch up to oral vocabulary until the seventh or eighth grade. Interestingly, then students read and write words that are more advanced than what they are able to use in common conversation.

Many classroom schedules include a time for the teacher to read out loud to the class, particularly in the primary grades. This activity is a wonderful way to build a positive classroom culture and expose students to appropriate fluency. When the activity is cognitively challenging with mind-engaging properties, it becomes a highly effective way to spend instructional time. Mind-engaging techniques for story time include reading the selection more than once, each time with a different incentive. The request could be to listen for new vocabulary, to look for a story line, to follow topic development, or to find the flow of information. Adult–child discussions are natural, as the strategy changes from being "read to," to being "read with," to being "talked about." *Talking about* happens through concentration-engaging questions that move beyond a *yes* or *no* or one-word response. Smaller groups of children, three to five in a group, can have a short but substantial talk directed by teacher prompts.

Teachers can have their classes look for targeted words from teacher read-alouds in other contexts, turning vocabulary acquisition into a game of word hunt that extends from the classroom to the neighborhood and beyond. Game activities may include crossword puzzles, student drawings of target words (remember a game from long ago called *Pictionary*), or "I spy a word that means . . ."

Vocabulary is not effectively expanded from materials that young children are able to read for themselves (Beck et al., 2013). With this knowledge, teachers select materials to read to children that are several levels above the children's own reading levels. Selections as much as two years ahead of the grade level are used to accelerate vocabulary growth.

## ANCHORING WORDS IN KNOWLEDGE NETWORKS

Vocabulary development, as we have seen, can become an engaging part of reading instruction. Playing with words in whimsical ways through puns, exaggerations, metaphors, idioms, or cartoons captivates students' attention. Vocabulary development, whether it is vocabulary for speaking, listening, reading, or writing, when provided in ways that are appealing and exciting, helps the child's brain to hold on to words, which are placed into neural networks for ease of capture and automatic recall.

Reading comprehension moves beyond the mechanics of word-by-word reading. Children's brains make new neural connections as they store information from classroom instruction, their experiences, and the environment in which they live. As children are exposed to new information, they unconsciously search long-term memory systems to bring previous, similar experiences to working memory. This memory system allows students to consider, use, and connect previously learned concepts to make sense of the new information.

Chunking is the process of combining several pieces of information into a single item that occupies one slot in working memory. Children use chunking of letters to form a meaningful phonological pattern or a word during decoding. Chunking a phrase or sentence allows the brain to conserve working memory space. Use of fairy-tale language—*once upon a time* or *and they lived happily ever after*—gives examples of how words are chunked as one memory space. To help a child organize information and ideas into conceptual chunks, teachers or parents can use strategies to tie new information to already acquired core knowledge. To capitalize on the brain's tendency to seek novelty, adults can add rhyme, rhythm, chant, or song to make information chunks firmly etched in working memory for practice and ultimately for automatic long-term storage and recall.

Chunking ability accounts for some of the differences teachers find between children who give simple responses to comprehension questions, and those who respond in detail using their wealth of available, previously stored background information. Children with an information-rich memory have developed the ability to make multiple connections from the words they read. They learn to chunk information while they contemplate it in working memory.

## DEVELOPING VOCABULARY FOR ENGLISH LANGUAGE LEARNERS

Earlier, strategies were provided for English learners (referred to as ELLs) to decode text. Think about it this way: phoneme awareness and phonics instruction are precise. They follow the structure of language and have rules. When a student is given systematic, explicit teaching and sufficient practice, decoding skills can be mastered. However, ELLs may be able to read with phonetic correctness and yet not comprehend a word of what they have read unless they have the background or experiences to understand the vocabulary. No program can teach all the words a child needs to know in Grade 1, Grade 3, or even Grade 12.

Vocabulary acquisition depends, as we have seen, on both direct vocabulary instruction and learning how to identify and categorize new words. ELLs tend to acquire much of their vocabulary outside of planned instruction, as they have conversations with peers and adults, listen to adults read, and read on their own. This is another situation for "talk, talk, talk." These older children, as well as the young children addressed in the first two chapters, have the same need for rich language experiences as they learn English. Provision of conversation-rich experiences both with adults and with peers is an important experience that is accompanied with specific instruction. There is a significant difference between proficiency for face-to-face communication, referred to as basic interpersonal communication skills (BICS), and proficiency needed to comprehend language in the educational setting, or cognitive academic language proficiency (CALP). Because of the difficulties that children who are ELLs may experience, these students need every minute of vocabulary development that school can offer.

A proliferation of research centers on the needs of a nation steeped with accountability issues and a diverse student population. Studies indicate ELLs require instruction in basic and academic vocabulary, academic language, and more sophisticated words (Collins, 2005). At the same time, these students need the same instruction all students need—definitional, contextual, analytical, usage, and elaboration. They need more practice and engagement through opportunities to talk using new vocabulary, responding to questions, learning songs, and acting out word plays. More than regularly progressing native English speakers, they must be prompted to speak, not simply to listen. Partner talk or work with small-group projects with native English speakers is highly engaging. This type of interaction provides needed social and academic interactions.

## ADDRESSING FLUENCY

Reading fluency, previously introduced, is a topic for Chapter 8. The standards expect a student to read with sufficient accuracy and fluency to support comprehension. Additionally, a second-grade student aims to read with accuracy, an appropriate rate, and expression while self-correcting using word recognition skills. Brain-compatible support for fluent reading is provided through continued timed readings that are conducted with the whole class, with a partner or group, or independently. Student paired reading provides oral reading practice for fluency, while teacher read-alouds model the appropriate prosody for oral reading.

# 4. COMMUNICATING THROUGH WRITING

Four distinct types of vocabulary—speaking, listening, reading, and writing—are accessed together and separately in the brain. For most children, the first two, speaking and listening, have an impressive start prior to school attendance. At school, teachers face instructional considerations based on their students' broad variability in the development of speaking and listening vocabulary. As children advance in school, their classroom experiences and leisure reading activities expose them to more and more words, and their active vocabulary for speaking and listening expands as students become writers.

## WRITING INDEPENDENTLY

To meet CCSS expectations, second-grade students learn to write opinion pieces, describe a narrative event in writing, and define personal thoughts and feelings, all with order and closure. How writing is developed—a different process from reading—is explained in neurological terms.

Vocabulary for writing is primarily learned at school. Instruction that includes specific teaching of words during reading is fortified through reexposure to the words during writing exercises. What is described as "novice writing" in the preschool years and "invented spelling" in first grade quickly advances to "independent writing" as students develop larger vocabularies and expand their understanding of orthographic and syntactic patterns.

Neurologically, the writing process is very different from reading, but it relies on some of the same brain structures. During reading, the brain responds first to visual stimuli, which then are processed into thoughts with meaning. When older children compose and write, the brain is commanded to start with internal thoughts. Brain structures connect in a reverse direction from reading to select appropriate vocabulary and then produce the symbols for these words in written format. In writing, the frontal lobes direct the motor cortex to coordinate arm, hand, and finger movements rather than to activate the mouth, tongue, and jaw as they do for speaking. As a child's fine motor movements become less tedious and more automatic, the cerebellum learns the writing procedure, allowing the child to produce print without concentrating on forming the letter shapes. This brain automaticity frees the child to concentrate on what is being written and communicated.

## HOW MANY EXPOSURES TO WORDS?

The amount of exposure that a child needs to move a target word into long-term memory for automatic recall depends on whether previous neural networks are available, or if they need to be developed to attach the word. When there is a very similar network (other words with the same orthographic structure, for example, or words that are synonyms) in long-term memory, the new learning can be linked or hooked to what is already there. The child may be able to read the word the next time it appears.

Assume the "hook" to previously stored similar words is not in the long-term memory system. Regardless of whether it is through conversation, reading, or writing, four exposures are not enough for children or most adults to remember or attach meaning to a new word (Stahl, 2003). In normal circumstances, 12 exposures to a new word are enough for most readers. Teachers find some children need to use a word 20 or more times before they are able to automatically recall it.

# 5. LANGUAGE

The use of adjectives and adverbs and ability to choose between them is specified in the CCSS. Children additionally need to be able to expand their writing, rearrange simple and compound sentences, and use adjectives and adverbs as words and in phrases for conversation and writing. Teaching the difference between these two terms is the initial activity. The use of these terms will take lots of practice in speaking and writing.

## TEACHING LANGUAGE THROUGH THE MEMORY SYSTEMS

Once again the reader is referred back to the systems for declarative and nondeclarative memory. The selected goal is to prompt the use of words, which are adjectives and adverbs, with the aid of the appropriate memory system (see Table 7.3).

The use of memory systems culminates this section. As a teaching strategy, using memory systems for most types of skill development prompts activities to fortify and cement learning. The memory systems are used as a guide for learning objectives from the CCSS. Practices to move learning objectives from working memory to long-term memory validate research provided by the science of reading. Understanding neurology provides the "how" and "why" for development of all skills for reading.

| **DECLARATIVE—CONSCIOUS (SEMANTIC, EPISODIC)** | |
| --- | --- |
| Semantic | Gives definitions; fills in the appropriate word; uses adjectives, then adverbs in speaking sentences; lists words that are adjectives and adverbs; finds and circles or underlines words that are adjectives and adverbs in narrative writing. |
| Episodic | Follows acting out a short story with identification of adjectives and adverbs to describe the characters and actions; watches a video and writes sentences using these two types of words. The teacher may read a story, and students walk two steps forward when they hear an adjective and jump three times when they hear an adverb. |
| **NONDECLARATIVE—UNCONSCIOUS (ROTE, PROCEDURAL)** | |
| Rote | Instantly identifies a word by saying its name, understanding words that are adjectives (or adverbs) so completely that the student can supply an adjective (or adverb) when the teacher reads and stops for a word to be supplied, or when given a narrative with adjectives (or adverbs) missing easily supplies a word with automaticity. |
| Procedural | The student writes or speaks fluently, with accurate sentences, including adjectives and adverbs, without stopping to contemplate a word to use. |

# COGNITIVE DEVELOPMENT

For second grade, there is one final listing on the chart of cognitive skills—this one is related to executive function. Note a child struggling with the complexities of learning to read may have one or more challenges in cognitive skill development. The chart of cognitive skills is a cumulative list, which results from a review of literature. The chart will be completed in the next chapter, and a comprehensive version appears in Appendix B.

## COGNITIVE SKILLS FOR LEARNING: AGE 7

Executive Function

| 7 Years | **Cognitive Speed**—Has the ability to reason through a problem and draw a conclusion with rapidity. Identifies unknown words. Engages with a timed reading task. Responds to questions. Reads a paragraph and identifies the main idea. When given a word, quickly uses the letters to form other words. Given a topic, lists words that relate. Identifies other words that start with two or three given letters. Completes this type of activity in timed segments, accompanied with progress charting.<br><br>**Preparation and Planning**—Has the ability to rationalize information or a problem to find and implement a workable solution. Develops questions to ask classmates when given an article from informational text. |
| --- | --- |

Teachers who command knowledge about the memory systems of the brain are likely to make sound instructional decisions about teaching reading. In all areas of teaching for second grade—phonemes, phonological processing, phonics, decoding, encoding, speaking, listening, writing, spelling, vocabulary, fluency, and comprehension—there are hundreds of decisions to be made, such as which ones, when, how often, how long, what strategies, what material, and with which children. Providing information about the memory systems in this chapter helps teachers to recognize when children have memory strengths and deficits. Semantic responses come from specific direct teaching. Episodic memory is formed by experiences from a heightened state that happens in the classroom with specific purpose, or as a chance happening. Rote memory is different from procedural memory and requires different instruction. By understanding the memory systems, teachers can develop instructional activities that are appropriate to develop each type of memory while meeting instructional objectives.

Vocabulary strongly depends on early oral language experiences. There is significant evidence that children who have decoding problems devote an inordinate amount of time and cognitive energy to the sounds of words. They are not able to concentrate on meaning. Some comprehension deficits could spring from limited instruction, but child-specific problems more likely result from a lack of long-term memory for background knowledge or vocabulary. In a classroom of 20 or 30 children, there may be several or even many who lack background knowledge about almost any new topic. Teachers use a variety of techniques to pretest children's knowledge of a new topic. If background experience is not evident, teachers then are able to provide the experience to prompt neural connections. New information is integrated into the child's memory systems. As children broaden their vocabulary, they progress also toward increased comprehension. Children who are able to comprehend text are more likely to be accomplished at a companion skill, fluency, which is a topic for the next chapter.

- The California Department of Education provides a yearly Recommended Literature List. This list is for Grades preK–2: bit.ly/3jSgJrF. Other lists are for Grades 1–5, 4–8, and 7–12. The CDE can be checked yearly for updates: www.cde.ca .gov/ci/cr/rl/.

- Chapter books for second grade are provided by Top10Best. How: bit.ly/3VPBQbv.

# Reflective Questions

1. This chapter is heavy with information about the memory systems: sensory, working, and long-term. Give your personal definition of each with its importance for a selected aspect of reading for a second-grade student. (Think about phonemic awareness; phonological processing; phonics for decoding, encoding, or writing; vocabulary development; reading fluency; and comprehension.)

2. What is declarative semantic memory? What are some strategies that you would suggest for second-grade teachers to use to strengthen students' ability to respond from semantic long-term memory?

3. It is suggested in this chapter that teachers occasionally withhold illustrations for some of the stories they read to students or stories students read themselves. Why would this strategy strengthen the brain's ability for comprehension?

4. Chunking information helps children to put more information into each available memory slot. How is chunking related to the development of reading comprehension?

5. Many adults prefer that children read hard, academically based books for their leisure reading. What are your thoughts on this preference? When would hard, academically based books be appropriate and even a best practice?

6. What strategies for teaching vocabulary do you find to be most useful for second grade? In what ways are these strategies brain compatible?

7. How do you see vocabulary development and comprehension skills as compatible? What are some second-grade teaching activities to encourage reading fluency?

8. **Bonus Question:** Select an instructional objective listed in the Common Core State Standards that you are interested in developing. Choose an instructional activity to teach this objective according to four different memory systems: semantic, episodic, rote, and procedural.

# CHAPTER 8

# Transition Time for Third-Grade Readers

Successful readers in third grade and beyond are able to rapidly scan lines of print and see every word but stop for few. These students seem to have an effortless ability to read. They spontaneously recognize familiar words and quickly, almost unconsciously, identify unfamiliar ones by applying their understanding of the orthographic nature of the English language. Students with reading proficiency additionally subvocalize appropriate verbal inflections to enhance the meaning of the sentences. Certainly, each teacher or adult who contributes to the mastery of skills for this level of reader must be delighted.

A student who reads with fluency, accuracy, and prosody is able to concentrate on the meaning of the words and sentences that are read. Brain circuits for word decoding in working memory systems are not being stressed, as word recall is handled almost automatically. The frontal lobes are free to concentrate on what the selection is about, not how it is constructed with individual words and their sounds. Generally, the science of reading promotes four principles for successful reading and comprehending: reading fluency, vocabulary, domain knowledge, and prosody for oral reading. This chapter investigates the speed at which the child's brain processes words during reading.

An additional component of building powerful information networks in students' brains is the habit of active engagement. The engagement strategies section of this chapter provides teachers with some not-too-frequently-used techniques as they relate to brain-friendly ways of doing teaching. Matching the way the brain learns with teaching that reflects the Common Core State Standards (CCSS) and research from the science of reading is a winning combination.

Third grade is the year for all the areas of reading competence to come together—cognition, decoding, encoding, comprehending, and fluency. Ideally, children master decoding and encoding during the first and second grades. Next, they develop networks of background information and vocabulary. By third grade, children's comprehension domain knowledge supports fluency. After third grade, instruction no longer focuses on learning to read. Rather, it shifts to using reading as a tool for learning. Word analysis instruction does occur in the upper elementary or middle school years; however, the emphasis on instruction to learn to read is diminished. More time is spent on *what* is read, not on *how* to read.

## READING AND LANGUAGE ARTS STANDARDS FOR THIRD GRADE

One of the expectations of our educational system is that every child will leave third grade with an enthusiasm to read and with the ability to read fluently, effortlessly, and independently. In 2001, Hollis Scarborough considered all of the skills that appeared to be in place in the areas of language comprehension and word recognition for students to become fluent, skilled readers (see Really Great Reading, 2015). For language comprehension, he listed background knowledge, vocabulary, language structure, verbal reasoning, and literacy knowledge. Word recognition holds three areas: word recognition, decoding, and sight recognition. Although the terminology may be slightly changed, his visual depiction, called the Scarborough Reading Rope, is now used to portray how all the skills for reading weave together to produce a coordinated process, a strong foundation, for fluent reading. (A Google search provides many versions of the Scarborough Reading Rope.)

## CHALLENGES FOR THIRD GRADE

When reading standards are addressed, they are not considerate of the fact that all students are not performing at grade level. According to the Nation's Report Card: Reading (2022), 32% of fourth graders performed at or above the National Assessment of Educational Progress (NAEP) proficiency in reading across the United States in 2022. As part of a recent podcast series, Jan Hasbrouck, a researcher and educational consultant for neurology and learning, made a bold statement. She claimed that approximately 95% of students can be taught to read at their grade level (Hasbrouck, 2022). Others have echoed this claim during professional development programs. There is quite a disparity between where students are in fourth grade (third graders were not tested), according to the NAEP results, and what is possible under ideal conditions. The problem lies with the reality that research does not translate into the real world that classroom teachers face. There is never enough time—specifically right instruction, support services, precisely appropriate instructional materials, or money for support resources—to teach each child in ways that exactly fit the student's needs. Now, as much as or more than ever, classrooms at all levels contain a group of students at varying levels of proficiency.

Notice the lack of specificity for developing phonics and decoding in the CCSS for third grade. One huge challenge for third-grade teachers is to assess and plan to cover and move forward with the CCSS for third grade while assessing and identifying skills that are underdeveloped and lacking proficiency with potentially up to 50%, or even more, of their students. Chapter 9 specifically addresses students who lag in proficiency for phonemic awareness, phonics, and word decoding, as well as those who lack attention, concentration, and memory for grade-level expectancies.

The Hasbrouck–Tindal oral reading fluency chart from 2017 has been recognized for establishing reading standards (Read Naturally, 2023). The standards were set as guidelines for teachers of Grades 1–6. Based on scores of 6 million readers, these standards guide teachers for reading fluency at the beginning, middle, and end of the year (Hasbrouck, 2022). See Table 8.1. This chapter targets development of fluency and reading processing speed. The content and proficiency standards for third-grade students cover the entire range of language arts skill development. Included here are some of the highlights from the CCSS for third-grade students in the areas of literature, informational text, and foundational skills. As in previous chapters, the standards have been summarized by the author.

| GRADE | PERCENTILE | FALL WCPM[a] | WINTER WCPM[a] | SPRING WCPM[a] |
|---|---|---|---|---|
| 1 | 90 |  | 97 | 116 |
|  | 75 |  | 59 | 91 |
|  | 50 |  | 29 | 60 |
|  | 25 |  | 16 | 34 |
|  | 10 |  | 9 | 18 |
| 2 | 90 | 111 | 131 | 148 |
|  | 75 | 84 | 109 | 124 |
|  | 50 | 50 | 84 | 100 |
|  | 25 | 36 | 59 | 72 |
|  | 10 | 23 | 35 | 43 |
| 3 | 90 | 134 | 161 | 166 |
|  | 75 | 104 | 137 | 139 |
|  | 50 | 83 | 97 | 112 |
|  | 25 | 59 | 79 | 91 |
|  | 10 | 40 | 62 | 63 |
| 4 | 90 | 153 | 168 | 184 |
|  | 75 | 125 | 143 | 160 |
|  | 50 | 94 | 120 | 133 |
|  | 25 | 75 | 95 | 105 |
|  | 10 | 60 | 71 | 83 |

**Source:** Excerpt from Hasbrouck & Tindal (2017).

[a] WCPM = words correct per minute.

## COMMON CORE STATE STANDARDS: HIGHLIGHTS FOR THIRD GRADE

**Reading Literature**

*Key Ideas and Details*—Ask and answer questions to demonstrate understanding by referring to text; recount stories, fables, folktales, and myths from diverse cultures.

*Craft and Structure*—Use terms such as *chapter*, *scene*, and *stanza*; distinguish one's own point of view from the narrator's.

*Integration of Knowledge and Ideas*—Explain how specific aspects of a text's illustration create mood; emphasize aspects of a character or setting.

*Range of Reading and Level of Text Complexity*—Read and comprehend literature at the high end of Grades 2–3 text complexity independently and proficiently.

**Reading Informational Text**

*Key Ideas and Details*—Describe the relationship between a series of historical events, scientific ideas or concepts, or steps in technical procedures in a text, using language that pertains to time, sequence, and cause/effect.

*Craft and Structure*—Use text features and search tools (e.g., key words, sidebars, hyperlinks) to locate information relevant to a given topic efficiently.

*Integration of Knowledge and Ideas*—Compare and contrast the most important points and key details presented in two texts on the same topic.

*Range of Reading and Level of Text Complexity*—By the end of the year, read and comprehend informational, history/social studies, science, and technical texts.

**Reading Foundational Skills**

*Decoding Words*—Use words with common Latin suffixes and multi-syllable words.

*Phonics and Word Recognition*—Identify common prefixes and derivational suffixes.

*Fluency*—Read with sufficient accuracy and fluency to support comprehension; read grade-level text and poetry with purpose and understanding at an appropriate rate; use context to confirm and self-correct; reread as necessary.

At this point, the summary is halted. Notice the dramatic drop in emphasis for reading foundational skills of phonics and decoding. The standards continue with writing, which is about opinion pieces and supporting a point of view. Writing is followed by speaking and listening, which features comprehension, collaboration, and presentation of knowledge and ideas. The area of language is extensive. Included are grammar of nouns (with plural and abstract nouns), pronouns, verbs, adjectives, adverbs, and coordinating conjunctions; punctuation; spelling patterns; and use of reference materials. Language includes knowledge of language along with vocabulary acquisition and use. It is easily seen that a dramatic change in expectations happens between second- and third-grade standards.

# WHAT IS KNOWN FROM NEUROSCIENCE?

Vocabulary and background knowledge were discussed extensively in Chapter 7. Now, the focus is on the speed at which the brain processes words when children read. Classroom practices follow to develop reading with automaticity, fluency, and consequently comprehension.

## THREE REASONS THE BRAIN CAN PROCESS WITH AUTOMATICITY

**Fluency**, which literally means *flowing*, has several components. In the context of reading, fluency means the ability to read fast, or to read a passage where the words are spoken spontaneously, with understanding, accuracy, and appropriate emphasis. All this is accomplished with seemingly a lack of effort. Fully developed reading fluency produces smooth, relatively effortless *oral reading* that is accurate and has an appropriate rate, including correct stress, intonation, rhythm, and word emphasis—all this *and* the student is able to comprehend text.

Reading fluency has been a topic of interest among educational and neurological researchers for several decades. Children move from being fluent decoders to strategic readers and finally to being expert readers, according to Maryanne Wolf (2007) in her book *Proust and the Squid: The Story and Science of the Reading Brain*. From this researcher/author's experience, there are three "brain" reasons readers can read with fluency and comprehension. First, following the adage "Cells that fire together wire together," neurons form cell assemblies or networks for the shapes, forms, order, and meanings of words. As a word is learned with familiarity, there are concurrent networks linked together and ready to activate as the reader gives recognition and meaning with an instant response.

Wolf (2007), as well as Simon Liversedge and Hazel Blythe (2007) from the University of Southampton, next describes the process the eyes follow during fluent reading. *It is assumed to be a smooth, fluid movement across the page, but research tells a different story.* It appears the eyes make small jerky movements to focus on a single word or to go back and reread passages that were elusive during the first glance. An automatic decision to refocus or dart back is executed unconsciously by the frontal lobes using the executive function and the attention systems. Realize these movements vary in duration from 50 to 200 milliseconds, which helps us to understand it is more like a briefly extended blink of the eye and barely discernable (Wolf, 2007). Furthermore, technology applied to the reading process revealed the reader's eyes are not always focused on the same letter or word. They may be two letters apart, but the brain is able to fuse the images to experience a single, clear visual representation during silent or oral reading.

While the first two neurological explanations for reading fluency result from clusters of quickly responding neuron circuits and rapid, darting eye movements, the third quality identifies a "word form" area in the occipital-temporal region of the brain. Neurons in this specialized area appear to learn orthographic patterns of the writing system for immediate recognition. Researchers Bruce McCandliss and colleagues (2003) describe changes of the visual cortex in expert readers. Initially, the area is designed for recognizing objects, such as a bus or snowplow, but the area is reconfigured in the reading pathway to also recognize letters, singularly and together in words. This trip through the neural networks happens with automaticity with the use of the procedural memory system.

In this instance, the brain quickly responds to letters as well as concrete words and phrases, much as the oral language pathway is co-opted to become the reading decoding pathway. For fluent reading, the visual association area is redesigned to accept representational forms and letters, and to place them on the fast track for identification as words and thoughts. Notice the absence of the precise pathway for decoding words, as there is no longer a need to access Broca's, Wernicke's, and Heschl's areas, which were required for early reading. The words retrieved during fluent reading are already packaged and delivered directly from long-term declarative semantic or procedural memory, aided by the cognitive ability of the frontal lobes and rapid processing in the cerebellum (see Figure 8.1).

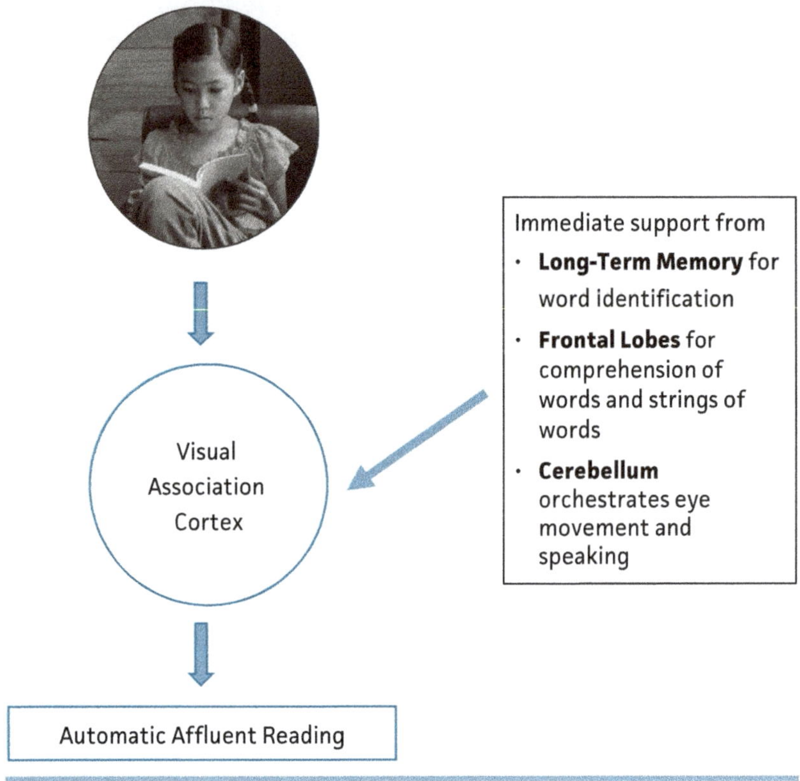



**Image source:** iStock.com/*t*:Six_Characters.

## SOME CHILDREN ARE FAST PROCESSORS; SOME ARE NOT

Decoding ability is an indicator for success in reading. The basic skill is being able to put sounds (phonemes) to letters (graphemes) and to apply phonetic rules to recognize words fluently, automatically, accurately, and with meaning. Theoretically, children who understand the rules for decoding and can produce the sounds of graphemes in words with automaticity will be good readers. There is another skill that, when accessed efficiently, works in tandem with phonological processes.

This skill is rapid automatized naming (RAN), introduced in Chapter 5, and can be defined as the ability to look at symbols, such as colored squares, simple objects, numbers, or words, and rapidly identify them. As noted earlier, reading teachers use RAN, or one-minute timing, as a very good indicator for reading fluency. In fact, researchers found that speed of naming, rather than accuracy of naming, differentiated between people who were good readers and those who were labeled as dyslexic (Wolf et al., 2000). A more recent study by Vander Stappen and Reybroeck (2018) validates RAN as a powerful predictor of proficient reading not only in English but across many languages. When a child lacks quick responses through automatic naming, reading suffers.

Phonological processing is a component of fluency. For example, when children respond to a simple perception task, such as pointing to the color red, there is no significant difference in rate of response between children who are impaired readers and children who are normal readers. However, when children are asked to observe a picture of a common object, recognize the object, determine the name of the object, say the name, and shift focus as quickly as possible to the next object, differences in timing between the two groups—good readers and poor readers—become significant (Wolf et al., 2000). Brain processing speed can be increased. George Georgiou and colleagues (2013) from the University of Alberta conducted a study with 65 children in Grades 2 and 6. This team determined RAN is related to reading success as reading requires the brain to simultaneously process and orally produce objects to be identified for reading (Georgiou et al., 2013).

## ORTHOGRAPHIC KNOWLEDGE

When students can read aloud with speed, accuracy, and proper expression, they can concentrate on the meaning of the text and are more likely to understand and remember what they read (Wolf, 2007). Attaining fluency depends on many factors, including automaticity in decoding, orthographic knowledge, the speed at which the brain connects, and the degree to which the brain has become wired to process print information.

Orthography, introduced in Chapter 5, can be defined. Students' brains, when structured to organize words in orthographic categories, are able to establish visual patterns within written language. They recognize graphemes, which are the letters and letter groups that correspond to a single sound. Remember that phonemes represent single sounds that are heard, not represented by letters. There are 44 phonemes. Graphemes, however, are estimated to be about 250 as they represent letters or letter groups that produce a single sound. Graphemes represent the sounds of language and are recalled with automaticity when processing words for their structure and for their meaning.

## WORD ATTACK: ANALYTICAL AND ANCHORED

This knowledge base is most effectively developed from two techniques: analytical and anchored. Mentioned in the previous chapter and emphasized again, *young students are not as likely to remember words that they identify through contextual clues.* Teachers might say, "Look at the rest of the sentence to see if you can identify (which means to guess) the word that is puzzling you." This approach may satisfy the current problem, but next time the student sees the word, they may be every bit as likely to be stumped by it. Teachers help students in the early grades when they ask the child to *analyze* the word, how it looks, what other words look similar, and how the letters are grouped or ordered. By engaging the child to critically look at the word itself, holding it in working memory, it is more likely that the next time the word appears the child will be able to identify it or think thorough its properties. *Anchoring* the word brings stronger interest and feeling; consequently, this effort is equally successful. In this instance, the teacher identifies the word and asks the child if this word creates any images or feelings. The child is asked for other words that may be similar or mean the same thing. The qualities of metacognition, or self-talk, are strong in both approaches. Both analysis and anchoring are most successful when they are fortified by having many immediate repetitions of the word (see Figure 8.2).

**FIGURE 8.2** ● Unknown word strategies: How to talk to a reader about the word. Notice to analyze and anchor are proven strategies, while addressing context is less likely to help the child remember the word next time it is seen.

| | |
|---|---|
| ANALYZE | • Look at the word. Identify the letters. What parts can you sound out? Do you know other words that are similar? What is the word? Notice the shape of the word. Say it again. |
| ANCHOR | • Talk about the word. How do you feel about this word? Use it in a new sentence, repeat it, then read the whole sentence. What do you want to remember about this word? |
| CONTEXT | • Does the word fit to make sense of the rest of the sentence? Read the sentence. |

**Source:** Reprinted from Nevills (2014).

The more times a child sees and recognizes words or word combinations, the more likely those words will be instantly identified, allowing reading to become automatic and fluid. Long-term memory is utilized for its rote and procedural processes.

However, children do not achieve automaticity with reading solely from constant word exposure. It is preferable that most words—with the exception of sight words and high-frequency words—not be learned by rote memorization. When all word call is from strong rote memory skills with no understanding of word foundations and variations, there is a false sense of reading ability. For children to process print with fluency, they begin their journey to become fluent readers by developing an understanding of the orthographic system that governs words. Fortunately, the orthographic rules for English are reliable and can be taught with their deviations. Rote memory is most appropriate for high-frequency words that do not behave and follow the rules.

Phonological processing, teaching predictable patterns in their written format, is at the very foundation of reading fluency. Beyond simple phonemes and extensive graphemes, the positions of different graphemes and syllables, particularly at the beginning and at the end of words, are taught through phonics instruction, mostly in first and second grade. As children address more complex words, they also learn to focus on syllables and come to understand how stress on one syllable rather than another affects word meaning. All instruction for phoneme awareness, phonics, spelling, and writing in the previous school years comes together as children address text with multisyllable words and long sentences. Proficient readers look at each grapheme and syllable that makes up each word, but pause for few, as they automatically recognize words for their orthographic properties and continue effortlessly reading with speed.

## ASSESSMENT FOR READING FLUENCY AND AUTOMATIC NAMING

Both *formative* and *summative* assessments are used to measure student reading achievement. Formative assessments are completed "along the way" to better understand the specific learning needs of students. Formative assessments direct instruction. Another dimension of testing is summative assessment, which certifies student performance. The purpose here is to look at student formative progress in building reading fluency.

Reading fluency may be assessed by measuring the speed at which text is read, followed by evaluating the quality of responses to comprehension questions. Teachers using informal reading inventories (IRIs), a graded series of passages with increasing difficulty, can identify children who process slowly when they read. More specific diagnostic information for fluency can help determine when a reading intervention is warranted. There are many tests for decoding and comprehension, and now assessment of fluency is identified as a continual part of reading development. For children in third grade, oral fluency and comprehension need to be tested separately. Due to the mental process of attempting to read as much as possible during a measured time period, students at this young age cannot do their best at understanding what they are reading. For assessment of comprehension, the person conducting the assessment can read the passages out loud prior to asking comprehension questions. Another method to measure comprehension is to allow the student to read silently and then respond to questions about the text.

**Formative assessment** is used with students to give feedback on reading progress. A quick screening or progress monitoring assessment, identified as a running record, uses brief passages to provide an oral reading fluency (ORF) target rate norm. The student reads the selected passage as accurately and rapidly as possible. As represented in Table 8.1, the number of words read correctly within a minute provides the ORF score. This useful tool allows teachers to identify how one child's oral frequency score compares to another student's. It gives an indicator of children who are at risk of reading problems. Another early indicator of reading speed, mentioned previously, is RAN. Because of the importance attached to early identification, a less formal assessment of RAN is suggested as early as kindergarten. Naming assessment is useful for identification of children who, at the very onset of reading instruction, show early signs of slow processing.

Formal diagnostic tools for formative assessment are available. One such tool is the Gray Oral Reading Test, fifth edition (GORT-5). It has 16 developmentally sequenced reading passages, each with five comprehension questions. While this timed assessment is appropriate for third graders, reading sections are leveled too high for children in the lower grades. Another assessment is the nationally normed Test of Word Reading Efficiency, second edition (TOWRE-2). This test measures word reading accuracy and fluency to monitor growth of reading skills. TOWRE-2 is designed to measure fluency in sight word reading and phonetic decoding skills using real and phonemically regular nonsense words. The assessment covers an age range of 6 to 24. A subtest of the Woodcock Johnson–IV Tests of Achievement measures oral sentence reading fluency to determine how well a student reads words in context. Students read out loud, and reading errors are recorded for diagnostic and instructional purposes.

## TEACHING METHODS TO DEVELOP READING FLUENCY

It takes only one painful experience with a slow and halting reader in a reading group to understand that this reader is not making the same reading progress as peers who are reading effortlessly. Teachers intentionally are more attuned to the needs of these readers. Rather than having them read out loud with the need for continual correction, another approach is given. Students who are not fluent readers actually benefit from additional oral reading practice. They simply need a safe place to read, not in front of the whole group. Fluent reading is developed with appropriate text through individual activities with the goal of successful reading out loud.

### REPETITIVE PRACTICE FOR OBJECT NAMING

All students, particularly slow, laborious readers, benefit from the three following approaches: repetitive practice for object naming; guided, repeated, modeled oral reading; and independent silent reading at an appropriate reading level. Regardless of the strategies teachers use, reading fluency is strengthened through deliberate, planned reading activities.

When children are fluent, accurate readers, they can devote their attention and energy to understanding what they read. RAN, mentioned earlier and now expanded by using sequentially more difficult letter configurations (e.g., letters, diagraphs, root words, or multisyllabic words), is a precursor to reading with fluency. Naming familiar objects and progressing to letter forms, clusters, and words are suggested for practice.

Fluency practice can be turned into a game. Children keep a record of how long it takes to name all the objects on a chart and then attempt to improve their own times. When one set of objects—for example, colors—is mastered within a target time, the child moves on to another set, such as a chart of words from the sight words list developed in the 1930s by Dr. E. W. Dolch. Each succeeding set is mastered with quicker response times than the previous one, and following charts can provide more difficult naming sets. During this process, the brain is primed to develop facilitated neural networks for rapid identification, naming, disengagement, and movement to the next object. The brain, particularly the cerebellum, is strengthened to respond with increasing speed.

## READ, REREAD, AND READ AGAIN

Processing speed for reading is undeniably more complex than it is for object identification. Reading puts demands on the brain structures for memory and complex recall, because reading requires decoding skills, orthographic patterns, and access to a knowledge base for comprehension. Strategies to strengthen the connections the brain needs to access for increased reading fluency call for guided, repeated, and modeled oral reading.

This practice for formative assessment is a tool to increase reading fluency. A total class strategy uses only five minutes of instructional time. Select a passage that all children are able to read and within which they can identify 95% of the words. Students read with one-minute intervals.

Here is the one-week design for this strategy. On the first day, the teacher reads the selected passage for one minute, while students follow with their own copy of the selection. Next, students read silently for one minute, followed by students in pairs each taking a turn to read for one minute. The listening partner provides corrections, as needed. Students record the last line and the last word that they read each day. This process is repeated every day for a week with the same passage. As children progress in their ability to read with fluency each week, the teacher monitors passages for progressive complexity. Vocabulary from the current lesson may be interjected into the target passage. Passage selection can include poetry, narrative text, or instructional text that is long enough that the strongest reader does not run out of reading material. The process becomes more challenging as the teacher requires passages be read with accuracy, prosody, and attention to the meaning of the words.

## EXPANDED PARTNER AND INDIVIDUAL READ AND REREAD PRACTICES

**Integrate focused activities to fill noninstructional time.** Creating pairs of readers using community volunteers, cross-age tutors, peer partners, or parents (possibly through take-home passages) provides a variety of opportunities to practice reading aloud.

**Use individual read-aloud techniques**. Set a goal, such as 85 words per minute. Students practice on their own. When they are ready to perform, they read the passage aloud to as many listeners as they can find at school or at home. When the reading speed target has been reached three consecutive times, they are "signed off" for this passage.

**Pair students, one who is a fluent reader and one who is a less fluent reader**. Partners read a selected passage several times together until the student who is less fluent feels comfortable reading independently. A record of accuracy and time is kept until a target is reached, then a new passage *and a new partner is selected*.

**Use an echo reading approach**. Partner A reads a sentence. Partner B then reads the same words. This first-and-follow routine continues, switching which partner reads first, through the selection until each partner can reread the passage individually or together at an increased rate. This technique is also used when the teacher reads, and the group follows with choral reading of the same passage. A variation of this technique is to use unfamiliar but easy-to-sing songs. The teacher sings or says a significant portion of the lines, so the children read the words from the song sheet to echo the response.

Teachers easily integrate strategies to build fluency practice into classroom schedules. Reading with individuals, pairs, and whole-class activities provides practice for fluency on a regular basis.

## INDEPENDENT READING

The last instructional technique simply, but effectively, helps children increase their reading rate through practice with silent reading. School is the best place for children to get books to read, as books can be leveled so that the difficulty of the text matches a student's ability.

### BOOKS, BOOKS, AND MORE BOOKS

Literature-based and **expository text** instruction makes a perfect contribution to reading development to increase practice and, ultimately, fluency. When schools include storytelling, read-alouds, poetry parties, book fairs, meet-the-author events, puppet shows, writing stories, acting out stories, and other wonderfully engaging book-related activities, children learn that reading is fun.

Children can be exposed to lots of books that capture their attention in whimsical and playful ways. Many books have endured the test of time. In the early grades, stories such as Julian Scheer and Marvin Bileck's *Rain Makes Apple Sauce* (1964) invite children to play with mouth-wallowing phrases about monkeys that mumble with a jumble of jellybeans. Young children gain reading confidence with stories that have repetitive phrases, such as the "everyone-is-sleeping" sequence from Audrey and Don Wood's *The Napping House* (2009).

Children find prose and poems to be appealing through authors such as Shel Silverstein. His style, which combines pictures that are a bit quirky with the unique phrases of his poetry, charms childhood audiences. Likewise, poetry with a magic twist captures the young reader's attention—for example, in "The Paper Doorway," Dean Koontz tells how it feels to be engaged and trapped within a book (see Koontz & Parks, 2001, p. 18). Books similar to Dr. Seuss's *Cat in the Hat* (1957), known for their appeal to early readers, are now available for primary readers as narrative-informational stories. Bonnie Worth's *Oh Say Can You Seed? All About Flowering Plants*, from the Cat in the Hat's Learning Library, is one such book. It contains the ever-present magic rhymes and has serious scientific information to teach (see Worth & Ruiz, 2001).

Joanna Cole's *Magic School Bus* series must be mentioned, again (see Cole & Degen, 1986–2020). This series features Ms. Frizzle, a zany, absentminded teacher. In *The Magic School Bus Explores the Senses* (Cole & Degen, 2001), for example, Ms. Frizzle moves through town, while her class tries to catch up with her in the magic school bus. During the chase, the bus and the children shrink, move inside the heads of different people and animals, and learn about the senses and the brain. J. K. Rowling's (1997–2007) Harry Potter series is yet another example of how books can capture young readers' interest, but may be too advanced for most in the third grade. It can be considered for a teacher read-aloud. With stories like these that are laden with whimsical words, serious information, and sometimes engrossing pictures, even children who have difficulty with reading can be enticed to pick up a book for independent, pleasure reading.

## SUSTAINED SILENT READING

Sustained silent reading (SSR) may be a practice that has diminished during the years. It was developed to provide daily time for children to be immersed in reading. *SSR can be very,*

*very good with appropriate implementation.* It can be a horrid experience if it is a "drop everything and read" strategy followed by an immediate return to the previous task. This latter, less productive interpretation of SSR frequently requires students to be engaged with any available reading material and to sit quietly and read for an extended period. Teacher direction and follow-up are nonexistent. When SSR is used without an instructional intent and without any rules for implementation, it runs the risk of becoming a waste of important instructional time.

What practices make this reading strategy successful? Author and teacher Janice Pilgreen (2000) studied SSR with high school–aged students who were English language learners (ELLs). While our target population is much younger students, Pilgreen made recommendations that speak to all grade levels:

- Children need access to huge numbers of books with an appropriate variety of reading levels.

- Teachers model how much they love to read for the children.

- A home reading program extends the time available for independent reading.

- Children are not held accountable for what they read (such as having to write a book report), but time is set aside to share reading experiences and recommend books.

An SSR time may be adopted by individual teachers or exist as a schoolwide program. In effective programs, students make selections from books that have been previously coded for their individual reading level. Children, however, are given freedom to read books that are more difficult when they have interest and desire to learn more about a specific topic. A variation to SSR is to have "reading buddies." The paired students select a book to read together or alone. When both have finished the book, they have a conversation about their reading experiences.

## TEACHING WITH BRAIN-COMPATIBLE PRACTICES

A proliferation of information about the human brain and how it responds in a learning environment has been provided. In literally most of their waking hours, students find opportunities to learn. At school, learning time can be designed to be not only efficient and effective, but also engaging and curious. Consider the following activities to heighten students' engagement with their working and long-term memory systems.

## FIVE-MINUTE WARM-UPS

Teaching occurs with an element of fun when teachers use five-minute warm-ups. This technique is effective when children need to be focused after recess or lunch or at a myriad of other times during the school day. Even at the very start of the school day, a warm-up can instantly engage students with a challenging question on the board or an opportunity to write on the board or chart a response to a strong opinion. The warm-up may be a quick talk among partners or triads to add something new to review statements from a previous lesson. Teachers are full of ideas for this type of activity. The caution is to keep the five-minute frame, or to know why it is being extended. For starters, Bea Green and colleagues (2003) assembled 84 examples, listed with references, in their classic book, *Five-Minute Warm-ups for Elementary Grades* in the areas of math, social studies, language arts, science, and self-awareness. For language arts, the topics include idioms, past tense, topic sentences, analogies, poetry, listening, irregular plurals, and much more.

## CLASSROOM ENVIRONMENT FOR ACTIVE ENGAGEMENT

Picture a learning environment that demands student engagement. Every student is connected to the lesson. Each one is in a constant state of readiness, for students know they are expected to think, respond, and learn. When students are engaged, learning potential is at its highest. While an active engagement classroom will not be the quiet, orderly, neatly managed environment some have come to expect, there is no doubt that the teacher is in charge. There is a planned lesson, and student responses are anticipated, even though there is no way to predict what they will need or ask or talk about to reach the lesson objective. Students bring to the classroom a wild range of information, a wide berth of needs, and a whimsical curiosity. The classroom can be anything but predictable when students are actively learning. Furthermore, they know and sense when a classroom is productive, and they savor the opportunity to be in these happening, active classrooms.

Traditional teaching requires students to pay attention and to *wait for the teacher to call on them or maybe not.* Teachers change this time-tried and somewhat antiquated process by expecting that every student will stay focused and at a continual state of readiness. Each student has the potential to be asked to contribute and respond out loud to the whole class, a small group, or a partner at any point of the lesson. This concept looks and sounds very different with expanded student responses. Students attend, remain engaged, and strengthen newly forming neuropathways in their brains to enforce learning and remembering. How do teachers reinforce this type of student engagement? The opportunities are endless, but two examples follow.

## CALL OUT RESPONSES

The teacher stops talking during a lesson and signals students to respond out loud. There are many ways this engagement can happen. The most common strategy is to have all students answer a question out loud in unison. A variation is to prompt responses from the right or left side of the class, boys/girls, tables, or rows. Students can also repeat what the teacher just said following a prompt, such as both hands being held out and open. Students respond by repeating the last sentence spoken.

A more advanced strategy requires students to listen attentively to one another, as if they are having a large-group discussion. This technique requires individuals to keep track of answers given by others, and wait for an opening to take a turn to talk. Note the teacher's role, instead of calling on individual students, is to expect attentiveness. A sign of approval is given by the teacher, such as a nod, an open hand, or a step toward the self-initiated speaker. If responses are not accurate or moving away from the topic, the teacher intervenes and redirects the discussion. When the discussion is exhausted, the teacher proceeds with the lesson. Students can also be asked to repeat someone's answer or add to it. These more advanced callout strategies expect students to be attending to what other students have to say. It requires some practice and not only enhances listening and learning skills, but fosters respect among students.

## HOLD IN WORKING MEMORY
## (FIRST, SECOND, OR THIRD CONCEPT)

In this example, the teacher announces there will be three (or another number) of key points the students need to remember. While teacher input is given, the teacher stops and asks the class to respond, "What was the first point (or second, or third)?" This questioning happens continually during the lesson to force students to hold important information in their working memories. Students can be encouraged to keep track of the big **concepts** from the lesson by taking individual notes, explaining the big ideas with a partner, or developing the concept in a small group. This type of engagement forces students to practice and rehearse information in working memory. If the neuron signals are strong and reinforced, it is more likely the student will be able to recall the information at a later time. Continuing this chain of thinking, the next section provides additional insights for memory capacity through engagement.

## EXPANDING MEMORY CAPACITY

When students transfer information into long-term memory, their working memory doesn't have to work so hard, and they are able to grapple with novel, complex topics more quickly and more efficiently. Learning becomes less of a struggle, and students may feel smarter and more confident. When students feel this way, they're more willing to stick with difficult concepts and problems—allowing deep learning.

Transfer from working memory to long-term (more or less permanent) memory can be relevant and interactive in many additional ways. Students at this age may not have the capacity to listen to a teacher "lecture" for more than 10 to 15 minutes at a time. Working memory is challenged to stay attentive during a "lecture" part of a lesson. The lesson can be stopped and mixed up by some of the following strategies.

1. **Turn and talk**—talk with a partner or triad about what you just heard. Or, identify questions that the partners all have to pose to the whole class.

2. **Model, demonstrate, or give examples**—incorporate "hands-on" practices intermittently, or ask for real-life examples.

3. **Summarize**—incorporate a picture, an organization map, or a drawing for students to discuss.

4. **Song or rhyme**—select words, phrases, or sentences to make into a limerick, or sing to the tune of a familiar song to sum up the lesson.

5. **Concept or story mapping**—create diagrams, charts, or sorting charts with teacher modeling and students making their own individually or in small groups.

A reminder about long-term memory: Although in this book long-term memory has been touted as permanent, teachers and learners alike need to know that even long-term memory can be fleeting over time. Rote memory is especially afflicted with memory loss, unless it is periodically revisited. Strategies that continue in this section help to maintain and cement long-term memories for declarative and procedural memory systems.

## QUESTIONING TECHNIQUES

There is a host of great teachers worldwide who ask really important questions. Questioning comes naturally for some, while others may plan and deliberate about questions that would be the most powerful during their lesson design. A really provocative question may linger only to be addressed at a later time or even may be more fully developed at a later grade level.

Jackie Walsh and Beth Sattes (2005) provide research-based practice through questioning that engages every learner. Jay McTighe and Grant Wiggins (2013) provide a teaching resource that is considered powerful in any teacher's toolbox. There is an acute connection between critical thinking skills, touted in *Thinking Critically*, twelfth edition, by John Chaffee (2018), and essential questioning. *Questioning, rather than telling, is a powerful teaching tool for reading in every school subject.*

With the CCSS, the use of questions as a teaching tool becomes critical. Questions that have previously permeated classrooms, or convergent questions, lead to a common set of responses. Questions of this type focus on narrow teaching objectives and prescribed answers. They center student thinking on knowledge, comprehension, and application levels of understanding. *With learning outcomes that are reflective of deeper thought, questioning techniques take on new importance.* Consider questions that are divergent and elicit a wide range of student responses and in-depth exploration. These big questions are carefully crafted and encourage multiple responses. Keys to developing a safe environment where students are willing to give responses require teachers to nurture these habits.

## PRACTICES FOR DIVERGENT THINKING

1. Honor wait time for students to gather their thoughts and hone their responses.

2. Resist repeating student responses to encourage students to listen attentively to their peers.

3. Insist that students speak clearly and loud enough for all to hear.

(Continued)

4.  Allow students to speak their complete thoughts without interruptions, as much as possible.

5.  Acknowledge that student contributions are important.

6.  Enrich discussions by asking other students to repeat, question, or expand upon a previous student's response.

7.  Redirect when information is inaccurate by positively acknowledging the response, but develop another question to redirect or prompt another thought.

*Essential questions* are defined as the use of provocative questions that interrogate the content. If the teaching content provides the answers, then what are the questions that help students learn? Students are led to well-known content answers, and then the topic is overturned to challenging the answers and deepening understanding (McTighe & Wiggins, 2013). Think about what is happening in the human brain when this inquiring type of learning technique is experienced.

## LEARNING FRAMES AND ORGANIZERS

There are a variety of visual aids to prompt thinking at the foundational and deeper levels. They include having students develop diagrams, tables, figures, and timelines; questioning and answering; and thinking through organizational maps. Some work with graphic organizers and mind mapping as learning activities ran their course, and have lost their prominence. Teachers now challenge student thinking with learning frames.

Learning frames help organize big ideas, major concepts, and important implications not only on a piece of paper, but also as a prompt for organization in the human brain for long term-memory. A basic frame is a series of boxes organized on a student's work paper. A key topic is identified and inserted at the top of the worksheet. In the simplest form, teachers direct students to think of two or three main ideas, each with several details. The main ideas are identified and recorded in frames located under the topic. Details are recorded under the ideas. The entire process culminates with a summary statement. The resulting frame looks like a chart and often fits on a single page. Children, as early as first grade, use frames to develop sentences. The process is an ideal tool to begin a short report or story for older students.

This strategy directs students to think deeply about the topic rather than to simply identify facts. The frame technique is accompanied by robust instruction, as the teacher introduces the process for developing the frame and completes one for the students to use as a model. With each succeeding exposure to learning frames, the teacher supplies less of the information, and the children fill in more, until students can use the frame independently. Children can use learning frames to organize a report, summarize a story or expository text, or take class notes in the upper elementary grades.

Organizers, as visual aids, work to embrace skills listed in the CCSS. Students select from a variety of formats, which encompass the traditional circle or bubble and also include a tree or bridge map. See Figure 8.3 for a variety of computer-generated shapes that can be introduced.

Students' organizers have specific qualities:

- **Consistency**—a format and symbols are selected and remain relatively the same throughout the frame development.

- **Flexibility**—the figure grows uniquely and incrementally with information and details of the selected topic.

- **Development**—the overall shape and design continue to emerge with various connections.

- **Integration**—during construction a new thought process may develop and need to be expressed by increasing the original design.

- **Reflection**—the final product is wrapped in a rectangular shape (or other designated shape) and ready for consideration by study partners, in a process group, or as an assessment tool for other students (adapted from Hyerle, 2004).

To move beyond the basic formats, teachers and students can use hand-drawn shapes or access the SmartArt tab available in Microsoft Word. Teachers introduce organizers or other visual aids by telling what they are thinking—for example, "What do I know about the sun?" or "If a cat is a mammal, what other animals may also be classified as mammals?" or "I wonder what characteristics these two heroes have in common." Letting students know how the teacher thinks is metacognitive modeling. This experience is followed by the teacher making a prototype through a visual aid or organized design. Powerful learning, the type of learning required in the Common Core, happens when students in third grade work on their own to determine the structure or format they need to

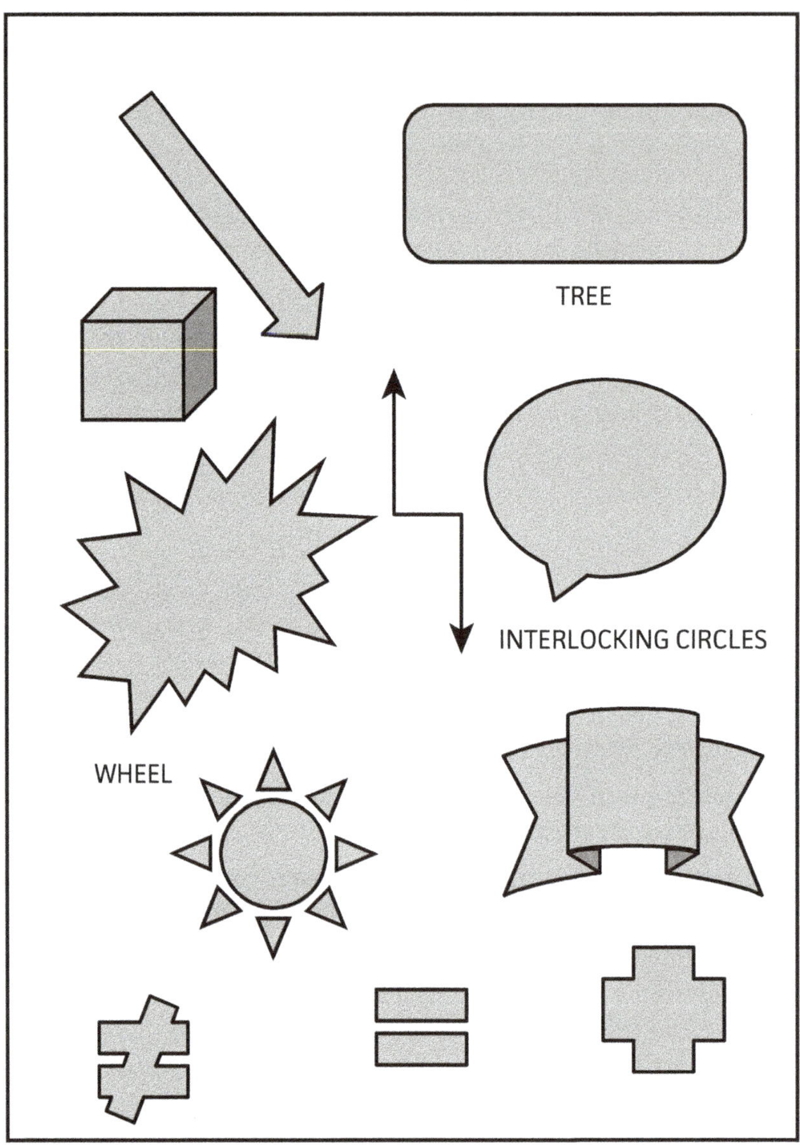



**Source:** Reprinted from Nevills (2014).

show information from their own unique memory systems. Figure 8.4 is a sample organizer developed by the author to produce and demonstrate a key topic in this book, student engagement.

Background knowledge fortified through organizers is super important for learning as children search for neural pathways in the brain for new information to connect to and strengthen. While thinking shapes and organizers can be a culminating activity, teachers can activate neural networks at the onset of

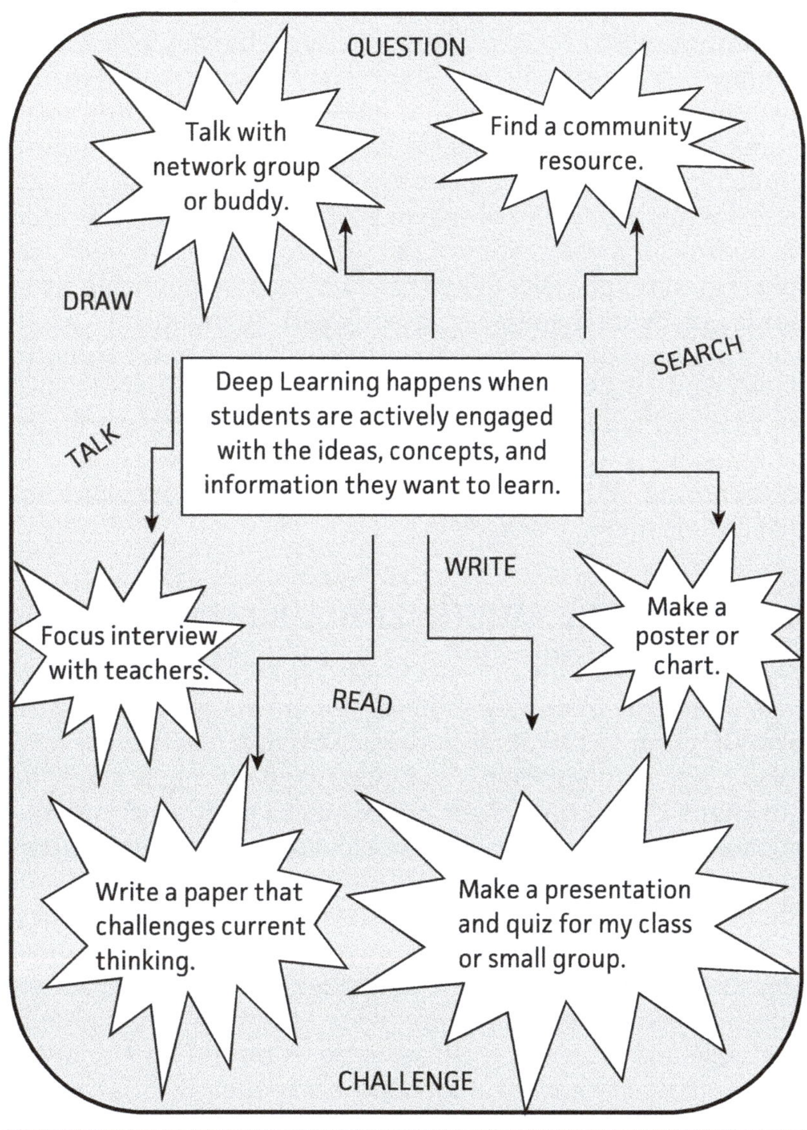


teaching new content or a new skill. Concept mapping, word webs, and KWL (Know, Want to Know, Learned) charts are additional concept thinking tools to awaken previous knowledge and stimulate the process of encoding new information. Programs like Kahoot! (a game-based learning platform with an online network of connected players) or Quizlet (an online source for learning tools) can be used to support learning and remembering. They are found by a Google search.

# A FORGOTTEN SKILL: CURSIVE HANDWRITING

According to Ray Reutzel (2015), an early literacy researcher, studies over several decades show that handwriting speed and legibility are critical skills that have been largely eliminated from early education. Reutzel touts that speed and legibility are predictive of quality and quantity of written compositions and note-taking. Students are able to produce high-quality written responses for a wide range of genres, required throughout the upper grades and reflective of the Common Core writing standards. Procedural memory is activated automatically when students employ cursive handwriting. It is a brain thing to develop cursive writing proficiency, as well as keyboard skills. As availability for computer writing and test taking continues to be more and more prominent, cursive handwriting and keyboarding skills are most likely to continue as topics for discussion among teachers.

# WHY WE LIKE MUSIC: IT'S A BRAIN THING

Teachers and parents are encouraged to contemplate the part music can play in children's lives—for encouragement and for overall brain activation—and particularly how *well-selected* music can calm emotions and enhance learning. It might be questioned, what type of learning could be positively impacted by music? For a few examples, consider these areas for reading/language arts: alliteration and rhyme, sound extensions for phonemic awareness, phonics rules, spelling rote memory, or procedural memory for a series of directions. Pick up some common music and put the task to work. All human brains are programmed to respond to the wide variety of music that is available and usable in the classroom. A reward for work well done is to make time for students to share their favorite music, prescreened by the teacher, certainly.

People have an interesting relationship with music, and it all results from brain activation. The children's reaction to a song makes a big difference in their emotional behavior. Teachers can consider all the ways the human brain responds to music and decide when and how to use this powerful instructional tool. A rundown of what happens in the brains of the students when music is introduced as a classroom tool helps to validate the role of music for instructional purposes.

The auditory cortex is stimulated when a new song is heard. If a child sings the words of the song out loud, the premotor cortex is activated. That's the frontal cortex area that backs up to the motor cortex strip. When children get up and dance or move to music, the motor cortex, sensory cortex, and cerebellum are involved. Listening to the lyrics stimulates the parietal cortex, and if personal memories are recalled, the frontal cortex becomes involved. All these brain areas are stimulated by music. How can music be used in the classroom to reinforce important instructional content?

For readers of this book who are intrigued by brain terminology, try this extended explanation. As all of these diverse brain parts are stimulated, emotional feelings, feel-good feelings, spring forth. In the primitive part of the brain, the thalamus has received stimulation and in reality has sent a continual stream of input to different parts of the brain for interpretation. As a result of activity in the orbitofrontal cortices in the frontal lobes and a strong accompanying response from the somatosensory strip behind it, the thalamus overreacts. It connects and responds to the amygdala, the emotional part of the inner brain, to order the release of dopamine, serotonin, oxytocin, and other chemicals that make people feel good. The more the song is enjoyed, the more likely the experience becomes a "neurochemical bliss."

## BRAIN BREAKS

Researchers recommend a brain-type break every 10 to 15 minutes for elementary-age children after concentrated study. An amazing thing happened following an intense learning time described by Leonardo Cohen and his colleagues (2021) as a *binding process*. Through the use of magnetoencephalography, a sensitive brain-scanning technique, *they discovered that stepping away from an activity while providing a physical disengagement with the lesson task is not a break in brain activity.* Rather, they observed a spike in brain activity that mimicked the neural activity during learning, but compressed twenty-fold. The brain subconsciously was replaying the events at a high rate of speed in the neocortex, where sensory and motor skills are processed, and sending it to the hippocampus, where memories originate over two dozen times in a period of 10 seconds. These researchers identify the process the brain uses as *neural replay*, as the brain rapidly cycles through the learning experience to compact, wire, and optimize the parts of learning that are important to the learner for memory recall (reported in Terada, 2022). This information is a strong support for giving students a break, a change in activities, not to quiet down neural activity, but rather to allow learning to jell and connect.

# COGNITIVE DEVELOPMENT

The cognitive skill development chart is concluded here. The entire chart, spanning ages 1–9, is provided in Appendix B.

## COGNITIVE SKILLS FOR LEARNING: AGES 8 AND 9

Memory Systems (Sensory, Working, and Long-Term)

| 8–9 Years | Places items from long-term memory into categories by sorting, ordering, defining, and identifying. When provided with a list of items or concepts, is able to find commonalities among the list to sort and organize. Moves known words into classifications provided. Responds to "if–then" order. Explains the function of nouns, pronouns, verbs, adjectives, and adverbs in general and their functions in particular sentences. (Grade level 3 from Language Standards, Common Core State Standards, California.) |
| --- | --- |
| | NOTE: Cognitive aspects from all Common Core State Standards can be identified, rephrased, and inserted within the cognitive skills areas, as examples. |

Executive Function, Listed in Expected Developmental Order

| 8–9 Years | **Problem Solving**—Goes beyond reasoning to develop a detailed plan and to implement the plan to its conclusion. Given a situation, how would the child respond to resolve the dilemma? For example, "If you have these items, how could you use them to create something new?" Or, "If this situation occurred, what are two possible ways to resolve the problem?" |
| --- | --- |
| | **Synthesis**—Analyzes multiple inputs and, drawing from long-term memory, strategizes and develops a plan, device, approach, or proposal that is unique. Given a situation at school, in the community, or even on a larger scale, the student is asked, "What are the possibilities for making the situation better, and what is the expected outcome as the plan is accomplished?" A research project might require students to use multiple resources and interviews with others knowledgeable about the topic, and culminates with a new idea, concept, or image. A speech, presentation, or demonstration may accompany the project. |

# CONCLUDING THOUGHTS ABOUT READING IN A THIRD-GRADE CLASSROOM

This chapter is bursting with teaching strategies based on how the brain learns through novel and challenging teaching strategies. It is the author's intention that readers will find many useful practices to add to their instructional skills "bag of tools." In spite of all that is done, there are still students who read slowly and lag behind their peers for reading fluency. Although children who read with difficulty may receive supplemental help or may receive the services of an intervention program, they still need the benefit of a complete reading program. This comment suggests that a skill development program only is not enough. Children with reading challenges or dyslexia need intervention *and* reading instruction with their normally progressing peers. Concurrently, they need to be exposed to reading and language arts standards and expectations for their grade level.

All primary-age children benefit when they are a part of the rich and varied classroom conversations that happen naturally between their peers and teachers during reading and language arts instruction. Teachers are the critical force to structure school environments where children construct their reading brains and attitudes about themselves as readers. Teachers orchestrate a delicate balance between instruction and student engagement with learning through conversation, practice activities, reading narrative and informational texts, leisure selections read aloud and silently, and active experiences that are shared with the class. The next chapter addresses students who are not proficient readers at their grade level. Children have a good opportunity to become fluent, efficient readers when instructional decisions are based on how children learn to read accompanied by an understanding of the development of the neural pathways in the human brain.

# Reflective Questions

1. How do or will the Common Core State Standards impact your teaching? What system do you use or suggest to others to keep track of student competencies? Is the system you use from the school district's plan, or have you developed your own?

2. What from Chapter 8 has impacted how you look at developing readers? How could you use that information to enhance your teaching practices for reading?

3. Reading fluency is a goal for the end of third grade. Explain what is happening neurologically for a student to move from slow methodical reading to reading fluency with comprehension.

4. Fluent, accurate reading depends on a child's understanding of orthography, the visual patterns of written language that feature graphemes, phonology, and semantics. Describe some ways reading programs could build teaching fluency into lessons for students in the third grade. Would you anticipate the need to provide supplemental instructional materials or practice and rehearsal activities? If so, what are they?

5. Prepare a list of strategies to share with parents to help children increase their reading fluency. What information would be appropriate to include for parents to understand what happens in the child's brain for fluent reading?

6. If you are reading this book as a part of a university course or study group, have each member explain something known about the reading brain that helps us to understand how children are able to read with automaticity, accuracy, fluency and comprehension.

7. Refer to the section on brain-compatible teaching practices to choose several practices you would like to use. How would you adapt the activities to your classroom?

# CHAPTER 9

# Assessing and Responding to Readers With Disabilities

Students in the elementary years are privileged to have high-powered, quick-thinking brains. It is estimated their neurons fire up to 225 times faster than the average adult brain during a similar thinking task (Kotulak, 1997). Teachers use this information to provide instruction that is meaningful, information laden, logical, and engaging. Children are building and constructing not brain structures themselves but, rather, organized connections and superhighways among existing structures for memory, recall, and cognitive function.

It has been estimated that reading can be achieved for 95% of children, yet high rates of reading failure are relatively common (Hasbrouk, 2022; Snow, 2021). Although there is not general agreement among researchers, the percentages for different levels of reading difficulties state about 30% of students can become readers without any instruction, while another 50% learn with explicit and direct instruction in the foundational skills from the science of reading. The additional 15% need intensive support over an extended time. The remaining 5% will likely struggle due to cognitive disabilities. Developing an understanding of how children's brains function during reading instruction will help the reader to understand and appreciate the work teachers and their students accomplish when they become proficient readers.

There are many reasons some children are not successful with the process for reading development. Some have a genetic tendency that forces their thinking to avoid brain structures that would allow them to build an efficient reading pathway. Other children lack early oral language stimulation or have a primary language that differs from English. Others have infrequent school attendance and do not receive sequential instruction for the development of all the skills necessary to become proficient readers. Still others are slow processors. Finally, some children lack what has been identified as priming and other cognitive skills to become proficient readers. Whatever the cause, when children struggle with any aspect of the reading process, their brains demand huge amounts of brain sugar—glucose. This need for energy in the neural cortex remains high anytime the child attempts to do a reading task. These children get tired of the reading struggle. They may become annoyed and disruptive with their peers who access the decoding reading pathway and read with ease.

The social-emotional impact of a reading deficit has received a vast amount of interest, and somewhat discouraging data have been collected. When children and parents learn a child's reading difficulties are attributed to **dyslexia**, it can be troubling. However, so much is known about dyslexia and reading difficulties in general that there are instructional strategies to help relieve or fix reading problems. It is advised that children get assistance with activities that build the student's brain for proficient reading. Additional reading strategies make changes in the reading routes children use to read, but it is very, very hard work for students.

Teachers most likely identify readers who experience reading disabilities by their behaviors, as well as by how they perform at their reading tasks. These students frequently act in ways that are disruptive or unacceptable in the regular classroom environment. When children tell us by their work or their behavior that reading is not progressing normally, school programs for assessment and intervention must be in place to provide the support they require. Programs can be initiated within the regular classroom, such as supplemental instruction in tandem with a core reading program. An additional or replacement reading program may be needed in the upper grades. These programs are tailored specifically to the needs of students with reading disabilities and are used to catch them up with their grade-alike peers.

# THE CASE FOR EARLY ASSESSMENT

Some children enter school already reading, some are ready to read, and others lack basic print awareness. The National Association for the Education of Young Children (1998) warned that "most children learn to read at age six or seven, a few learn at four, some learn at five, and others need intensive individualized support to learn to read at eight or nine" (p. 30). Basically, children have not changed greatly from that time. This means that, as early as kindergarten, there may be a three-year variation, or more, in reading readiness or ability in a classroom. The number can expand by third grade. A range of potential abilities, coupled with differences in background experiences, interests, personality, and temperament, challenge teachers. The public expectation is for every child to read proficiently in a predetermined time frame based on grade-level standards. With a large variation in language abilities even among 5- and 6-year-olds, teachers find they must identify children who are at risk for academic failure as early as the first year of school. This discrepancy can be determined as early as 4 years of age.

This chapter approaches formal reading instruction with the trust that all children are ready for beginning reading instruction when they reach kindergarten, and then discusses assessments for successful and emergent readers. Specific activities and program modifications are identified, and **individualized instruction** is provided, to meet the varying needs of children who are at risk of reading failure and for those who stumble along the way. However, this book differs from others that describe reading interventions as added insights from neurology are provided. With this approach, children are assessed for their ability to pay attention, focus, concentrate, and access memory. Added to these priming skills is an in-depth look at cognition including auditory, visual, and other attributes that could be preventing the student from achieving at expected levels. Brain-based interventions delve into what neurological problems the child is experiencing: (1) lack of early language stimulation; (2) infrequent school attendance accompanied with lack of sequential instruction; (3) brain structures that have not been co-opted or added from the oral language pathway to the reading pathway; (4) slow processing skills; (5) deficit attention, concentration, organization, and memory development; and (6) other cognitive skill development. Each of these areas is addressed. In some instances, the reader may return to a previous chapter to review the area of concern, thus expanding their teaching options through identification of variations from more traditional teaching patterns.

# NO WAITING ALLOWED

Neuroscientists using **PET scans**, or positron emission tomography, have identified critical developments in the brain between the ages of 4 and 12. During this time, learning appears to surge. Imaging technology follows the brain's consumption of glucose, which is the fuel nerve cells use when they are active and making new connections among themselves.

Prize-winning science writer Ronald Kotulak (1997) describes this energy spurt in his book *Inside the Brain: Revolutionary Discoveries of How the Mind Works* as a time "when the brain seemed to glow like a nuclear reactor, pulsating at levels 225 percent higher than adult brains" (p. 36). Kotulak speculates this is a time that the brain determines to keep regularly traveled neural pathways or prune connections from deserted routes as it eagerly responds to stimuli from the senses.

The years from birth through age 8 are furthermore considered to be critical for literacy development in terms of cognition. During the primary years, children are extremely responsive to instruction with malleable brains—brains with plasticity that make them more open to new learning than at any other time during their formal education. Educators' responsibility to students, particularly during this period of rapid brain development, is to make learning accessible and challenging for students. Also, they aim to provide appropriate interventions for those who do not keep up. Children must have their learning needs met, even when necessary intervention programs are costly due to intensive time and personnel investment.

 STUDENTS WITH DISABILITIES

Students with disabilities in the United States are protected by law to receive educational services described in an individualized education program (IEP). The program students receive, furthermore, is to be in the least restrictive environment, which is usually a general education classroom placement. A concern has been voiced about an extraordinate number of children of race or ethnicity different from white being placed in special education services outside the regular education classroom. The particular worry is for an overrepresentation of Black and Hispanic students in these placements.

In response to claims and concerns, a team of specialists led by Paul Morgan evaluated race and ethnic bias in special education placements by analyzing data from two independent samples of students with disabilities. The number of cases was

590 for one sample and 1,130 students in another (Morgan et al., 2022). The analysis began with kindergarten students and followed the individuals' attendance in first, third, and fifth grade. The surprising result from the study, reported in 2022, is that academic difficulties in both reading and math realized in kindergarten, not racial or ethnic disparities, were the primary indication that special education services would be required outside the general education classroom in later elementary years. The results were similar across the nation. A large number of referrals for special education services for students who are learning English as a second language pose another concern.

## ENGLISH LANGUAGE LEARNERS

This is a good time for the education of English language learners (ELLs). Students who are identified as English learners (ELs) have a variety of language assistance programs to help them attain English proficiency, and to meet state standards in all areas expected of all students. ELLs and ELs are the same students, but their designation is not used consistently in the United States. An increase in numbers of ELLs from 9.2% in 2010 to 10.4% in 2019 is reported by the National Center for Education Statistics (2022). Amplify (2020) reported 27% of children in the United States, or approximately 5.1 million schoolchildren, were Latino/a in the 2018 school year. The organization further reported that more than 1 in 4 elementary students in the United States are Latino/a and that this population provided more than half, 52%, of the population growth between 2019 and 2020. In current times, the number of bilingual people in the United States is at an all-time high of 65 million people ages 5 and older (Waterford.org, 2019).

Long-standing social issues are often claimed to be the cause for students who are primarily Spanish speakers to have lower reading scores than those who speak English only. Other statistics are equally as illuminating. It is predicted that as many as 77% of Latino/a students are likely not to be proficient readers by the fourth grade, and the percentage of Hispanic students served in special education for having a learning disability could be up to 42% (National Assessment of Educational Progress, 2019). A wealth of reports and information is available, and the education system is paying attention. Major ethnicities present in the nation's school system are white, Black, Hispanic, Asian, Pacific Islander, Native American, and children of two or more races. Spanish appears to be the predominant second language in many of the schools in the United States. However, the home languages of children from other ethnicities must also be considered as teachers prepare for their students. There are important language and cultural implications to be acknowledged and considered.

As an educational practice, Spanish speakers, as well as other students whose primary language is not English, are assessed in their home language to create a level playing field for all students. The skills that matter most for reading proficiency are not unknown. They include phonological awareness, alphabetic understanding and breaking the reading code, vocabulary, background knowledge for comprehension, and reading fluency.

## EARLY, THOROUGH ASSESSMENT

In an ideal educational environment, students whose first language is not English are assessed for English language skills *and* for skills of their native language upon entering the school system. For non-English-speaking students, assessments in their native language let educators know how to support the transfer of skills from one language to the other. Assessments that determine the level of competence a student possesses in both English and the child's primary language are needed. Some additional questions, listed in Table 9.1, can add meaningful information to help classroom and resource teachers make insightful instructional decisions.

A student's fluency in English and the primary language, along with an assessment of available school resources, are used to determine the language of initial reading instruction.

**TABLE 9.1** ● Questions and Observations

1. What language is spoken at home?

2. Do parents or family members who primarily speak a language other than English help the child with English reading activities?

3. What was observed when the student read out loud in English? In the primary language?

4. What behaviors or interpersonal interactions have been observed in the classroom, in the lunch room, or on the playground?

5. Does the child's primary language have a written form with a Roman alphabet?

6. Does the primary language contain phonemes, and how do the phonemes compare to English language sounds?

7. Does the student speak, read, and write with the primary language?

8. Is the level of speaking, reading, and writing in the primary language proficient for the student's age-appropriate grade level?

9. How can staff, programs, and resources be supportive of this student?

For students who are not proficient in English, answers to the previous questions prompt decisions about the type of program—primary language, English only, or bilingual (integrated primary language and English)—that will be appropriate, when these choices are available. Grade-level instruction in the child's native language for all school subjects is important so the student advances in background information with age-appropriate peers.

## BASIC INTERPERSONAL COMMUNICATION SKILLS OR COGNITIVE ACADEMIC LANGUAGE PROFICIENCY

Due to significant work by James Cummins, groundbreaking and essential theories about second language acquisition have been uncovered. Cummins's (2000) language learning theories break out the significant difference between basic interpersonal communication skills (BICS) and cognitive academic language proficiency (CALP). According to this researcher, whose work is featured in many publications, the most effective way for learning a new language is the cognitive route, particularly if the student already has a firm grasp of the native language. This theory supports BICS happening in a social context, playground, lunch room, or sports environment but *not* as a replacement for a strong academic program. Communication skills will become more fluent through social interactions between six months and two years after children enter the school program. However, the progress of social communication is not the academic language proficiency required for the student to become a competent reader in English.

CALP can be defined as the skills essential to learning academics in school, which include listening, reading, speaking, and writing. A student needs to be competent in all subject areas for their age-appropriate grade, with proficient, strong academics. Chapter 7 has an extensive section, "Developing Vocabulary for English Language Learners," which explains the importance of CALP for young students.

Children who come into the formal education system already speaking and reading well in their native language may be placed in a regular classroom that provides an English-only program. The background information about language that they already possess provides a foundation for instruction in an English-only program. These programs are particularly successful when they have instruction provided in a varied format that actively engages students in speaking, reading, and writing. Sound educational practices provided in earlier chapters are appropriate for students learning English; simply put, they need more of *everything* that reading instruction has to offer at the early stages of learning.

During the time English language is developing, the issues for learners whose primary language is not English are diverse. Although their needs for decoding are similar to those of their English-speaking peers, ELLs may need additional practice and modified instruction through the regular education program. One difficulty ELLs experience is that the sounds of English phonemes are often different from those in their native language. For example, Spanish-speaking students are familiar with the similar sounds of the consonants *b, d, f, l, m, n, p, s,* and *t* in their primary language. However, the vowels are pronounced differently. Vowels in Spanish are pronounced the same as the short vowel of English. Additionally, Spanish has a consonant sound that does not have an English equivalent: *rr.* Other consonants make different sounds from English, including *ll* and *ñ.* Punctuation rules are different, and vowels sometimes have accent marks that identify the stress in the voice inflection.

Important notation—if parents are not native speakers of English and are not proficient English speakers, it is suggested that they continue to interact with their child in both languages—talking, reading, singing, and playing. However, when the sounds of the English language, through phonological processing and phonics, are being taught, children can be confused when non-native English speakers attempt to help them with their school work.

## SPECIAL EDUCATION REFERRALS AND ENGLISH LANGUAGE LEARNERS

School districts strive to have appropriate assessment instruments and trained personnel to determine if a child has English language acquisition needs, or if those needs occur in tandem with a learning disability. Special education programs in certain districts show an overrepresentation of ELLs. To counteract overrepresentation of students whose primary language is other than English receiving special education services, schools seek to identify children with limited or no English ability early. School environments with proven instructional strategies for at-risk students are created. What Works Clearinghouse (2022) identifies reading programs that have been validated for success with students who are learning English.

Prior to referral for special education services, two supportive instructional strategies that are relatively easy to implement in the regular classroom are suggested. First, **peer tutoring** assigns partners (an English-speaking, possibly older tutor and a younger tutee who is learning English). The pair read together and complete assignments. A second practice, **peer response groups**, gives a group of four to five students shared responsibilities for completing an assignment. Both methods have high improvement indices for ELLs and their classmates (What Works Clearinghouse, 2007, 2022).

One question consistently perplexes neuroscience: Is there a critical time period for acquisition of a second language? Many students are introduced to a second language for the first time in middle or high school. How does this timing match with brain development?

#  SECOND LANGUAGE ACQUISITION

Here is a deviation from the topic of readers with a disability to another type of consideration. Teachers and parents alike wonder when there is a choice for children to learn two languages. This choice may be for a child speaking a language other than English. In this case, it is a decision of when English is most appropriate, how much English is appropriate, and how much of the primary language is appropriate. When an English-speaking child has an opportunity to become a part of a dual-language immersion program, for example, is that the best choice? Furthermore, when is it best for a child speaking any language to learn an additional language? While these questions cannot be answered without additional information about the unique situation of an individual child, there is some helpful information to make that kind of decision.

## APPROPRIATE AGE FOR LEARNING A SECOND LANGUAGE

Information from Johnson and Newport (1989) indicates the ideal time for second language acquisition is between birth and 7 years old. Other recommendations for age yield a variety of responses:

- Begin at ages 3 to 5 or shortly thereafter
- Start between ages 10 and 18
- Learn a second language from early infancy to puberty
- The most receptive ages are 2 to 13

Most reports claim there is a steady decline in the ease or accessibility for dual-language learning that levels out at about age 17 where the potential rests. Interestingly, it appears that in this domain of language young children are superior learners when compared to adult learners' potential. The results do not indicate that adults cannot learn a second language; rather, it is a more difficult process, and the availability of speaking like a native speaker is almost lost. The level of expertise for pronunciation and mastery of grammar is sensitive to age and limited by the auditory system's development, which occurs during a child's early years.

Some parents and family members desire bilingualism for their children. Infants learning two first languages simultaneously will remain receptive to both languages for a longer time than children who learn one language. This means the young ones must be able to separate the nuances for each language. The number of people in the infant's environment speaking each language is important. Most who are knowledgeable about dual-language acquisition suggest one person—a mother, for example—only speaks one language. Concurrently, another adult—possibly a father or close grandparent—only speaks the second language. The relationship separating the two people allows the little one to mentally isolate the properties of each language. This process is an area of relative interest, and certainly one of importance as more elementary schools offer dual-language immersion programs (Kuhl, 2012).

## BILINGUALISM AS A PATHWAY TO ADDITIONAL LANGUAGE ACQUISITION

A benefit for students who learn more than one language simultaneously is that other cognitive skills advance. In future years, this translates to mean that they can learn a third or fourth language as they age. Additional languages become progressively more attainable. How can that be? Here is where neurology helps to make sense of second and even third language acquisition. Research supports that bilingual students pick up some prereading skills faster than their monolingual peers (Foreman, 2002). Being bilingual at a young age has cognitive benefits, such as stronger multitasking skills, creativity, easier access to working memory, a larger vocabulary, and access to metalinguistics. Metalinguistics is the verbal understanding of a language's structure. Verbal understanding ultimately allows a child to read and write using their understanding of word structure (Waterford.org, 2019). In terms of the reading brain, children who learn in two languages have heightened abilities for frontal lobe executive thinking, have an expanded working memory for practice and rehearsal of concepts, are better able to multitask, and have advanced skills for abstract thinking at a younger age.

#  CHALLENGED READERS

This section looks first at regular education classrooms where some students are not progressing according to the Common Core State Standards. Ongoing formative classroom assessment allows teachers to identify children who are not progressing in one or more skill areas. Often, additional instruction time or skills practice will remediate a perceived problem through ongoing regular classroom interventions.

Teachers frequently use strategies of preteach, teach, reteach, modify, model, and adjust as they respond to the diverse needs of their students. While there are many skill development designs that involve whole-class instruction, teachers find flexible classroom groupings often meet the needs of their varied student population. Usually, teachers decide to assess and reconfigure their instructional groups many times, even during the kindergarten year. When teachers find they need to work with small groups, it is important that the rest of the children are able to work independently. Teachers may spend a considerable amount of time—four weeks or more—at the beginning of the year to set up classroom procedures for primary students to work independently. As the rest of the class works at their desks or on projects at learning stations, the teacher is free to target instruction to meet the varying needs of students in a small-group setting.

The brains of children who cannot read easily most likely are working very hard. There are huge demands in the brain for glucose (energy) as poor readers struggle with reading tasks. But the students' hard work does not yield successful reading results. Good readers have integrated, smoothly functioning connections among the structures of a well-defined decoding system for reading. In contrast, readers with disabilities, often identified as dyslexic readers, use ancillary connections among structures and frequently do not activate areas in the brain that effective readers use. These alternate connections may allow struggling readers to accurately read words, but do not permit them to attain and recall mental models for words to allow fluent and automatic reading. Six different neurological causes of reading deficits are explored.

# 1. LACK OF EARLY LANGUAGE STIMULATION

A primary theme for the beginning chapters of this book is language development. As much as is known about the importance of early language experiences, that knowledge is not prevalent among all families. With the proliferation of communication through the media, on the Internet, and through school outreach programs, it is hopeful that all parents and caregivers will be encouraged to provide enriching language experiences at home for infants, toddlers, and young children prior to the time they enter formal schooling. The oral language pathway developing in a young child's brain is critical to future reading success.

Teachers can quickly identify children who lack the ability to speak with a varied vocabulary and in complete thoughts and sentences. The response to this lack of language stimulation is simple. Teachers can provide an abundance of oral language opportunities in school for these children. Fortunately, children are resilient, and most will catch up as a result of their teacher's intention to provide more and more oral language opportunities and experiences.

# 2. INFREQUENT SCHOOL ATTENDANCE OR A LACK OF SEQUENTIAL INSTRUCTION

Teachers may have students who lack a strong background in prereading or reading instruction due to infrequent school attendance or reading instruction that was not based on the science of reading principles. Understanding that the human brain learns and remembers what is taught explicitly, sequentially, and with organization is key for these students.

Most students who are struggling to read are initially helped in their regular classroom. Interventions provide reading instruction for students who are slightly below expected reading levels. Frequent assessments and interventions direct instruction to correct deficits when they are identified early. Teachers may select from value-added materials that provide additional practice with the same concepts that the whole class learns for students who are not making adequate progress. Many instructional strategies, provided in the previous two chapters, help children develop academic reading and cognitive skills. Often the lack of attendance or inconsistent instruction can be corrected with classroom modifications of additional materials or intensified instructional teaching methods for children who deviate minimally in their progress to become readers.

# 3. BRAIN STRUCTURES FROM THE ORAL LANGUAGE PATHWAY NEED TO BE CO-OPTED INTO A READING PATHWAY

In her research with **functional magnetic resonance imaging (fMRI)**, Sally Shaywitz (2003) found very different brain reactions between readers who exhibit disablities and those who read with ease. Although all beginning readers used the parietal and temporal lobes of their brains, called the parieto-temporal area, as they became skilled readers they automatically switched to an express pathway through the occipito-temporal area. Refer back to Figure 2.2 in Chapter 2 for the locations of the lobes within the brain's cerebral cortex. Both areas, parieto-temporal and occipito-temporal, are located toward the back of the brain. Children who were unsuccessful with reading developed a very different ineffective route by accessing the frontal lobe area. Shaywitz and other reading specialists (2002) define struggling readers as dyslexic, a hidden disability that simply means "having a hard time reading." What they saw through fMRI gives validation to practices that teach reading systematically. More recent information from neurology confirms the work of Shaywitz, but indicates there are even wider areas of right- and left-hemisphere involvement than those named in earlier neuroscientific studies (Bradshaw et al., 2020).

Reading disabilities can be overcome at the time of early reading instruction, as if they never existed, even for children who may have predestined, generically influenced reading problems. Teachers who understand the workings of the human brain during reading are equipped to respond before a reading glitch becomes a reading problem.

Differences between children who are fluent, proficient readers and those who have a reading disability or dyslexia are brain based. Students who advance through school with reading deficits, but without corrective reading intervention, continue to read slowly, even when they are in college. If they were observed by fMRI, it would be apparent that they access mainly the frontal and right anterior areas to decipher words. This slow reading pathway works for them, *but with much difficulty*. A student with a normally developed reading pathway mostly accesses the left anterior area of the occipital and temporal lobes. The right temporal and frontal areas are also minimally involved during fluent reading.

## BASICS: FROM SLOW TO GO READING

Students who are slow, inefficient readers frequently have a deficit relating to phonological processing, particularly the ability to decode and recognize words and to encode words through writing and spelling. According to Roxanne Hudson and her colleagues (2007), identification of children who experience dyslexia is difficult. The term can be broken into two parts: *dys*, meaning difficult or not happening, and *lexia*, meaning involvement with words and language associated with reading. Shaywitz (2003; Shaywitz et al., 2002) and medical personnel, researchers, and clinicians tend to identify all readers who are not proficient as dyslexic. Reading specialists use a variety of descriptions. Commonly used terminology includes *poor readers*, *children with special needs*, *struggling readers*, and *disabled/impaired readers*. Classroom teachers, too, would tell us that there is a range of children who struggle with reading. Some children have minimal skill deficits, while at the other end of the continuum children are identified with learning disabilities and qualify for special education services. Special education services or placements are provided so all children have access to a free and appropriate public education. There is not agreement among educators on a single term that adequately defines the variety of readers who are unsuccessful, nor do they agree on the intensity of reading problems children experience.

Known is that reading problems are neurobiological, meaning they result from problems located physically in the brain. Difficulty reading is not solely caused by speech or hearing impairments, a developmental delay, or a low socioeconomic background, although these characteristics may contribute to a higher risk for reading problems (Hudson et al., 2007). Based on the uniqueness of each child's brain, there is not a simple cause, nor is there a single instructional response to reading problems.

Regardless of terminology, many children who experience reading problems have been exposed to regular reading instruction and may exhibit strong abilities in higher-order reading skills of vocabulary, syntax, and reasoning discourse. Yet, they lack the ability to decode and read rapidly. These students each require a thoughtful, thorough plan for reading instruction, hopefully before they begin to experience defeat and feelings of helplessness.

## IMPACT OF PHONEMIC AWARENESS SENSITIVITY

The inability to discern and manipulate abstractions associated with phonemes has been identified as a significant cause of many reading failures. A lack of exposure to phonemic awareness practices that appear playful and fun to do is one causal factor. Another is that some children are genetically predestined with an inability to hear and process the difference between sounds. Intense phonemic awareness activities followed by explicit teaching of phonics and other decoding skills often help a student to develop awareness of distinct differences in the sounds of words. The reading pathway is constructed as all structures used by successful readers can be accessed. As was discovered in Chapter 5, one structure that is an essential addition to the oral language pathway is the angular gyrus. First know that the term *gyrus* means one, but then recognize this area has convoluted folds rising above the surface of the cerebral cortex with a plural form of *gyri*. The angular gyrus as a type of structure then consists of irregular folded brain matter that is located at the junction of the occipital, parietal, and temporal lobes. It is at this location that the letters of written words are translated into the sounds of spoken language. This structure, when added to the oral language pathway for early readers, allows the students to progress in reading skill development using a completed reading pathway.

In some cases, the need is greater than what can be accomplished by intensifying regular instruction. Often a supplemental program that is strong in phoneme sequencing and explicit phonics instruction is provided. Some intensive programs successfully engage struggling readers with their senses. Children feel how sounds are formed with their mouths. They watch how their lips and tongue form sounds by using a mirror to discover and label the oral-motor movements of the phonemes in words (Lindamood et al., 1997, 2020). Older students who appear to have missed the opportunity in the lower grades to read proficiently can still be taught to read with intense, lengthy therapy. It is never too late to learn to read, but there are developmental windows where certain cognitive skills are easier to achieve. If a student has missed the "best time" to learn those skills, they can still learn—it just takes more effort.

A relatively small number of emergent readers do not respond to regular or extended classroom interventions for phonemic awareness and decoding deficits. Even as these children are given additional instruction and practice and they continue to fall further behind their classmates, they may have cognitive differences (see item 6) that block their ability to even think about phonemes and the variation of sounds they represent.

# 4. SLOW PROCESSING SKILLS

All children do not learn to read at the expected rate. First, here is a grade-level range for how many words are read with a one-minute timing. A number of factors may influence reading rates. Although the rate of oral or silent reading may be quite similar during the early grades, for third graders the gap between reading aloud and reading silently may be significant. In third grade, some children with slow reading rates may need instruction in the basics for phonological and orthographic processing. They may not have mastered the skills to identify, manipulate, produce, and recall speech sounds. Other children exhibit difficulties with reading rates due to a lack of word recognition, vocabulary, comprehension, or processing speed deficits. Unsuccessful readers at any grade level, as identified in Chapter 7, need assessment to determine a remediation plan that addresses their specific deficits. An increasing number of commercial programs address reading fluency. "Read, reread, and read again" shows up as a strategy in many programs. Refer back to the Hasbrouck and Tindal (2017) oral reading fluency data provided in Chapter 8 in Table 8.1 for one-minute timings for words per grade level.

## REPETITIVE PRACTICE FOR OBJECT NAMING

Interestingly, even though flash cards for rote memory word recognition have been dubbed by some as "drill and kill," flash cards are useful practice for reading single words, particularly those that do not follow orthographic patterns or rules, called sight words or high-frequency words. When these words are found in text, readers identify them with improved speed using the rote memory. Rote memory is a part of the unconscious, nondeclarative memory system, discussed in Chapter 7, that happens with automaticity. Words have been practiced so thoroughly that responses are produced without any mental effort. Likewise, pictorial flash cards of objects show promise as one type of remediation practice for children with slow response rates for naming. In this case, children use flash cards with objects, pictures, or words that they already know. Students can work with partners to quiz each other, since demands to turn over the flash cards could interfere with the target process of rapid naming. The desired outcome is certainty, accuracy, and, most important, speed. Recording times and engaging children to beat their own best time provides motivation for this type of flash card activity.

Here, also, is a place where the computer is suited to provide repetitive practice. Programs are designed specifically to present images for identification at varying speeds. Children learn to respond quickly and to prime their minds to make connections rapidly. A word of caution about electronic teaching programs. Choose a program with a person's speaking voice rather than a robotic one that may be misrepresenting natural phonemes and sounds. Once the concept of naming speed is understood as a developmental skill used by readers to attain fluency, other classroom activities can provide this type of practice through repetition.

## 5. DEFICIT IN PRIMING SKILLS

In Chapter 6, cognitive priming skills were developed that need to be in place for the emerging reader. These skills, particularly attention, concentration, memory, and organization, may not be identified through traditional classroom testing. Traditional assessment determines what a child is able or unable to do, not necessarily what cognitive skills may be interfering with reading progress. Careful observation and note-taking by an adult other than the teacher can aid in determining if a child is having difficulty with one or more priming skills. Practices that support increased skills are listed:

- **Attention**: Acknowledge the need for shorter work times and more physical activity. Generally, children can pay attention to one task for two to five minutes per year of age, so pick the lower number to start. Have a chart and timer for another adult to mark the amount of time the child attends to work. Observe the child's work habits with work that is not too hard for the child to do on their own. Confer with the child on the observation results. Make a plan to increase attention to classroom tasks.

- **Focus**: Be reasonable about time expectations, decrease distractions, and break big tasks into smaller pieces through task analysis. Practice focusing with games, such as "name all the objects in the room that are square shaped," "count the number of desks or books," or "name the children in our class from a class picture or other pictures."

- **Concentration**: Check the student's amount of sleep, home routines, and diet. Select seating carefully. Attach visual, auditory, and kinesthetic facets to lessons, as possible. Redirect as possible. Make note of the amount of time the child concentrates on self-selected activities to have an idea of how much concentration is possible.

- **Memory**: Card games like Memory, Go Fish, and Uno increase short-term memory for objects and rules; try also memory board games. A small-group oral exercise is "I'm going to the beach [or another outing], and I am taking . . ." One child names something that starts with an *a*, the next child names the word for *a* and adds a *b* word, and each subsequent child must provide the previous list and name a new item according to the sequence of the alphabet.

- **Organization**: Personal space and classroom organization can be taught. Children need to know where school supplies are kept, where finished work belongs, and where their personal items are stored. Cleanup needs to be taught. Getting ready to learn—what does it look like? Post a daily class schedule and refer to it often. Pair a child with good organization skills with one who is learning to organize to work together for a learning project. Use charts for vocabulary. Sorting objects from science or math mimics the way the brain categorizes and stores information in declarative and nondeclarative memory systems.

## 6. COGNITIVE SKILL DEVELOPMENT

Traditional classroom assessment does not provide information about how the brain is structured for reading when we look at students who are struggling with cognitive differences. P. G. Aaron (1995), a university professor of psychology, suggests a "deeper elusive problem with cognitive processes that underlie reading" (p. 345). An example of one such problem could be visual processing. In this instance, a child is unable to concentrate on or focus on tracking words to make the necessary conversions from the visual input to a sound or word output. Neuroscientist Guinevere Eden, director of Georgetown's Center for the Study of Learning, and colleagues as long ago as 2004 studied a group of 80 students identified as dyslexic readers and have updated their research based on ongoing studies of students with dyslexia (Reading Rockets, 2019). Phonological awareness was earlier identified as critical to the learning-to-read cycle. Eden and colleagues also uncovered that children with dyslexia rely on visual perception more than phonological cues for reading (Reading Rockets, 2019). At initial reading stages, visual cues are dominant for all prereaders. Children who experience reading success switch emphasis to rely on left-brain tasks for deciphering sounds of language (Turkeltaub et al., 2005). Here, again, there is a signal to educators that the left hemisphere is used for successful readers, while struggling readers continue to rely on right-hemisphere structures that are not as efficient.

Much of the information currently received about aberrant brain function during attempts at reading come from studies neuroscientists are conducting that compare brain imaging of successful and nonsuccessful readers using fMRI technology. Hudson and her colleagues (2007) reviewed studies on structural differences in the brains of children who are successful readers and those who are identified as having a reading disability. Their report identifies the differences between white and gray matter. In the brain, gray matter is the neurons (nerve cells) themselves, which are responsible for processing information. Counterparts in the brain, the white matter, represent the neuron's axons coated with glial cells, which communicate with a myriad of dendrites. The white matter is located deeper in the brain and is responsible for passing information to all the various parts of the brain. Reports indicate that people with dyslexia have less gray matter *and* less white matter in the area of the brain identified earlier as the angular gyrus, the sound-to-letter area in the parieto-temporal lobe junction in the left hemisphere (Hudson et al., 2007). Hence the strategy of practice, practice, practice that is inherent to intervention programs results in the development of new neural connections and pathways, increasing gray and white matter in children's brains.

It is not feasible, nor would it be suggested, that a child having reading difficulties undergo a brain scan. The technology and the professionals and assistants required to run the equipment are cost prohibitive and unnecessary for education. Additionally, reports of findings are based on group outcomes and are not deemed reliable for individual diagnosis. Educators who are consumers of information from brain studies increase the depth of their assessments and have a greater understanding of their observation methods. Understanding differences in a reader's cognitive function leads educators toward a more informed course for remediation.

## AN EXAMPLE OF INTENSE INTERVENTION

An example of the many programs with intense assessment and observation for reading intervention was developed by Lindamood-Bell (Lindamood et al., 2020). Pat Lindamood and Nanci Bell developed a program to identify and treat individuals with reading deficiencies through sensory-cognitive function. Assessments done by clinicians use standard tests of reading progress and additionally check a child's ability to manipulate phonemes. Different from and more intense than many interventions, a cognitive tactile/sensory approach is used. Children learn to pay attention to sounds by feeling what is happening with their mouths and to identify how they form sounds with labels such as "lip poppers" or "tongue tappers." This methodology progresses from oral sounds to having the child represent sounds with colored blocks. Ultimately, children move to letters and words. This sequence of instruction appears to activate the child's brain for attending to sounds through a tactile approach and stimulate a pathway to the brain's language centers for sound identification. By strengthening the tactile senses, students initially approach phonemic awareness and phonological processing of sounds through feeling. The slow and intense process finally redirects students to develop and use the traditional reading pathway successful readers use that begins with visual input.

## AN ADDITIONAL TOOL: CHART OF COGNITIVE SKILLS TO BECOME A LEARNER

To extend understanding of the complex processes that happen in a student's brain, a list of cognitive functioning expectations was developed by the author. Charts for cognitive function begin in Chapter 2 and continue to be developed through Chapter 8, with the exception of Chapter 4. The chart is available in its entirety in Appendix B. A caveat to this list is the caution that the list has *not* been field tested, nor has it experienced scientific inquiry. Rather, this list resulted from a comprehensive review of expected learning standards for reading, developmental charts, descriptions, observations, online resources, and feedback from people who are present with children at the ages corresponding to the chart.

Why this listing? Cognitive learning expectations give teachers and diagnosticians an observation tool that is different from other informal assessment documents. How is it different? The descriptions and examples relate to demands on students' brains at different developmental levels. Examples given may be forged into instructional responses to strengthen weak areas of cognitive skills—all of which are encompassed in the process of reading according to the keystones identified earlier by the science of reading: phonological awareness, phonics instruction, decoding or breaking the reading code, vocabulary development, comprehension, encoding or writing, and fluidity.

Teachers and other readers are encouraged to use the comprehensive cognitive skill development chart, located in Appendix B, to better understand students' brains as they advance in age and approach reading tasks with increased difficulty. Children with cognitive functioning deficiencies challenge educators to look more closely at the way these students interpret sensory input the brain receives for reading. When children experience serious reading difficulties, assessments administered by a psychologist or speech and language specialist provide in-depth information about the prerequisite cognitive functions required for reading.

## UNSUCCESSFUL READERS MUST HAVE INTERVENTION

For educators, there is a strong message. The longer a child continues to struggle with an inefficient system for reading, the more urgent it becomes that intervention begins. Observation of this long-term effect, not by brain imaging, but by substantial research supported by the National Institute of Child Health and Human Development (NICHD, 2019), provides stark evidence. *Without systematic, focused, and intensive intervention, the majority of children who enter school at risk for reading failure are rarely able to catch up with their peers who are nonimpaired readers.* It is education's challenge and responsibility to select reading intervention strategies and programs that will correct the weaknesses individual children experience with their language systems. Intensive reading programs appear to change the neural networks in a child's brain and activate the brain in different ways to create an effective pathway for word and sound recognition and ultimately for fluent, comprehensive reading (NICHD, 2019).

## SPECIAL EDUCATION SERVICES

As indicated earlier in this chapter, students who have not been successful readers during regular classroom interventions may need special education services. Responsible parties, including parents and educational support staff, meet together to decide if the child meets special education criteria. If so, the child is identified for services, and an individualized education program, or IEP, is developed and designed to address the child's individual reading needs. This plan identifies the child's strengths for reading as well as areas of deficit. Included with a child's IEP are global reading goals, benchmarks for progress, and specific objectives that will pave the way for grade-level-appropriate reading development.

The U.S. Congress reauthorized the Individuals with Disabilities Education Act (IDEA) in 2004 and amended the original law in 2015 with P.L. 114–95, the Every Student Succeeds Act (U.S. Department of Education, 2022). At this time, a child who needs reading intervention is no longer tested for a severe discrepancy between achievement and intellectual capacity. Prior legislation used the discrepancy model for receiving services from a special education program. Current law requires school programs to determine if a child will respond to a scientific, research-based intervention as a part of the evaluation process for children. The services may be provided within the general education program. Funding was authorized from the federal government through 2021. In July 2021, the U.S. Department of Education released more money for children and youth, ages 3–21, with disabilities. These Reading Recovery funds are available from state-funded competitive grant programs.

## CONCLUDING THOUGHTS ABOUT ASSESSMENT AND RESPONSES FOR AT-RISK READERS

The reading challenge is to close the gap between what researchers tell us is needed for readers who are not proficient and what is provided in our schools. Teachers are ready to react and be effective. Teacher preparation at universities can provide effective preservice methods and practices to prepare future teachers. Understanding that children's brains are designed for oral language, not for reading print, is critical knowledge for teachers to have before they are assigned to a preschool or elementary grade. Finally, if school-level support is in place, educators are ready to help children who are challenged by normal and unique reading demands. Strong preservice education and on-the-job professional development support for primary teachers, and for all teachers who provide reading instruction, is the best protection to prevent children from becoming *curriculum causalities*. Moving forward, Chapter 10 has a unique challenge for teachers. What if children are invited to understand their reading brains and become responsible learners during their reading development?

## RESOURCE

EAB. (2019, March 21). *How our brains learn to read* [a chart to understand how the science of reading and neurology fit together to support readers]. bit.ly/3GGmh1k

# Reflective Questions

1. Educators believe it is urgent that children at risk for reading failure be assessed and receive intervention promptly. Provide supporting information that leads educators to take this stand.

2. Some children enter school with a small oral vocabulary. Why is oral language development so important to the reading process, and how can teachers respond to the needs of children with vocabulary weakness?

3. What are some important considerations for assessing children who are English language learners? Describe what is meant by basic interpersonal communication skills (BICS) and cognitive academic language proficiency (CALP). How do these two instructional proposals differ? Which one honors the way the brain learns? Explain.

4. What are the advantages for children who learn a second language? What benefits result from dual-language programs in the elementary school years?

5. If you are reading this book as part of a study group, describe one or more interventions for a school to implement that are responsive to the needs of all children, particularly those who are unsuccessful readers or are learning English.

6. Morgan et al. (2022) studied the overrepresentation of ethnically and racially different (nonwhite) children placed in special education services outside general education classrooms. Their conclusion, available from https://doi.org/10.1177/00222194221094019. did not support bias in schools. How would you explain the different response these researchers discovered?

7. How would you decide whether to recommend a reading intervention for a second-grade child who can decode words and comprehend text but is not able to read fluently?

8. Select a current research study on a topic of reading development that is of interest or important to you. Describe how the study outcome influences or could influence teaching reading in a primary classroom.

# CHAPTER 10

# Teachers and Students as Learning Partners

Students can be invited to understand how they grow and develop *and* how they learn, even at an early age. They need to know that terms like *smart*, *gifted*, *stupid*, and *dumb* may not be appropriate at home or at school. Students receive praise for their specific efforts, progress, improvement, and strategies, rather than comments regarding innate intelligence or propensity for learning difficulties. Students are assured that while the work at school can be hard and challenging, they are able to succeed.

This easy-to-read and easy-to-implement chapter provides basic brain information for a second- or third-grade student along with some unique learning strategies. Some of the content and suggestions may be too advanced for your students, so teachers are encouraged to pick and choose or modify content from this chapter. The chapter is intended for teachers and parents to encourage and connect with the children in their care as they discover how their very young but miraculous brains are designed to learn. Students are excited when they know their developing brains can be coaxed to learn more from paying attention, concentrating, and practicing. A partnership between adults and students can lead to the children's acceptance of responsibilities as learners for the years of schooling ahead.

Students can be fired up about learning; it is a brain thing. When they understand how the 3-pound mass of neural cells works, they are able to take some responsibility for their own learning. Teachers can begin by reading and talking about what children's brains can do with a story or picture book such as *Your Fantastic Elastic Brain*, written by JoAnn Deak and illustrated by Sarah Ackerley (2010), and *How Your Brain Learns to Read* by Denise Eide and illustrated by Ingrid Hess (2022). Taking time with this one or similar books can help children to understand brain concepts and apply new learning to their own situation.

Children can be challenged to learn more with the following information and questions. Teachers may decide to use all or parts of these ideas, depending on the developmental level of their students. The important goal is to explain the fascinating brain each child owns. During the process, children will begin to understand how they can make learning easier.

## WHAT DO YOU KNOW ABOUT YOUR BRAIN?

1. How much does an adult brain weigh? Your brain now is over 80% of its full size. How much is that? Want to know more? Check this website: bit.ly/3WXIePg.

2. What are the five senses that give our brains information? What part of your body is important to receive each of the senses? See Figure 10.1 for how one student pictured the senses. When you were a baby, some of your senses were better developed than others so you could begin learning. Look at Figure 10.2 to see the strangely shaped baby. The senses that are fully developed or working are enlarged. Notice the young artist pictured the small legs and feet. A baby is not ready to stand and walk. The brain is also not ready to direct crawling, standing, or walking. There are too many other parts of the body that are building. What senses does a baby depend on at the beginning of life? Why did you give that answer? During the first two years of life, all senses are completely working. You have senses that are fully working. What if all your senses were blocked and not sending information to your brain? You'd have nothing to think about. Talk about how important your senses are for you to be a

learner. (*Teacher Reference:* Chapter 1 for a detailed discussion of the five senses.)

**FIGURE 10.1** ● A student drawing of the five senses and their locations. Notice how the body receives the sense of touch.

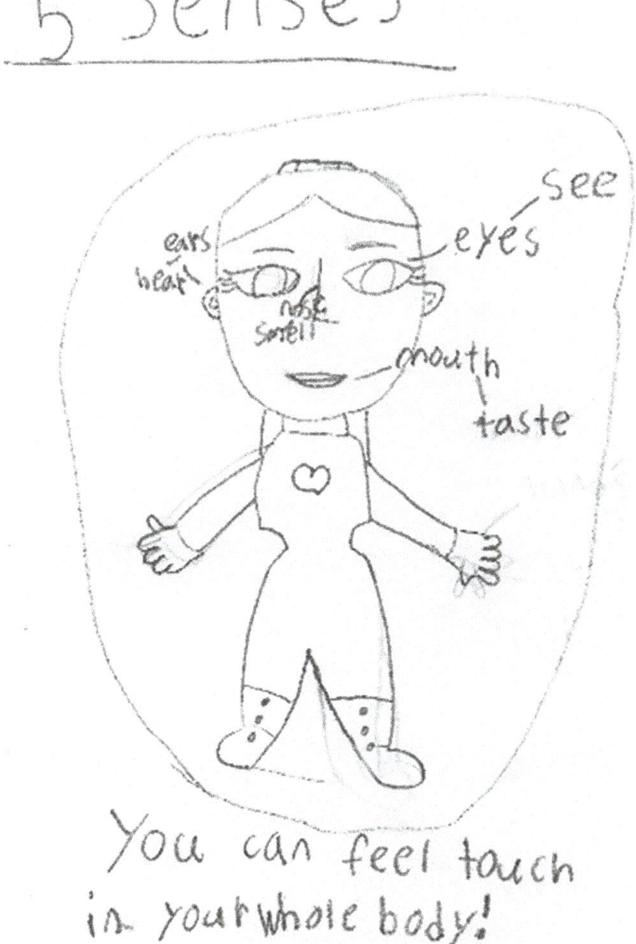


**Source:** Ayla Grace Nevills. Used with permission.

3. You are unique! There is not now, nor has there ever been, someone exactly like you. Everything you do and the way you do it are only your ways. What are some things about you that make you *you*? (Think about your favorite foods, free-time activities, sports, how you like to dress, and your family, for example.) Even though we will learn what parts of the brain are

(Continued)

*(Continued)*

the same in all people, when we learn specifically about *your* brain, there will be differences.

**FIGURE 10.2** ● An infant would look very strange if the body shape represented the senses used to learn. This figure is a child's drawing of how a "sensory-dependent baby" could be imagined. During the first two years of life, all the senses complete their development.

**Source:** Ayla Grace Nevills. Used with permission.

4. There are parts of your brain that do different things and have complicated words to describe them (*cerebral cortex*, *cerebellum*, and *brain stem*, for example). Look at a picture of the brain divided into three different parts. What information can you find about each of these parts of the human brain? Describe in your own words what each brain part does for you to be who you are. (*Teacher Reference:* See Figure 2.1 in Chapter 2 for a depiction of the cerebral cortex, cerebellum, and brain stem.)

5. Neurons are teeny tiny cells that exist all over your brain. They act as messengers. Neurons are most numerous in your brain,

but are located also in other places. Actually, they are all over your body to get messages to and from different parts of your brain. Remember the brain stem at the back of your brain? One job it does is to send messages to other parts of your body.

Just as you are unique in the way you look and act, neurons for different parts of your body are different, too. Look at Figure 10.3. One child drew models of differently shaped neurons. Notice the shape of the sensory neuron, which sends and receives information from the senses. Neurons send messages to different parts of the brain. When you read a book, the messages are going to different parts of your brain so the words have meaning. When you ride your bicycle, many parts of the whole body send messages to and receive messages from the brain. How does it feel when you are working very hard to ride your bike to the top of a hill? Are the feeling messages different when you ride down that same hill?

**FIGURE 10.3** ● Pictured is a student drawing of a sensory neuron and other shapes that neurons can have.

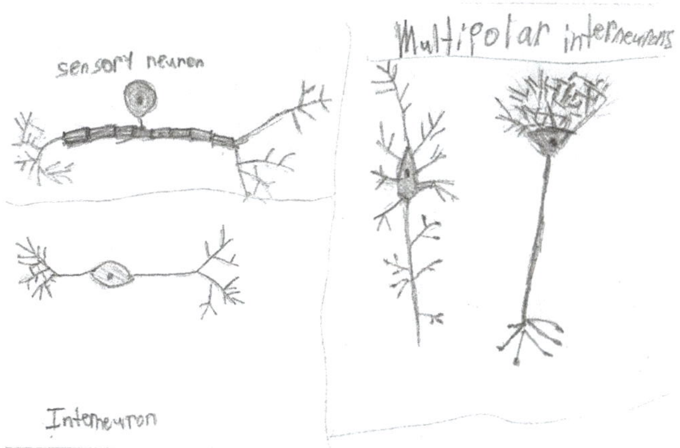


**Source:** Abigail Nevills. Used with permission.

6. A student drawing of a common neuron and its body parts is provided in Figure 10.4. People have the same body parts (head, trunk, arms, legs—you get the idea), but those body parts are shaped differently for each person. Neurons have the same body parts as other neurons (axons, cell body, nucleus, and dendrites, for example). Just as our bodies look different from one another, neurons are differently shaped and connected to one another as well. Their size and structure are determined by

(Continued)

where they are found in the body. Can you find another picture of some of the different shapes that neurons have? Can you find the body parts of differently shaped neurons—axons, cell body, nucleus, and dendrites? (*Teacher Resource*: Neurons and their body parts are pictured in Figure 1.1 in Chapter 1.)

**FIGURE 10.4** ● This is a mature or complete neuron drawn by a student. The myelin sheath on the axon tail makes the messages between neurons move quicker, and helps you think faster.

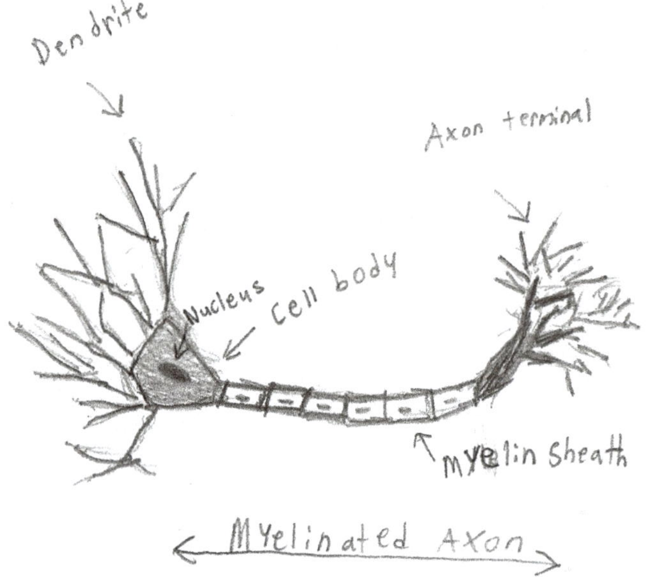


**Source:** Abigail Nevills. Used with permission.

7. Look again at Figure 10.4. Notice the area of the neuron's axon labeled as a **myelin sheath**. This sheath is a fatty material that covers the axon tail. It makes messages travel faster from one part of your brain to another, or even to another part of your body. This covering helps you to think faster. Before the myelin sheath was developed, messages moved slowly. You worked hard to think. Picture the messages connecting by walking from one part of your brain to another. When the neurons are complete and the axon is coated with the sheath, it is like the messages travel on a fast train. You think quickly. You cannot make the sheath grow. Your brain commands it to happen when you pay attention, concentrate, and practice to learn new things.

8. Neurons are very, very, very small. You cannot see a neuron without an extremely high-powered microscope. You have about 100 billion neurons in your body. Write that number.

That is an extremely large number, just as large as the unlimited number of stars in the sky on a very clear night.

9. It is important to run and play for fun, or for sports to build strong muscles. You also stretch and strengthen your brain by practicing, rehearsing, and repeating words or information that is important to learn and remember. What are some things that you are learning at school that are important to remember? When you have to remember and recall something important in your schoolwork, what do you do to practice?

10. Your brain is different from every other person's brain because it is built on all the experiences you have had during your life. Even though you and your friend have the same brain parts or structures, your brains are wired or connected differently, uniquely. That is why some work that is easy for you might be hard for someone else. Or you may be working hard at learning, and another friend may think it is easy-peasy. Wiring in your brain means the way neurons connect to each other to form neuron networks. Every single person in the world has a differently wired brain, even people who have an identical twin sister or brother.

Now, write some sentences to tell what you know about your brain. What picture could you draw? (*Teacher Insight:* Chart what children know about their brains, such as by using a KWL chart, introduced in Chapter 4, to display what students *know, want* to know, and have *learned*. You may also chart and record what students want to *R*, or *remember*.)

#  TEACHERS MODEL LEARNING

In previous chapters, strategies to encourage student engagement have been numerous. Teaching methods and practices have been provided as teachers choose, direct, and support student learning. What is different as students care and share the responsibility for learning, and how can teachers move into this type of partnership? Realize interest in teaching children how they learn began to grow in popularity in the 2010s. Many books challenge students to know more about their brains.

Among the brain books that can be considered for brain-curious students and their teachers, you might try a current book by Leanne Boucher Gill (2021) called *Big Brain Book: How It Works and All Its Quirks*. Note, however, the reading level is for ages 10–13, so this might be considered for a teacher read-aloud. Other examples include *The Human Brain—Biology for Kids,* which is part of a series by Baby Professor (2017). Some older books—*Look Inside Your Brain* by Heather Alexander (1991); *Brain Surgery for Beginners*, written by Steve Parker and illustrated by David West (1988); and *Understanding Your Brain*, written by Rebecca Treays and illustrated by Christyan Fox (2004)—although written a while ago, continue to be obtainable.

A simple beginning strategy is for the teacher to overtly demonstrate "thinking out loud" strategies, known among educators as **metacognition** (Noland et al., 2022). Most likely, this strategy is not in teaching manuals, but its strength is a foundation for teachers to reveal to students their thinking for the process of learning. Teacher self-reflection about how learning happens in their brain might sound like this: "I am confused by . . ."; "If I need to remember this, I will . . ."; "Before I thought . . . , but now I know . . ."; "If I want to remember these four steps, I will . . ." The metacognition process encourages children to think out loud or quietly subvocalize as they are introduced to new words, ideas, sequences, or concepts they are learning. Metacognition can be used to evaluate text, identify what might be confusing, remember vocabulary, build background knowledge, problem solve, or meet the Common Core State Standards outlined for second or third grade.

Another strategy to begin this practice is to choose a book to share with students, such as *Why I Sneeze, Shiver, Hiccup, and Yawn*, written by Melvin Berger and illustrated by Paul Meisel (2000), or, as previously recommended, *Your Fantastic Elastic Brain* (Deak & Ackerley, 2010) or *Big Brain Book* (Boucher Gill, 2021). Teachers model how reading works in the brain's working memory as they articulate what they are thinking during the reading process. To get started, teachers may predetermine their questions and place sticky notes on the selected book's pages to remind them to stop and verbally model what they are thinking. Teachers may use a think-aloud metacognition process to identify text or vocabulary that could be a barrier or to wonder what the author means. Pictures or diagrams provided in the book might give cause for teachers to model what is seen and what is meant in their way of thinking.

## CLASSROOM ENVIRONMENT STRUCTURED FOR LEARNERS

Teachers show students how important learning is for them personally when they use the think-aloud practice. They also model how the classroom is the place for every student to be a successful learner by structuring class rules or a class

Our teacher plans, teaches, shows us what to learn and how we can learn best, and . . .

Students are in charge of what they learn. **Let's Do It!**

We use ways to activate our brains to learn. **We'll Try It!**

We help each other to understand and complete class work. **Together We Learn!**

agreement that aligns with this goal. Statements like those provided in Table 10.1 might be used.

To encourage reinforcement of this type of classroom agreement, it is important for the teacher to watch for and identify when students act in ways that are stated. Noticing and acknowledging actions of individual practice and rehearsal, keeping track of work assignments by note-taking, and supporting a peer who is struggling with a concept are examples. Reinforcement of these statements at the onset, possibly for several weeks, will encourage these responsible and respectful processes to become part of the classroom routine.

Previously learned topics, vocabulary, and problems solved are charted or available in other ways to support students as they take responsibility for reinforcing long-term conscious memory. The classroom emerges as a treasury of previously acquired, newly acquired, and waiting-to-be-discovered learning.

## MEMORY SYSTEMS FOR REMEMBERING

The brain receives information to think about or to enjoy. Children can be reminded that their brains also want to remember people's names, exciting experiences at home or in school, or a birthday party, for example. Students can be asked, "What is something that has happened in the last day or two that you would like to remember?" A way to introduce young students to memory systems is with the following suggested conversations, which may be used for several teaching periods. Props, charts, illustrations, and books are helpful for these topics. Consider if the following topics would be helpful for your class.

We all want to remember important events, things, and people in our lives. There are different kinds of memory systems in your brain to help you remember, recall, and retell those things. Even neuroscientists (scientists who study the brain with machines or microscopes) cannot find the memory systems in the human brain. Each person has a different pattern of wiring for neurons to connect to each other. Everyone has different experiences they would like to store for memory. Neuroscientists know how you use different parts of your brain for different jobs, but they cannot identify exactly where you store things to remember. What is known is that you put things into your own unique long-term memory system in four different ways.

**Four Ways to Remember, Tell, and Show**

1.  You can learn something and be able to tell or write about it. Here are some examples. You practice to learn and use a rule from phonics to pronounce a new word. You tell about facts you learned in science about the planets. You write a story about your favorite uncle. To get information into this memory system, you most likely need to practice, rehearse, talk out loud, or connect new information to something else you already know. When you do things like this, you use your brain's memory system to give responses and share information. It may be to answer quiz or test questions. This type of memory allows you to tell or write what you have remembered and learned. We can call it your *remember and tell memory*. How have you used your remember and tell memory today?

2.  Some learning happens with a lot of excitement. You feel joy and excitement when you have a birthday party. You may feel scared if the classroom alarm goes off and a fire engine arrives at school. Or, a parent may come to the classroom dressed like a character in a book and read the story to you, and you most likely will feel amused and interested. Memory that comes with excitement can have a range of emotional feelings from very happy and excited to sad or scared. Usually, important experiences at school help us to learn key facts, information, or ideas. What are some experiences you have had at school that have been exciting and have helped you learn something new? When you feel a lot of excitement, either with joy or with concern, your experience memory becomes activated.

What you remember may not be exactly what happened. The message game is a good example of how this type of memory may not be correct. A group of children sit in a circle and pass a message by whispering it from one child to the next. When the message has been passed to everyone, the last child tells what was heard. What do you think happens to the message? Let's try it. What happened to the starting message? When you tell or write what happened after an exciting experience, you are using memory from experience. It can be called your *experience memory*.

So far we have talked about two kinds of memory. These systems for remembering are for thinking and telling facts or ideas. What are they? *Hints:* To use the first type of memory, you need to practice and rehearse to be able to use the r_________ and t_________ memory. Can you give an example of this type of remembering?

The second memory type remembers good or bad excitement. It is e_________ memory. Can you give an example of this one?

Follow this review by writing a class description of each memory type. (*Teacher Resource:* Refer to Chapter 7, in particular Figure 7.2 and Tables 7.1 and 7.2, for more on these types of memory.)

3. There are times you have to recall small bits of information or a fact. These items are usually a one-word answer, like a word you use a lot when you write, the answers when practicing your multiplication tables, or the name of a friend. After a lot of practice, you can give the answer without thinking about it. This type of memory is used when you are reading and you know words without sounding them out. You just know them. We can call this *rote memory. Rote* is the word scientists use to identify this type of memory. How do you practice to remember something for your rote memory?

4. The last type of memory is an easy one because you use it all day long. You use it to get dressed, to eat your breakfast, to walk to the car or to school, and even when you read. These are tasks or everyday happenings that you do without even thinking about it—there are hundreds of them. Can you name some more? (If not identified, explain how procedural or process memory is an important task for reading quickly and with understanding.) *Process memory* relieves the brain from the hard work it took to learn how to read so the reader can focus and concentrate on what is being read for understanding.

How does your brain do process tasks? You practice and practice until a sequence of activities is so well learned that a special part of

(Continued)

*(Continued)*

your brain, the cerebellum, takes over and directs the actions you need, without you even thinking about how to respond. You most likely can remember how hard it was to learn to ride a bike. After so much practice, and maybe some falls, you finally got the hang of it. And now, you don't even need to think about what your legs are doing to pedal, what your hands do to steer with the handlebars, or how your body maintains balance. It all just comes together thanks to your cerebellum.

Find the cerebellum, the small brain at the back of your head, in a picture and place your hand on your head where it is located. We use this term to remember this type of memory: *process memory.* (*Teacher Consideration:* Would *action memory* be a more appropriate term for your class?)

Let's see what we remember. What are the first two types of memory that we have to think about [*remember and tell* and *experience memory*]? Give an example of each.

The second two memory types happen without you having to think hard. The answers you give or what your body does just happens. What are these types of memory called [*rote memory* and *process memory*]? Give an example of each.

Follow this review by writing a class description of each memory type. (*Teacher Resource:* Revisit Table 7.3 in Chapter 7 for examples of activities that allow students to demonstrate their understanding of adjectives and adverbs using each of the four types of memory available to the brain.)

##  STUDENTS AS LEARNERS

Teachers can keep the different types of memory systems in mind as methods and activities for teaching are determined. If this is new thinking for you, begin by asking yourself what you want children to remember and be able to recall. What type of memory system or combination of memory systems is needed? Then you can explore teaching strategies to match that system or combination of systems.

Teaching strategies should match the learning need, and teacher-determined learning strategies can be turned into student strategies. Teachers know how to plan for direct instruction, repetitions, engaging activities, and assessment

| Self-talk and metacognition | Talk to and with yourself. Rehearse and practice to move important concepts or ideas into long-term memory. Ask yourself questions out loud or quietly subvocalize them to direct your studies. "What do I need to remember from what I just read?" Or, "How could I explain to my friend what I just learned?" |
|---|---|
| Graphing or charting | Look for the main topic or thought and gather other smaller bits of information that fit into that topic. Draw a model to represent what you learned. (*Teacher Resource:* Refer to the "Learning Frames and Organizers" section of Chapter 8 for some organizing tools and maps.) |
| Learn note-taking | Use words or phrases to help you remember what you want or need to learn. Use colored pencils, markers, or highlighters when taking notes to draw your attention to what you want to know. |
| Take notes with drawings | Making pictures is a brain pleaser. You can develop quick sketches to practice this technique. Notes with words, phrases, and drawings are creative and friendly for memory-making. |
| Remember lists with a song | Chose a favorite song with an easy-to-remember melody to list steps, sequences, or spellings. Your brain loves to remember melodies and can reproduce them with the things you want to remember spontaneously. How about a song for spelling the word *spontaneous*? Might the song also give a definition? |
| Make a picture in your mind | Select real or ridiculous images to remember lists or the order of items. Learn the basic parts of the brain by stating the name of the area and picturing what that area allows you to do. The brain's hippocampus allows you to remember what you have learned. Picture a hippopotamus sitting on a file cabinet. The hippo has control of what you have learned. It is all filed neatly in different parts of your brain so you can find what you want to remember. Remember the cerebellum, often called the "small brain," at the base of your brain. The cerebellum allows you to do activities without thinking about doing them. Picture the cerebellum sitting on your bicycle seat, enjoying the ride as it automatically self-directs the legs or hands to move and the eyes to search for danger. You always need your cerebellum to be active when you ride your bike, as well as during many school learning tasks. |
| Use mnemonics | Use a catchy saying to remember a list or details. To learn the parts of the brain cells called *neurons*, each of which includes a *nucleus*, a *cell* body, *axons*, and *dendrites*, the mnemonic might be "Naughty Nancy Calmly Ate Dirt." Or, "My Very Educated Mother Just Served Us Nachos" can be used for the order of the planets in the solar system (Mercury, Venus, Earth, Mars, Jupiter, Saturn, Uranus, and Neptune). |

methods. What do students know about their own learning? Table 10.2 presents some practice activities to prompt students to support themselves as learners. Using these memory-supporting strategies, students pick up ways to take pieces of information or concepts and chunk them into larger units to remember.

In this learning environment, the teacher is doing what teachers do while following and teaching the specified grade-level standards, but students take responsibilities as well. Students will be unique in the strategies they use most successfully. Teachers can encourage students by having them experience many different strategies for long-term memory and then acknowledging what works best.

In addition to the brain-type learning responsibilities, students need to be aware of how they care for their bodies. Here the focus is on what children need to be healthy learners. They identify the importance of eating regularly and well, and getting enough sleep to arrive at school on time and *ready to learn*.

## TAKING RESPONSIBILITIES FOR PRIMING SKILLS

Priming skills support cognitive thinking. Children can be taught what the priming skills are and how they can become effective students by developing these skills, which include organization, paying attention, concentration and focus, and practice and rehearsal.

*Organization* is a priority as students record and complete assignments at school and at home. *Paying attention* can be a learned concept as students monitor their own time-on-task behavior. Students can be encouraged to understand *concentration* and *focus* as they stop their work and self-check how much time they have devoted to a task *and* recall what has been accomplished or finished. Taking responsibility to *practice and rehearse* can be associated with a diagram or picture to remind students of the memory systems their unique brain uses. A child's version of the model of memory systems from Figure 7.3 in Chapter 7 can be developed. Students realize that a lot of work goes into getting information into the brain's long-term memory system for instant recall. They might be reminded from time to time of the different memory systems: remember and tell, experience, rote, and process.

## HABITS OF MIND WITH COMPASSION

Students find it *motivating* to learn how others work to learn. They each develop *habits of mind* that work. They can be directed to realize and value the variances of ways to learn among their class of age-alike peers. Understanding others and *having kindness* and *compassion* for each other wipes away the need for name-calling or bullying others. Differences can be identified and accepted for the benefits each student brings to classroom projects. Who can imagine the brilliance of a single child's brain for compassion and acknowledgment of differences, all the while learning to value others?

# WHAT CAN PARENTS AND CAREGIVERS DO?

Parents, other family members, and caregivers are encouraged to remain involved with what and how their child is learning. They can contemplate and find out what they can do to support and connect new learning to real-life situations when they are aware of units of study. Home activities could include checking additional information about a science topic with "Mommy or Daddy and Me" time. It could be a trip to the grandparents' house to learn more about the cultural backgrounds they bring to the family. Field trips, such as attending a play, visiting the library or a museum, or going to a sporting event, are family activities that can be related to school study topics and create episodic, experience memories.

## QUESTIONS, QUESTIONS, QUESTIONS: FOR PARENTS

Parents discover important responses when they question themselves about their child's learning habits (see Table 10.3).

Teachers can gain parent support with suggestions for how they can help. This communication happens naturally at Back-to-School Night and Open House activities. Other ways of communicating can include weekly work packets, social media

**TABLE 10.3** ● Questions for Parents About Habits of Learning

1. How does my child learn? Or, how do my children learn? What are the different needs for learning among my children?

2. What learning strategies does my child use—self-talking, repetitive practice, rehearsal, putting learning strategies to song, or saying learning concepts rhythmically? Others? Are they successful?

3. Is there a specific place where, and time when, homework is completed? Is it independently done or with help and supervision? When is supervision needed? Can my child work independently? Does my child need to have an assignment review before doing homework?

4. Do I value and support my child to adhere to deadlines and completion of work?

5. Am I consistent about good eating habits, family routines, and bedtimes?

messages, and even a surprise phone call or text message to share some good classroom news.

Teachers who provide resources for parents to use at home might additionally suggest computer applications that can be downloaded or accessed for free and provide educational benefits. For example, Wordie is a "guess the word" app on Google Play, and Script Academy is a JavaScript computer coding programming course to learn how to make your own computer games. The potential for students is too important to miss the opportunity for teachers, other important adults in a child's life, and the student to work together as a team for learning proficiency that will last a lifetime.

## CONCLUDING THOUGHTS ABOUT TEACHERS AND STUDENTS AS LEARNING PARTNERS

This is a unique plea for teachers to share their knowledge about the teachable, learning brain that is housed in each living being. Children can understand how they learn to develop "habits of learning" at a young age to serve them well all their lives. The human brain is known through the science of neurology. Children can use their brains to understand themselves.

### RESOURCE

Wilson, D., & Conyers, M. (2014, February 11). *Engaging brains: How to enhance learning by teaching kids about neuroplasticity.* Edutopia. bit.ly/3Zckg4d

# Reflective Questions

Teachers are encouraged to consider these questions if a learning partnership with their students is desired.

1. What is the potential to develop a partnership with students in your classroom to strengthen learning outcomes, if this is not a current practice?

2. Are there behaviors in your class that could be supported or eliminated through approaching learning in this way?

3. What instructional supports or materials could be used to introduce students to the concept of understanding their own brains?

4. What suggestions in this chapter would be implementable this year in the classroom with this group of students?

5. How could parents be included in this learning practice? What is already in place to enlist the support of parents?

6. The chapter is designed for second- or third-grade classrooms. For teachers of younger children, what would be appropriate from this chapter for your students to experience?

# CHAPTER 11

# Conclusion

## A Dozen Key Learnings

Anyone who has ever been involved in a construction project knows that it's rarely a simple process. The plans need to accurately convey a vision of the final product, the materials must be available, the builder must be skilled, and the cost must be within means. If there are no unexpected factors—and there always seem to be—the final product will meet the needs for which it was designed, and the effort and time will be well spent.

Building the reading brain is also a construction process. As in building a structure, many steps are involved, and many factors need to be controlled for the final product—the child's brain—to become one that reads accurately, with fluency and understanding, and also for enjoyment. This final chapter summarizes what has been learned from educational research, the practice of teachers, and, more specifically, research from cognitive science and the neurosciences to direct the best building practices for a child's reading brain.

Some of what is known about the development of reading comes from scientific brain research about neural structures and their functions, while other knowledge comes from information gleaned from clinical reading research and practice. A scientific perspective can be applied to understand the developing brain as children learn to read, why the learning time is prolonged to build the reading brain, and how neural plasticity supports the entire process. Findings may come from research or experience outside the field of neuroscience; however, information about the brain and how it learns is helping educators understand why certain instructional processes and strategies are more effective than others. And, importantly, direction is found for why some children benefit from a certain program, while others proceed with reading development more readily with another approach.

## A CHILD'S BRAIN AND READING: A DOZEN KEY LEARNINGS SUMMARIZED

Responses to questions in this book's Chapter 1 are given as a summation of key learnings. Some readers may have accepted the challenge to find the answers along the way as they completed each chapter, even though the questions are not answered in a chapter-by-chapter format. Congratulations if you did, as you have developed some semantic declarative responses to some difficult-to-answer queries. Here are responses from the author.

1. **Children learn to speak naturally, so why is learning to read so difficult?** The brain is not innately wired for reading; there are no naturally designated neural structures for reading. The brain must co-opt structures designed for other purposes, most specifically for oral language.

Children are born with a brain that has a built-in pathway for oral language. If they are exposed to the native language in their environment, barring any neurological disability or disorder, they will learn to speak that language with little difficulty. The same is *not* true of reading. In a sense, reading is an unnatural act for the brain. There is no built-in pathway for reading. While raising children in print-rich environments is important—especially in the early years—most children do not learn to read through exposure; they must be taught.

Teaching materials that match the methodologies identified through extensive, thorough research, identified as the science of reading, are used for direct, explicit teaching. Purposeful teaching prepares young students to identify sounds they hear in oral language in their smallest form as phonemes. Teaching progresses as children learn how to combine and manipulate sounds, and eventually to match sounds to the letters that make the sound. This type of instruction continues through all aspects of beginning reading as children learn to decode words, and then encode as they become writers. This book emphasizes how the student's brain functions during the development of a reading pathway by changing and coercing the naturally forming language pathway.

2. **How do a baby's experiences shape the brain?** Neuroplasticity is a characteristic of the brain that allows it to be shaped by experience.

How can a brain, which is not wired for reading, eventually accomplish this extremely difficult task? The answer lies in a unique characteristic of the brain called *neuroplasticity*. The reason humans learn habits and skills that are not innate is that the brain is "plastic" throughout life. This means that it can adapt to new circumstances and requirements, literally changing the function of certain brain cells, neurons, and their connectivity. This ability to adapt to its environment, to sculpt itself depending on the demands of the environment, is one of the most amazing characteristics of the human brain, beginning right at birth.

3. **How can potential reading success be determined when a child is only 3 years old?** Many factors have been shown to be strong predictors of eventual reading success.

Because language is a precursor to reading, the size of children's vocabulary, their expressive language, recognition of the letters of the alphabet by name, the ability to name the letters rapidly, and knowledge of the purposes of books are all key predictors of later reading success. Reading aloud to children with interactive dialogue is one means to help children develop these skills before they are able to read on their own. Writing (or scribbling), reading's reciprocal action, supports the development of skills that will be important in learning to read and write. Listening to and repeating songs, jingles, or rhymes are additional ways to develop children's emerging literacy at the young age of 3.

4. **Why is there interest in cognitive skills for focus, concentration, and attention even for very young children at 1 and 2 years of age?** Priming skills for reading, which include paying attention, being able to focus and concentrate, putting order and organization to thinking, and holding information in working memory, become critical attributes that need to be in place in the early school years.

Teachers find that when they identify children who struggle with these attributes, they can make relatively simple instructional adjustments to encourage and essentially force children to become better at listening and repeating. Holding information in their conscious memory for contemplation and rehearsal strengthens working memory. Instructional adjustments for priming skills also affect students' motivation to learn, and ultimately how well they store and retain information critical to successful reading.

**5. What is the importance of sounds, called phonemes, in terms of the child's cognitive development for reading?** Essential to learning to read is the understanding that sounds (phonemes) can be arranged to formulate many different words. Alphabetical principles and early phonics instruction direct children to realize that spoken language can be represented by print.

Children pick up an understanding of the sounds of letters by combining sounds for words on their own through a language-rich home environment and/or a language-oriented preschool environment. Ultimately, phonemes can be explicitly taught. Phonemic awareness has been proven through scientific study to be an essential skill prerequisite to decoding print and to learning to read. In addition to phonemic awareness, children must be able to recognize and produce rhymes, break words into sound syllables, distinguish parts of syllables (onsets and rimes), and determine root words, prefixes, and suffixes of words. *Phonological processing* is the umbrella term given to this broader array of skills, which includes phonemic awareness.

**6. Why are some teaching strategies for decoding less effective than others?** Some strategies commonly used to teach children to decode have proven to be less effective than others. Information on how the brain learns best can assist teachers to select the most brain-compatible strategies.

The content that children practice needs to be as logical as possible since the brain seeks patterns to make sense of the task with which it is engaged. Many commonly used word walls, letter-to-sound approaches, and orthographic rules seemingly have no patterns or logical sequence. They are confusing to the young child's brain. Word walls need to be sound-to-letter(s) based. Orthographic rules with examples, discussion, and jingles or songs as meaningful practice are more likely to be stored in and retrieved from the brain's long-term memory. Students need lots of activities that cause contemplation, rehearsal, practice, and recall to move important learning from working memory, where it can be literally dumped, into long-term memory where it can be recalled consciously, by rote responses, or through access processes, such as reading with automaticity, without conscious thought.

**7. Why is there so much interest in teaching children to read in kindergarten? What helps to determine if a young child is ready to learn to read?** Assessment as early as kindergarten has proved to be effective to determine which children are ready to begin reading development, and which ones will require early intervention or simply more time.

The conventional wisdom has been that some children are ready to read in kindergarten while others won't be ready until later, indicating that reading instruction should wait until children are ready. Many factors determine whether or not children appear to be ready to read.

Children who have limited exposure to print—those who have not been read to, learned nursery rhymes, or been exposed to a language-rich environment—may enter school without the emergent literacy skills necessary to learn to read. Neurological developmental factors may also play a role. Early assessment to identify these environmental and biological factors is essential to select an appropriate prereading or reading preparation program from the many that are available.

8. **Why do some children experience difficulties when they try to read?** Difficulty in learning to read (e.g., dyslexia) can occur from several factors.

Some reading problems are the result of a neurological decoding "glitch" in the reading pathway of the brain. This problem may be a genetically programmed error—generally an underactivation in the angular gyrus and Wernicke's area. Or, the situation may be more environmentally influenced, such as by a lack of early stimulation or intermittent schooling. Other problems seem to stem from cognitive skill development, as well as physiological, socioeconomic, ethnic, and/or second language factors. Regardless of the source of the reading problem, nearly all deficits can be overcome with a reading program that is matched with the child's assessed reading deficit. The selected program is based on direct, explicit instruction, with teaching practices that fortify the memory skills needed to recall and comprehend. Universal agreement among educators is that there is no waiting allowed; students need early intervention.

9. **What is happening in the brain when children read with fluency and comprehension?** Recognizing whole words (and eventually some phrases) with automaticity is essential for fluent reading and comprehension.

As children become more proficient in decoding print, they begin to see common groups of letters as words. How does this happen? When a certain configuration of letters is processed numerous times, the brain begins to store this configuration as a single bit of information, a word. This chunking process is how the brain overcomes its limited processing space, identified as working memory. Without this ability, there would be insufficient "space" in conscious memory for comprehension of what is being read.

Processing speed is another requirement for students to be able to read fluently. When a child recognizes words and moves with ease from the identification of one word to the next, the ability to think about comprehension is possible. The reading pathway in the brain is complete and operates with automaticity.

Additionally, children who read words and phrases with ease are able to read silently while comprehending what they are reading. Note the requirement to read out loud, pronouncing each word and word phrase, requires the reader to pay attention to prosody. Prosody is more than the ability to decode text. It requires the normal rise and fall of pitch. Reading out loud may suggest fluency, but comprehension may suffer as conscious effort goes to the reading-out-loud process.

10. **How do children move from "learning to read" to "reading to learn"?** Since reading has a purpose, comprehension can be considered an end product of reading instruction.

As important as it is to develop the ability to decode print, it is not of much use if students do not comprehend what they read. To comprehend what is being read, students' brains must be able to decode automatically and unconsciously without effort. As words are identified automatically, the conscious processing functions of the brain are totally available to connect the words being read to previously acquired information about the words. The brain instantaneously accesses associations stored in long-term memory, and the reader is able to understand the content of the print. This information does not mean to wait until all decoding is automatic before beginning to teach and practice reading with comprehension.

11. **How do students develop an understanding of word vocabulary?** The size of children's vocabulary and their comprehension of what they read are highly dependent on their school and personal experiences.

Recall that the brain sculpts itself based on the input it receives from the environment. Children who are actively engaged with learning by practicing, rehearsing, talking, experiencing, responding, creating, or making products are more likely to remember words and develop expansive vocabularies. Additionally, they are able to attach new learning to neural networks that were previously established.

Teachers help children to organize their thinking by giving them activities that require them to organize, sort, compare, list, find differences or similarities, mind map, or develop a big picture or gestalt. Through these activities, children's minds form a way to organize and store words and information that is important enough to remember. The human brain moves information from working memory to long-term memory when the student has been engaged with the information through practice and rehearsal in working memory. Once words are moved to long-term memory, they can be recalled with no conscious effort.

12. **What proficiency for reading is expected at the end of third grade? How do children's brains function during proficient reading?** Attaining skills for fluency and comprehension in reading by the end of the third grade is the ultimate goal of reading instruction during the primary grades.

When children can read with speed and accuracy, they are able to concentrate on the meaning of the text. However, if they must devote considerable energy to the mechanics of reading, their focus on the meaning is diminished. The ability to read fluently is dependent, therefore, on each of the following:

- How automatic decoding is (using the decoding reading pathway)
- How familiar children are with the orthography of language (accessing the visual association areas of the brain)
- How expansive the neural networks are for vocabulary and background information
- How quickly neural activity happens among the structures of the brain that have been developed and reinforced for reading

Reading proficiency by the end of third grade allows a student's reading brain to change from the work of "how to read" to the dynamic task of "what to read to learn more."

## CHALLENGE QUESTIONS FROM CHAPTER 5

**Is there a relationship between priming skills and cognitive skill development?** Yes, there is a relationship and a dependence between the skills identified as priming and those called cognitive. Furthermore, note that developmental benchmarks describe highly observable beginning learning processes.

Cognitive skill development is dependent first on the developmental benchmarks identified in the early chapters of this book, and concurrently on priming skills that begin developing during the preschool years and continue during elementary school. Priming skills are identified as habits of mind. Cognitive skills are the academically related processes of learning. For example, a young reader may use the priming skills of attention and concentration to decode an unfamiliar word. Cognitively, the child is accessing the concepts of visual recognition and sequencing.

The learning sequences (developmental benchmarks, priming skills, and cognitive skills) develop simultaneously and some in succession. During the early years of a child's life, the developmental benchmarks are the highlights of the brain's work. Prior to school, children begin to refine their thinking habits of mind to support more complex learning. During the school years, cognitive development is accentuated as academic skills prevail and build. There are exceptional growth periods for each, separately and together, depending on the uniqueness of each child.

**What is the purpose of providing cognitive skill development? How can teachers use this information?** Some children do not develop reading as expected. They appear to have a "glitch in the system."

Reading intervention programs may focus on phonological processing, phonics, or the plethora of other decoding and encoding processes, unique to the needs of an individual child. However, there may be cognitive or executive (brain processing) skills that are underdeveloped. Cognitive skills development charts with an increasing progression of skills provided at the end of Chapters 2–3 and 5–8 are available for teachers to use with students who experience reading difficulties (see also Appendix B for a comprehensive version of the charts). Cognitive skills are likely to be assessed and identified by a school psychologist. Teachers who are aware of the complicated cognitive skills accessed during reading are able to provide instruction respective of the cognitive attributes of the child's reading challenges. Often, the Common Core State Standards identify cognitive skills needed to acquire reading proficiency. The charts provided in this book are a sampling of these skills provided by the author as examples, and not intended to be complete.

#  CONCLUDING THOUGHTS

A theme reiterated from the introduction to this book and validated through its chapters is the essential purpose of reading instruction. Reading well for children is more than a legislated priority; it's an ethical and professional imperative. It is with hope that this book will provide an understanding of how neuroscience gives a broad understanding of the complex process called the science of reading. Furthermore, it is hoped that outcomes from studies that include neural imaging of both learning and reading tasks are supportive of and match with results-based research from education's behavioral science. May this book be a guide to parents, families, care providers, and, most importantly, teachers as together we strive to give children the reading legacy they deserve and desire.

# Continuum of Developmental Benchmarks: Birth to Age 5

| 1 Month | Watches objects and faces at 12 inches or more, even when moving. Moves by arching back, kicking legs, or flailing arms when startled by noises. Hearing is developing. Sense of smell is the only sense that is fully developed. Turns head toward mother's breast. Recognizes scents such as handwashing fragrance. |
|---|---|
| 2 Months | Eyes follow an object. Begins to recognize familiar people. Becomes fussy when awake and is unstimulated. Seems happy when parent approaches. Makes sounds other than crying. Holds head up when on tummy. Moves both arms and legs. Opens hands briefly. Looks at a toy for several seconds. Sense of vision is becoming more acute. |
| 3 Months | Recognizes source of food: bottle or breast. Beginning to develop interest in taste. Turns head to identify sounds. Tries to push up when on tummy. |
| 4 Months | Communicates if happy, sad, or irritated. Watches faces, particularly during feeding. Good head control. Pushes up onto elbows/forearms when on tummy. Reaches for toys and can bring a toy to the mouth (sense of taste). Better motor control and the sense of touch is developing. Chuckles when others laugh. Opens mouth if hungry and sees food source (breast or bottle). Brings hands to mouth. Makes sounds back to you when you talk. |
| 6 Months | Good control of hands and hand-to-mouth activities. Moves items from one hand to the other. Reaches for items that are out of reach. Knows familiar people. Looks at self in a mirror. Takes turns at making sounds with another. Makes the "raspberry" sound. Closes lips when does not want food. Rolls from tummy to back. Leans on hands to support when sitting. |

| 9 Months | Plays peekaboo. Can pick up small items with precision. Turns pages of a book. Watches as an item is hidden and seeks it. Able to move arms and limbs to hold body in crawl position or picks self up when holding on to a table or chair. Is shy around strangers. Looks when name is called. Reacts when care provider or parent leaves and reaches for the person. Makes a lot of different sounds, such as "mamamama" and "babababa." Lifts arms to be picked up. Can move into a sitting position and sits without support. |
| --- | --- |
| 12 Months | Moves items from container to container. Points to pictures of words known and stored in long-term memory. Claps and bangs items together. Can drink from a cup, pick up a book, brush own hair, and poke with index finger. Can pick things up with thumb and pointer finger, like small pieces of food to eat or a crayon to make marks. Stands upright alone or with support. May be able to navigate walking or moving from one object to another. Waves "bye-bye," and understands "no." |
| 15 Months | Copies other children. Claps when excited. Hugs dolls or other stuffed toys. Shows signs of affection with hugs, cuddles, or kisses. Tries to say one or two words for common items. Follows simple directions, such as "Clap your hands." Attempts to use common items, such as a phone, cup, or book. Can walk somewhat on own. Uses fingers to eat finger food, such as Cheerios. Scribbling and coloring may include blocks of color and more definite marks and patterns. Stacks at least two things or blocks. |
| 18 Months | Holds a crayon or pencil to scribble. Begins to identify body parts. Can follow one oral direction. For example, if an adult says, "Stop," the child ceases the activity. Can identify by pointing to common objects: cup, spoon, brush, book, phone, and so on. Enjoys singing, following stories in a book, and listening to simple stories without a book. Is interested in toys and can pretend play with a stuffed toy. Puts hands out to be washed. Walks without holding on. Climbs up on a chair or couch. Can drink from a cup without a lid. Tries to use a spoon. Crayon strokes represent something to the child. Swirly loops may be a puppy, or bold lines may be Daddy. May have a tantrum when does not get what is wanted. (Respond or not to tantrums, but be at eye level if a tantrum is addressed.) |
| 2 Years | Builds with blocks. Explores how toys work. Can follow simple two-step directions, such as "Pick up the blocks and put them in the box." Plays make-believe games. Can name pictures in a book. (*Side note:* This is a complex task to recognize an abstract picture of a physical item.) Speaks in simple sentences and recites rhymes. Kicks a ball, runs, and walks up a few stairs without help. Eats with a spoon. Can point to at least two body parts. Increases the use of gestures like blowing a kiss or nodding yes.  Notices when others are upset. Recognizes books by their cover. |
| 3 Years | Can fit three to four pieces to complete a puzzle. Enters into make-believe play. Has the concept of one and two items. Sorts objects by shape and/or color. Can open a door using the handle. Plays next to other children and sometimes with them. Follows simple routines. Pretend plays, like reading a book, flying like a bird, or feeding a doll. Turns the pages of a book one at a time. Handles books a specific way. Can label known objects in books, including characters. Looks at specific print, such as letters in a name. Occasionally distinguishes between drawing and writing. Talks well enough for others to understand. Can identify animals, their actions, and sounds they make. Draws a circle with instruction. Can help with getting dressed. |

| 4 Years | Copies simple shapes. Follows instructions with two or three steps. Knows the concepts of same and different. Has some understanding of time. Can count and may be able to identify numbers 1 to 10. Knows body parts, and possibly where the brain is. Draws a person with four body parts or more. Uses blunt scissors. Copies letters and can identify some. Listens intently to a story read aloud and can predict what will happen next. Pays attention some of the time when other children talk. Can visualize and answer questions about a person or a thing in memory without seeing a picture first. Can write own name. Can recite days of the week and possibly the months of the year. Active with conversation at home, at school, and during play activities. Makes early writing and reading attempts. Has a sense of before, now, and after. Can sequence up to four pictures in order of occurrence. |
| --- | --- |
| 5 Years | Demonstrates one-to-one correspondence of items up to or exceeding 5. Can identify everyday items. Reads words from cards taped to items in the environment: *chair*, *bed*, *orange*, *truck*, *door*, and so on. Begins printing. Draws a picture of a person with at least six parts of the body. Follows three or more steps or directions. May be able to read books with repetitive words. Begins to establish a sight vocabulary of words. Works extensively with sounds of the language and can identify same beginning sounds, middle sounds, and endings. Changes beginning, middle, or ending sounds to make new or nonsense words. Identifies number of phonemes in long or complex words. Begins writing with simple vocabulary and "made-up" spelling. Remembers phone number, address, and birthday by month and day. Plays simple board and card games. Acknowledges and plays with other children. |

Available for download at
**https://resources.corwin.com/BuildingtheYoungReadersBrain3E**

# APPENDIX B

# Cognitive Skills for Learning

The cognitive areas to support learning are addressed for children as they advance from ages 1 through 9. Cognitive development occurring in the brain is difficult to assess. This appendix represents a cumulative account, from many sources listed in the reference section, of a synthesis of learning tasks needed for developing readers, and represents teacher and parent input. The following chart has not been validated by a scientific review. Rather, the stages of cognitive development are representative of the way a child's brain develops *and* represents the skills needed for reading growth. The chart can be shared with parents, as they search for ways to help their child progress. Note that some developmental areas cover a two-year period to accommodate learning variances among children.

## Attention

| | |
|---|---|
| 1–2 Years | **Visual and Auditory Sustained Attention**—Sustains interest without adult intervention for an elongated period of time. Watches the lips of a speaker and attempts to reproduce the same sound. Tracks and follows the actions of another person. Engages in play alone or with another child for a sustained time. Explores toys and moves around. Tries switches, knobs, and buttons on a toy. Holds something in one hand while using the other hand for a task. |
| 3 Years | **Visual and Auditory Selective Attention**—Screens out distractions for focused attention. Attends to a task in a place where visual and/or auditory interferences are happening. (For example, Mommy and Daddy are having a conversation and may be moving around, but the interesting thing at hand is more important to the child. In a preschool classroom many other children are talking and moving around, but the drawing the child is doing is more important for the child's focus.) Calms down within 10 minutes. Joins other children to play. Asks *who*, *what*, *where*, and *why* questions. Can identify actions in a picture book. Knows to say own name. Talks well enough to be understood. Draws a circle. Avoids dangerous things. Can mostly dress self. Uses a fork. Can string beads. |
| 4 Years | **Divided Attention**—Can attend to two activities alternatively at the same time (e.g., listening to music and drawing; riding a trike and paying attention to not ride into another child; listening to the teacher's directions and cleaning up from the last task). Can take on another character when playing. Asks to join in play. Comforts others if sad or hurt. Likes to be a helper. Changes behavior based on environment (e.g., library, classroom, playground, church, or grocery store). Says sentences with four or more words. Answers simple questions. Names a few colors. Tells what happens next in a known story. Can follow an auditory story (no pictures) and respond to questions. Maintains attention to the task at hand. |
| 5–6 Years | **Attention Flexibility for Visual or Auditory Input**—Can focus and refocus with rapidity. Follows Random Automatized Naming (one-minute timed identification). to focus, say the name of the item, detach, refocus, name, and detach over and over again. Begins with shapes and advances to letters, numbers, simple sight words, and beginning number facts. Follows rules, and takes turns. Sings, dances, or acts for others. Tells a story with at least two events. Counts to 100. Understands words about time (e.g., *yesterday*, *tomorrow*, *last week*, *morning*, or *evening*). Pays attention for more than 10 minutes while blocking out unimportant sensory stimulation (screen time not included in the time limit). Writes complete name. Can identify by name all the letters of the alphabet in first grade. |

# Visual Processing

| | |
|---|---|
| 3 Years | **Visual Discrimination**—Distinguishes differences among items, including objects, shapes, and colors. More advanced, *but not necessary* at this age, identifies some letters, numbers, sight words, and larger numbers beyond 1 and 2. |
| 4–5 Years | **Visual Figure Ground**—Puts attention on the focus item and disengages from disruptors or the visual distractions in the background. Finds specific items in a picture. Finds shapes within the images in a picture. Picks the one that is different from a group of similar items.<br><br>**Visual Recognition**—Identifies an object regardless of its size or orientation. Can identify one letter, either lower or upper case, in various sizes and angles among other letters. Identifies letter names when letter is produced in different fonts.<br><br>**Visual Span**—Names objects from memory, such as the number of letters in a word. Learns a phone number or an address by singing or repeating a rhyme. Recites the letters in own name.<br><br>**Visual Sequencing**—Recognizes a string of three or four letters kept in a certain order to name a sight word. Picks out the target word among others. Can put 5 to 10 numbers in sequence. |
| 5–6 Years | **Visualization**—Has the ability to look at words or listen to words, sentences, or a complete story and form a unique vision in the mind from what is heard or read. Responds to questions without individual picture prompts. (Note this is an extremely important skill for comprehension.) Recognizes and accepts different responses as the teacher questions other children. The child may draw a picture to demonstrate understanding. Upon seeing the beginning of a high-frequency word, the child is able to complete the word by adding the missing letters. |
| 6–8 Years | Can look at a series of letters, identify the letters as words, and recall and pronounce the word correctly. Recognizes a cluster of words as phrases to be identified, read, and comprehended. Can write words and ideas with automaticity and accuracy. |

## Auditory Processing for Phonological Awareness

| | |
|---|---|
| 3 Years | **Discrimination**—Distinguishes differences among sounds. Listens and attends to simple nursery rhymes. Listens to words to identify if they start or end with the same sound—for example, *man, monkey, milk* or *funny, sunny, bunny*. Can say individual sounds for two- and three-letter words, such as *c-a-t, d-o-g*, and *s-a-t*. Notice this cognitive activity is about sounds from spoken words, and about sounds, *not letters*. |
| 3–4 Years | **Recites** simple nursery rhymes.<br><br>**Produces** a rhyming word. When given *bat* can produce *hat* or *mat*.<br><br>**Recognizes** alliteration (e.g., understands that beginning sounds for *sun* and *smile* are the same, but *sun* and *man* are different). |
| 4–5 Years | **Sequencing**—Retains verbal sounds or words in a sequence. Can hold and repeat three to five different words in a sentence. For example: Repeat—"I am full." "The car has four wheels."<br><br>**Processing**—Processes verbal directions and follows with action. For example: "Put one hand on your tummy and pat your head with the other" or "Open your book to page 5."<br><br>**Identification**—Segments a word into syllables (e.g., *moun-tain, air-plane, eat-ing, hap-py, hap-pi-ness*). Segmentation may be accompanied by clapping. |
| 5–6 Years | **Identification**—Recognizes phonemes in words with four or more phonemes (e.g., *d-o-g-h-ou-se, k-i-ch-en, p-u-m-k-i-n*). Identifies words when phonemes are given (e.g., *a-ni-mal* for *animal*).<br><br>**Substitution**—Uses a different beginning, middle, or ending to form a new word or a nonsense word. This response is for sounds of words only, not letter association (e.g., "Say *mother* without the *m* sound"; "Change the *b* sound in *boat* to a *g* sound"; "What word is different—*turtle, money, toys,* or *tumble*?"). |

# Sensory-Cognitive Processing

| 3–4 Years | **Imaging**—Forms a picture in the mind after hearing a word. For example: "See the cat." The child is able to identify what a cat looks like by pointing to a cat in a book. "Where is Daddy?" The child finds Daddy in a picture with other people." |
| --- | --- |
| | **Predicting**—Determines what will happen next. For example: "The boy let go of the string tied to the balloon." The child responds that the balloon will go up or away to the sky. "Mommy set out a plate of cookies." The child responds that everyone will eat a cookie. |
| 5–6 Years | **Imaging**—A simple story is read without any pictures. The child imagines the story and is able to answer simple questions not given in the story about objects or people. For example, in a story about a leprechaun, the leprechaun is not described. The child is able to answer questions about the size of the leprechaun, his clothes, whether he is wearing a hat, and whether he would be a good friend. |
| | **Predicting**—A new story is read, but stopped before it ends. The child is able to tell what could happen next, or how the story might end. For added value, other children express their endings—acknowledgment that each child processes thinking uniquely. |
| 7–9 Years | **Concept Imagery**—Can take verbal or textural input and formulate a concept of understanding or comprehension. This complex skill allows a student to read a chapter book and follow its development. Subject matter textbooks are understood with diagrams, figures, or pictures. |
| | **Application**—Information from written sources, observations, or interviews is accessed. The student is able to develop a paper, report, model, and/or speech to demonstrate learning. |

# Memory Systems (Sensory, Working, and Long-Term)

| | |
|---|---|
| 3–4 Years | **Sensory Input**—Can determine what information received from the senses is important or worthy of attention. (Notice this is an observed ability.)<br><br>**Short-Term Memory**—Moves interesting information from sensory memory that is deemed important for further thinking. (Note: It is available for recall for about 24 hours and is then dropped unless reviewed or practiced again.) Can follow two or more directions.<br><br>**Long-Term Memory**—Moves input that has been practiced, rehearsed, and associated with other familiar items to long-term memory and can recall this input at will. For example: "Who are people you see at school?" The child's responses include friends, teacher, teacher's helper, and so on; "What toys do you like at school?" The child's responses include the play kitchen, the trucks, the trikes, the sandbox, and so on. Has memory for songs, rhythm, and body movements. May share "what I like to do at the park" or "at Grandpa's house." |
| 5 Years | **Memory Manipulation**—Moves words, items, and concepts from long-term memory into working memory to create something new. Makes a sound and attaches a letter, beginning with consonants. Uses a category, such as colors, food, or animals, and names items that would go into that category. |
| 6–7 Years | Takes a root word that is known and manipulates it with a prefix, suffix, or plural. Takes what is known about planting seeds and growing from long-term memory and expands it with new information, such as harvesting and eating. Takes what is known about their home neighborhood and expands that information to where their school is located.<br><br>Draws on several or many items or concepts from long-term memory to contemplate and add new information or to change misconceptions. For example: What is the job of the school principal? What is the job of a cafeteria worker? How is the breakfast or lunch prepared?  Why does our community have police officers? What activities are available for children in our community? |
| 8–9 Years | Places items from long-term memory into categories by sorting, ordering, defining, and identifying. When provided with a list of items or concepts, is able to find commonalities among the list to sort and organize. Moves known words into classifications provided. Responds to "if–then" order. Explains the function of nouns, pronouns, verbs, adjectives, and adverbs in general and their functions in particular sentences. (Grade level 3 from Language Standards, Common Core State Standards, California.)<br><br>NOTE: Cognitive aspects from all Common Core State Standards can be identified, rephrased, and inserted within the cognitive skills areas, as examples. |

# Executive Function (Listed in Expected Developmental Order)

| | |
|---|---|
| 4 Years | **Working Memory**—Has the ability to draw thoughts and combine information from long-term memory into working memory for a purpose. Can recall a parent's phone number and then identify instances when it would be important to know the parent's phone number. Recalls names of siblings with their birth order and tells something special about each person named. Engages in organization of manipulatives, simple organization or charting of tangible objects, and making associations. Answers questions or makes inferences from hearing a story. |
| 5 Years | **Cognitive Flexibility**—Takes action to change an idea or plan when the input from other sources changes. Realizes that furry animals with four legs can be many types of mammals. Names different types of transportation. Knows the difference between food that is grown on a tree and food that grows in the ground. Has print awareness, holds a book correctly, and knows the cover, title page, and story pages. |
| 6 Years | **Reasoning**—Logically works through complex or competing information (family relationships, for example: "My father and my uncles and aunts have the same parents, who are my grandparents"). Uses mathematics reasoning to talk through story problems. Provides an answer to a question, and talks to explain the solution. Talks through playground problems and develops a list of potential solutions. |
| 7 Years | **Cognitive Speed**—Has the ability to reason through a problem and draw a conclusion with rapidity. Identifies unknown words. Engages with a timed reading task. Responds to questions. Reads a paragraph and identifies the main idea. When given a word, quickly uses the letters to form other words. Given a topic, lists words that relate. Identifies other words that start with two or three given letters. Completes this type of activity in timed segments, accompanied with progress charting.<br><br>**Preparation and Planning**—Has the ability to rationalize information or a problem to find and implement a workable solution. Develops questions to ask classmates when given an article from informational text. |
| 8–9 Years | **Problem Solving**—Goes beyond reasoning to develop a detailed plan and to implement the plan to its conclusion. Given a situation, how would the child respond to resolve the dilemma? For example, "If you have these items, how could you use them to create something new?" Or, "If this situation occurred, what would be two possible ways to resolve the problem?"<br><br>**Synthesis**—Analyzes multiple inputs and, drawing from long-term memory, strategizes and develops a plan, device, approach, or proposal that is unique. Given a situation at school, in the community, or even on a larger scale, the student is asked, "What are the possibilities for making the situation better, and what is the expected outcome as the plan is accomplished?" A research project might require students to use multiple resources and interviews with others knowledgeable about the topic, and culminates with a new idea, concept, or image. A speech, presentation, or demonstration may accompany the project. |

Available for download at
https://resources.corwin.com/BuildingtheYoungReadersBrain3E

# Quick Reference Guide for Memory Systems

It is not expected that readers of this book will learn all the specific memory categories. However, an understanding of the functions of sensory memory, working memory, and long-term memory provide a helpful guide for teachers to structure teaching activities. Teachers who understand that learning is measured by what children can retrieve from long-term memory are more likely to select instructional methods to engage children in activities that mirror the way students learn, as they to move items, concepts, and processes into long term memory, located in different areas of the human brain. Here is a summary/guide:

1. **Sensory Memory**—information from the five senses. Most input from the senses is dropped from memory, very little passes to working memory. What is forwarded to working memory is considered as important and interesting by the child.

2. **Working Memory**—items are held in working memory for about 24 hours. Actions and activities of learning can happen through rehearsal, practice, repetitions, taking notes or writing, and sub-vocalization. These actions continue to happen over an extended period of time, particularly if the information is new or does not relate to previous knowledge. At some point automaticity of remembering will be accomplished.

3. **Long-Term Memory**—when automaticity is achieved, items, concepts, processes, and events can be recalled without effort. There are two basic types: Declarative and Non-Declarative. There are four sub areas:

a.  **Declarative/*semantic***—talk, write, or identify by
    some other means the facts, information, concepts,
    procedures, or problem solving that is learned
    behavior.

b.  **Declarative/*episodic***—memory for events or
    experiences that can be recalled due to a high
    emotional identifier or experience.

c.  **Non-declarative/*rote***—speaking or writing a
    response with no conscious thought effort, such as
    word spelling or responding to a flash card.

d.  **Non-declarative/*procedural***—engaging in a natural
    process that is accomplished with automaticity.
    Examples are:  the process of handwriting, reading
    fluently by identifying each word, but pausing for
    none, or turning the pages of a book, reading from
    line to line, and moving from left to right.

Available for download at
https://resources.corwin.com/BuildingtheYoungReadersBrain3E

# Glossary

**Academic vocabulary** The ability to use general or content-specific words or terms for acquiring understanding, knowledge, or skills to respond to school assignments or to interact with others using the terms to impart information to others.

**Alliteration** Reoccurring sounds, often consonants or clusters at the start of a string of words (*rabbit, rainbow, run* or *tree, trick, trunk*).

**Alphabetic principle** The basic understanding that segments of speech are represented by letters.

**Amygdala** A response system to the thalamus when it perceives something dangerous or something that might be pleasurable. The amygdala is able to activate the motor cortex or the body's muscular system without direction from the frontal cortex.

**Angular gyrus** A brain structure located at the junction of the occipital, parietal, and temporal lobes. It is here that the letters of written words are translated into the sounds of spoken language.

**Arcuate fasciculus** A band of neural fibers connecting Wernicke's area with Broca's area.

**Association cortex** An area of the brain that may also be called the prefrontal cortex. As one of the last brain structures to completely develop, it allows higher-level thinking skills by associating input from all other lobes in the cerebral cortex including access to long-term memory.

**Attention** A cognitive act of focus on a particular object, event, or happening while ignoring other environmental or personal stimuli.

**Auditory cortex** An area of the brain located in the temporal lobes and provides the ability to listen to sounds or words, holds them in working memory, and pulls sounds together to make a word.

**Auditory memory** The ability to listen to sounds or words, hold them in working memory, and complete a task, such as repeating a string of words or putting the sounds together to make a word.

**Automaticity** The ability to perform a skill or habit automatically or unconsciously. Much of the work happens through the cerebellum.

**Axon** One of the two appendages that protrude from a neuron's cell body. Axons seek to connect with the other appendage, a dendrite, from a neighboring axon through a chemical interaction.

**Brain stem** One of three distinctive parts of the human brain. It is the stalk-like feature that includes the midbrain, pons, and medulla. It sits at the base of the cerebral cortex and connects it with the spinal cord.

**Broca's area** The central brain region for the production of speech and processing of syntax. This work is mostly completed in the left hemisphere.

**Central nervous system** Consisting of the brain and the spinal cord, this system controls thinking, emotions, movement, and other actions that can be conscious or unconscious. The skull and spongy layers are safeguards for the brain. Bones and membranes protect the nerves that travel to other parts of the body from the brain.

**Cerebellum** Often called the "little brain," this structure is located at the base of the cerebral cortex and is a super support system for automatic movement, balance, and many learned actions, such as writing, reading, and walking, that happen without conscious direction from the frontal lobes or motor cortex.

Cerebral cortex The deeply folded outer layer of the cerebral hemispheres that is responsible for perception, awareness of emotion, planning, and conscious thought. Also called the neocortex.

Cerebrum The largest part of the human brain, which includes the cerebral cortex, the lobes, cortices, and even the innermost portion of the brain, the limbic system. For most purposes, it can be called the human brain. Accompanying the cerebrum is the brain stem to form the central nervous system.

Cognitive neuroscience Provides an explanation of what neurological activity occurs in the human brain when a child performs a task, such as speaking or reading.

Cognitive psychology Being mindful is to hold concepts and ideas in a conscious thinking state for consideration. Although difficult to observe, cognitive psychologists watch for attention, concentration, evidence of memory through recall, and concept development.

Comprehension The process of attaching meaning to written or spoken language by accessing previously stored experience or knowledge.

Concentration An extended period of attention in which the brain focuses on information and enters into a state to develop understanding or remembering.

Concept A general idea developed through interpretation or generalization to make sense out of the world. It may be a pattern, an organized thought with specific attributes, a summation of experiences, outcome identification, or determination of similarities and differences.

Corpus callosum A large bundle of myelinated fibers (axons) that connects the left and right hemispheres of the brain.

Declarative memory Explicit memory to allow storage of information in an organized manner so it can be subsequently recalled by speaking or writing.

Decoding The ability to recognize a sound–symbol relationship when translating a written word to speech or to decipher a new word by sounding it out.

Dendrites Extensions from the cell body of a neuron that seek messages from other neurons by receiving chemical substances (neurotransmitters) from a neighboring axon.

Dialogic reading A nontraditional adult–child reading activity where the adult asks questions, prompts the child for additional information, and describes pictures.

Dyslexia A cognitive deficit relating to phonological processing, particularly the ability to decode and recognize words.

Emergent literacy Skills that begin to develop during early infancy through meaningful activities with adults and include oral language, print knowledge, and phonological processing.

Encoding Writing and spelling words using sounds to attach to letter patterns.

Episodic memory Long-term memory of a happening or occurrence that is accompanied by strongly felt emotions.

Explicit instruction Programs that provide precise, systematic directions for teaching.

Expository text Written selections that include essays, paragraphs, textbook chapters, professional articles, and newspaper editorials that are used for reading instruction.

Fluency During silent or out-loud reading, a child is fluent when the words are identified at a regular pace. If out loud, they are spoken with prosody.

Formative assessment A process to provide specific feedback to teachers about students' continuing reading progress. This assessment prompts teachers to adjust ongoing teaching.

Frontal lobes The largest of four major divisions of each hemisphere of the cerebral cortex located in the front part of the brain and responsible for higher-level cognition. These structures are directly involved with every other functional unit in the brain for response and recognition activities.

Functional magnetic resonance imaging (fMRI) A technique for imaging brain structure and activity by measuring oxygen use of the cells.

Glial cells Provide a vast system of support for the neurons in the brain. Oligodendrocytes, one particular type of glial cell, wrap themselves around an individual neuron's axon to restrict sodium from slowing down messages between neurons.

Grapheme Printed representations, letters, that represent a phoneme.

Heschl's gyrus (or area) A small left temporal brain region where auditory input is rapidly processed as speech or language, rather than sounds not relating to words.

Hippocampus A pair of brain structures located under the surface of the temporal lobes that hold information temporarily until it is dropped or moved to long-term memory for storage and recall.

Implicit instruction Incidental teaching that occurs when an opportunity arises. For phonics instruction, teaching would happen by opportunity, not by an explicit, systematic plan.

Individualized instruction Instruction responsive to the unique needs of each child in a classroom regardless of the lesson setting (whole class, small group, or one-to-one).

Inhibitory neurons Brain cells designed to siphon, detain, and drop unnecessary sensory stimuli from memory as if it had not been received.

Letter–sound relationship The relationship between the grapheme and its corresponding phoneme.

Limbic system A portion of the brain that is located deep inside and is considered to be a more primitive part. It is involved with behavioral and emotional responses, especially when the safety of the person is involved. The "fight or flight" response originates in this system.

Long-term memory Unconscious storage of information for long periods of time, which can be recalled through declarative or nondeclarative memory systems.

Memory How and where the human brain stores information to be recalled at will or automatically. Declarative memory is consciously sought and produced, while nondeclarative memory is recalled by rote response or by engaging in a procedural action. The very essence of teaching is to encourage the learner to hold information or actions for practice and rehearsal in working memory so the brain can develop neural pathways to the declarative or nondeclarative system for recall.

Metacognition A teaching practice that models for students what the teacher is thinking during a learning activity. The teacher vocalizes questions and statements to represent progression of thoughts during process of concept development.

Mindfulness The action or deliberate practice of paying attention, considering, and concentrating.

Mirror neurons A specific type of neuron, discovered unexpectedly, which is amply present in the language system as well as other parts of the human brain. These nerve cells allow a person to activate brain areas while watching another person, as if the observer is actually performing the act.

Morpheme The smallest unit of language that has meaning.

Morphology The study of the language of words and how they are ordered to have meaning.

Motor cortex The lateral part of the frontal lobes that extends from ear to ear across the roof of the brain. It governs coordination of movement and some cognitive processes. The motor cortex may also be referred to as the *motor strip*.

Myelin sheath Glial cells provide a fatty coating for the axon tail of a mature neuron. Myelination allows neurons to fire rapidly, and connections among neurons to become efficient.

Myelination A maturation process in structures and areas of the human brain where one type of glial cell wraps itself around axons and results in speedy transmission of neuron connections.

**Narrative text** A written selection that tells a story and includes children's picture books, fairy tales, fables, myths, tall tales, short stories, and novels.

**Nervous system** The brain, the spinal column, and the complete network of nerves that connect the brain to all parts of the body.

**Neuroanatomy** The branch of neuroscience focused on the *structures* of the system.

**Neuron** A nerve cell in the brain containing a cell body, which metabolizes and synthesizes proteins; numerous dendrites, which receive chemical messages; and one axon, which transports impulses to excite other nerve cells with proteins.

**Neurophysiology** The branch of neuroscience focused on the *functions* of the system.

**Neuroplasticity** The characteristic of the brain that allows it to reorganize itself by forming new neural connections and to adjust their activity in response to new situations or changes in the environment.

**Neuroscience** An understanding of the nervous system.

**Nondeclarative memory** Responses that consist of habits and skills that have been practiced to the point that they can be performed automatically without conscious thought (procedural) or with a prompt (rote).

**Occipital lobe** One of the four major divisions of the cortex located in the back of the brain and responsible for the processing of visual stimuli.

**Oddity tasks** Activities for building phonemic awareness that require a child to "find the one that is different" from a series of sounds or words. Generally the list contains three examples, one of which does not belong.

**Onsets** The initial consonants or blends in the syllable; not every word has an onset.

**Organization** In reference to brain development, the way the brain is systematically connected among neural networks and brain structures for long-term memory recall.

**Orthographic mapping** A process used to permanently store words in long-term declarative memory, available for rote recall.

**Orthography** Written language's visual patterns that account for features of graphemes, phonology, and semantics.

**Parietal lobes** One of the four major divisions of the cortex, located in the upper back part of the brain between the occipital lobes and the frontal cortex. The lobes are responsible for sensory integration and give humans their sense of opportunities and dangers.

**Peer response group** A group of up to five students who have shared responsibilities to complete an assignment. English learners benefit from working with the group.

**Peer tutoring for English learners** An English-speaking older student reads with the younger English learner to complete assignments.

**PET scan** A radioactive material is injected, which emits energy. The activation of different parts of the brain is detected. A PET scan, or positron emission tomography, helps neuroscientists to determine areas of the brain that are activated during different tasks, such as reading.

**Phoneme** The smallest sound of speech that corresponds to a particular letter of an alphabetic writing system.

**Phonemic awareness** Conscious understanding that words are made of individual sounds (phonemes) from speech and that these sounds are representative of the alphabet. Phonemic awareness activities include rhyming, alliteration, oddity tasks, phoneme segmentation, phoneme blending, phoneme manipulation, and syllable splitting.

**Phonics** A system used in alphabetic writing that is representative of speech sounds, which can be referred to as instruction for sound–symbol reading or a phonics approach to reading.

**Phonological awareness** Awareness at all levels of the speech–sound system, including stress patterns, onset–rime units, syllables, and phonemes. It includes both phonemic awareness and a systematic approach to phonics instruction systems.

**Phonological processing** The process used to identify, manipulate, produce, and remember speech sounds, which includes word pronunciation; use of memory for naming word, syllable, and rhyme; and phoneme segmentation blending and manipulation.

**Phonology** The study of rules that govern how speech is identified for individual sounds and bringing the understanding to a conscious level.

**Priming skills** Cognitive development to pay attention, concentrate, remember, and organize thinking. Practices for development also include attending to tasks, sustained focus, and getting set to listen.

**Principles of print** The understanding of written language, including reading from left to right, reading from the top to the bottom of the page, that spaces separate words, and that writing conveys a message.

**Print conventions** The organizational scheme for writing, which goes from left to right and top of the page to the bottom, and has different forms for different writing genres.

**Print form** During the development of understanding writing a child identifies units, letters, and words as having names and being organized in specific ways.

**Print function** An awareness that printed materials provide meaning.

**Print interest** This developmental stage is attained when a child realizes print is stimulating and worthy of attention.

**Print knowledge** Understanding that words are represented by print, that letters of the alphabet are represented in different ways (e.g., upper- and lowercase letters), and that letters can represent multiple sounds or that the same sound can be represented by different letters.

**Print part-to-whole relationships** A final stage to understand print function, as the child realizes letters can be combined to make words and words are grouped together to create larger meaningful units.

**Procedural nondeclarative memory** A long-term memory system that allows the individual to perform a task with automaticity and without involving language systems.

**Processing speed** The rate at which a task, such as reading, occurs through accessing brain structures that are developed for this function.

**Prosody** The stress and intonation patterns, rhythm, and emphasis given to words during oral reading.

**Receptive vocabulary** Words or groups of words when received through the oral language pathway that are understood or comprehensible to the listener.

**Rhyme** The correspondence of ending sounds or lines.

**Rime** A vowel and the following consonants that make a syllable—letter combinations previously referred to as phonograms or word families.

**Schwann cell** In the peripheral nervous system these cells produce the myelin sheath around neuronal axons.

**Semantic memory** Words, phrases, sentences, or other forms of text recalled and articulated through speech or writing, which are reflective of the individual's background information and experience and recalled through declarative memory systems.

**Semantics** The meaning of words, phrases, sentences, and text as reflective of the individual's background information and experience.

**Sensory memory** The initial processing of stimuli coming into the brain from internal or external sources.

**Sensory neuron** A specific type of neuron to transport messages from all parts of the body, which include information through seeing, hearing, smelling, tasting, and touching. These messages are routed to the sensory cortex.

**Somatosensory cortex** An area of the brain located behind the motor cortex that receives information through the five sense, also called sensory memory.

**Source memory** Episodic memory that retrieves what happened, where an incident happened, and when it happened following a highly emotional experience. Details, although vivid in the mind, may lack accuracy.

**Subvocalization** A conscious process of holding the string of words or other information to be repeated over and over.

**Synapse** The physical space or void that allows an electrochemical connection between neuron axons and dendrites.

**Syntax** A rule system that functions unconsciously to order words in phrases and ultimately in sentences that correspond to accepted rules for grammar.

**Systematic phonics instruction** A plan for teaching that is carefully designed around a set of sound–letter relationships following a logical order for explicit instruction.

**Telegraphic speech** Short phrases containing basic information such as "All gone" or "Daddy play ball."

**Temporal lobe** One of the four major divisions of the cerebral cortex, located on the sides of each brain hemisphere. It is responsible for auditory processing and some aspects of memory.

**Thalamus** A relay station in the central, inner area of the brain for incoming signals from all the senses, except the sense of smell, and an output mechanism for sensory stimuli as it is sent to areas of the cerebral cortex for interpretation or to the amygdala for response if sensory input appears to indicate danger or pleasure.

**Visual cortex** Located within the occipital lobes, this area of the brain sorts visual images, associates the images with known background knowledge, and sends the signals to other cortical areas to be interpreted.

**Visual memory** The ability to receive images through the vision center of the brain and hold the images in working memory to complete a task, such as identifying a word from its letters or identifying a series of symbols.

**Wernicke's area** The language center responsible for comprehension of speech. It is typically located in the brain's left hemisphere.

**Word recognition** Identifying groups of letters or meaningful units, morphemes, such as prefixes, suffixes, and inflectional endings, to determine an unknown word.

**Working memory** The conscious processing and recall of information. May be called short-term memory.

# References and Resources


Aaron, P. G. (1995). Differential diagnosis of reading disabilities. *School Psychology Review*, 24(3), 345–360.

Acredolo, L., & Goodwyn, S. (1996). *Baby Signs: How to talk with your baby before your baby can talk*. Contemporary Books.

Alexander, H. (1991). *Look inside your brain*. Grosset & Dunlap.

American Speech–Language–Hearing Association. (2023). *Hearing loss at birth (congenital hearing loss)*. https://www.asha.org/public/hearing/congenital-hearing-loss/#:~:text=Genetics%20is%20the%20cause%20of,hearing%20loss%20in%20your%20baby

Amplify. (2020). *The importance of dual language assessment in early literacy*. https://amplify.com/wp-content/uploads/2022/02/mCLASS_Lectura_Infographic_022323.pdf?utm_campaign=FY22_ElemLitSolutions_symposium_National_biliteracysymposium&utm_medium=email&_hsmi=214360263&_hsenc=p2ANqtz-8GqHJYGAGQdinaIJz9K4zJmeU6f7rc_rrI74yuaqMsFcO5bxb6FKu-lNoiCFHgHQ45CYLMOLRphvk8tkMeETRGrSUxgQ&utm_content=214360263&utm_source=hs_automation

Armstrong, S. (2008). *Teaching smarter with the brain in focus; Practical ways to apply the latest brain research to deepen comprehension, improve memory and motivate students to achieve*. Scholastic.

Baby Professor. (2017). *The human brain—biology for kids*. Baby Professor.

Backpack Books. (2003). *A treasury for three year olds: A collection of stories, fairy tales, and nursery rhymes*. Backpack Books.

Baker, M. (2019). Playing, talking, co-constructing: Exemplary teaching for young dual language learners across program types. *Early Childhood Education Journal*, 47, 115–130. https://doi.org/10.1007/s10643-018-0903-0

Beck, I. L., McKeown, M. G., & Kucan, L. (2013). *Bringing words to life: Robust vocabulary instruction* (2nd ed.). Guilford Press.

Bell, N. (1991). *Visualizing and verbalizing for language comprehension and thinking*. Gander.

Bell, N. (2013). *Sensory-cognitive instruction and the Common Core, a new opportunity for all students*. https://lindamoodbell.com/lassets/Common_Core_Executive_Summary.pdf

Bennett, C. (2019, October 29). *Blog: The importance of nursery rhymes in early childhood*. PACEY. https://www.pacey.org.uk/news-and-views/pacey-blog/2019/october-2019/the-importance-of-nursery-rhymes-in-early-childhoo/#:~:text=Nursery%20rhymes%20provide%20bite%2Dsized,rhythm%20and%20patterns%20of%20language

Berger, M. (Author), & Meisel, P. (Illustrator). (2000). *Why I sneeze, shiver, hiccup, and yawn* (Let's read and find out science–2 edition). HarperCollins.

Berninger, V. W., & Richards, L. R. (2002). *Brain literacy for educators and psychologists*. Academic Press.

Boucher Gill, L. (2021). *Big brain book: How it works and all its quirks*. Magination Press.

Bradshaw, A. R., Bishop, D. V. M., & Woodhead, Z. V. J. (2020). Testing the interhemispheric deficit theory of dyslexia using the visual half-field technique. *Quarterly Journal of Experimental Psychology*, 73(7), 1004–1016. https://

journals.sagepub.com/doi/epub/10.1177/1747021819895472

Bruce, M., Miyazaki, Y., & Bell, M. A. (2022). Infant attention and maternal education are associated with childhood receptive vocabulary development. *Developmental Psychology*, 58(7), 1207–1220. https://doi.org/10.1037/dev0001365

California Department of Education. (2008). *California preschool learning foundations* (Vol. 1). Retrieved from https://www.cde.ca.gov/sp/cd/re/documents/preschoollf.pdf

Cambridge Neuroscience. (2016, April 18). *Foundations of the educated brain: Infancy and early childhood* [Seminar]. Lucia Windsor Room, Newnham College, Cambridge, England. https://www.neuroscience.cam.ac.uk/events/event.php?permalink=b3bfb5c006

Centers for Disease Control and Prevention. (2022a, December 29). *CDC's developmental milestones.* National Center on Birth Defects and Developmental Disabilities. https://www.cdc.gov/ncbddd/actearly/milestones/index.html

Centers for Disease Control and Prevention. (2022b, July 21). *Data and statistics about hearing loss in children.* National Center on Birth Defects and Developmental Disabilities. https://www.cdc.gov/ncbddd/hearingloss/data.html

Chaffee, J. (2018). *Thinking critically* (12th ed.). Cengage Learning.

Chan, J. (2022, March). *Common misconceptions about high-quality instructional materials.* EdReports. https://edreports.org/resources/article/3-common-misconceptions-about-high-quality-instructional-materials?utm_medium=email&utm_source=pardot&utm_campaign=hqim-misconceptions-mar-2022

Cherry, K. (2022, November 14). *What is the cerebellum?* Verywell Mind. https://www.verywellmind.com/what-is-the-cerebellum-2794964

ChildCare. (2022). *Ratios and group size.* https://childcare.gov/consumer-education/ratios-and-group-sizes

Chugani, H. (1998). A critical period of brain development: Studies of cerebral glucose utilization with PET. *Preventive Medicine*, 27, 184–188.

Coby, B. (2021). *Black and white baby book.* Independently published.

Cohen, L., Buch, E. R., Claudino, L., Quentin, R., & Bonstrup, M. (2021). Consolidation of human skill linked to waking hippocampal replay. *Cell Reports*, 35(10), 109–193. https://www.cell.com/cell-reports/fulltext/S2211-1247(21)00539-8?_returnURL=https%3A%2F%2Flinkinghub.elsevier.com%2Fretrieve%2Fpii%2FS2211124721005398%3Fshowall%3Dtrue

Cole, J. (Author), & Degen, B. (Illustrator). (1986–2020). *The Magic School Bus* (Book series). Scholastic.

Cole, J. (Author), & Degen, B. (Illustrator). (2001). *The Magic School Bus explores the senses.* Scholastic.

Collins, M. F. (2005). IRA Outstanding Dissertation Award for 2005: ESL preschoolers' English vocabulary acquisition from storybook reading, *Reading Research Quarterly*, 40(4), 406–408.

Common Core State Standards Initiative. (2010). *Common Core State Standards.* http://www.corestandards.org/

Common Sense Education. (2022, March 30). *Young kids and screens: Workshops for families with kids age 0–8* [Video]. YouTube. https://www.youtube.com/watch?v=oH3qnCU_EvA

Cristelow, E. (2010). *Five little monkeys* (6-book set). Scholastic.

Cummins, J. (2000a). *Bilingual children's mother tongue: Why is it important for education?* www.iteachilearn.com/cummins/mother.htm

Cummins, J. (2000b). *Language, power, and pedagogy: Bilingual children in the crossfire.* Multilingual Matters.

Cunningham, A. (1990). Explicit versus implicit instruction in phonemic awareness. *Journal of Experimental Child Psychology*, 50, 429–444.

Curriculum Associates. (2021a, November 4). *New research report from Curriculum Associates: More students are starting the school year behind.* https://www.curri

culumassociates.com/about/press-releases/2021/11/fall-results-2021

Curriculum Associates. (2021b, November). *Understanding student learning: Insights from fall 2021* [Research brief]. https://www.curriculumassociates.com/-/media/mainsite/files/i-ready/iready-understanding-student-learning-paper-fall-results-2021.pdf

D'Souza, K. (2022a, March 9). *Has the pandemic worsened the literacy crisis?* EdSource. https://edsource.org/updates/has-the-pandemic-worsened-the-literacy-crisis_

D'Souza, K. (2022b, March 11). *Will the pandemic leave a lasting mark on baby brains?* EdSource. https://edsource.org/2022/will-the-pandemic-leave-a-lasting-mark-on-baby-brains/668664

de Bellefonds, C. (2021). *When babies begin to smell. What to Expect.* https://www.whattoexpect.com/pregnancy/fetal-development/fetal-smell/#:~:text=years%20to%20come.-,Can%20babies%20smell%20in%20the%20womb%3F,smelling%20throughout%20the%20third%20trimester

Deak, J. (Author), & Ackerley, S. (Illustrator). (2010). *Your fantastic elastic brain: A growth mindset book to stretch and shape their brains.* Little Pickle Press.

Dell'Erba, M. (2020, February 19). *Engaging the arts in 2020's top education policy priorities.* Americans for the Arts. https://www.americansforthearts.org/2020/02/19/engaging-the-arts-in-2020s-top-education-policy-priorities

Dewar, G. (2018). *Baby sign language: A guide for the science-minded parent.* Parenting Science. https://parentingscience.com/baby-sign-language/#:~:text=They%20claim%20that%20babies%20taught,effectively%20at%20an%20earlier%20age

Diamond, M., & Hopson, J. (1998). *Magic trees of the mind: How to nurture your child's intelligence, creativity, and healthy emotions from birth through adolescence.* Penguin Books.

Dickinson, D. K., Golinkoff, R. M., & Hirsh-Pasek, K. (2010, May 1). Speaking out for language: Why language is central to reading development. *Educational Researcher, 39*(4). https://doi.org/10.3102/0013189X10370204

Dickinson, D. K., Hofer, K. G., Barnes, E. M., & Grifenhagen, J. F. (2013). Examining teachers' language in Head Start classrooms from a systemic linguistics approach. *Early Childhood Research Quarterly, 29*(3), 231–244. https://www.researchconnections.org/childcare/resources/27156

Dieleman, L. (2022, March). *How to use brain activation to combat learning loss: The life raft for your classroom* [Webinar]. Sponsored by BrainAhead. https://home.edweb.net/webinar/brain20220323/

DiTullio, G. (2021, September 9). *How to engage students' memory processes to improve learning.* Center of Excellence. https://www.fmucenterofexcellence.org/bestpractice/ditullio-g-2021-september-9-how-to-engage-students-memory-processes-to-improve-learning-edutopia-retrieved-march-9-2022/

Dobbs, D. (2006). A revealing reflection. *Scientific American Mind, 17*(2), 22–27.

Dr. Seuss. (1957). *The cat in the hat.* Random House, Houghton Mifflin.

Dr. Seuss. (1974). *There's a wocket in my pocket!* Random House Books for Young Readers.

duopress labs & Mora, J. (Illustrator). (2016). *Hello, baby animals: A durable high-contrast black-and-white board book for newborns and babies* (Illustrated ed.). duopress.

Durkin, K., Lipsey, M. W., Farran, D. C., & Wiesen, S. E. (2022, January). Effects of a state-wide prekindergarten program. *Developmental Psychology.* Advance online publication. https://my.vanderbilt.edu/tnprekevaluation/files/2022/02/Effects-of-a-Statewide-Prekindergarten-Program-on-Childrens-Achievement-and-Behavior-through-Sixth-Grade_10_20_21.pdf

Dwyer, J., & Harbaugh, A. G. (2020, June 1). Where and when is support for vocabulary development occurring in preschool classrooms? *Journal of Early Childhood Literacy, 20*(2), 252–295.

Eckart, K. (2020, February 3). *Not just "baby talk": Parentese helps parents, babies make "conversation" and boosts language development.* UW NEWS. Retrieved from https://www.washington.edu/news/2020/02/03/not-just-baby-talk-parentese-helps-parents-babies-make-conversation-and-boosts-language-development/

Eide, D. (Author), & Hess, I. (Illustrator). (2022). *How your brain learns to read.* Logic of Reading.

Eliot, L. (1999). *What is going on in there?* Bantam Books.

Ferrandio, T., & Zaryczny, V. (2021). *Handwriting: The secret foundation for academic success* [Webinar]. edWeb. https://media.edweb.net/edWebinar/?view=20210930edweb62

First Things First. (2017, October 15). *The baby brain* [Video]. YouTube. https://www.youtube.com/watch?v=-ijGVM1h1nU&t=4s

First Things First. (2023). *Brain development.* https://www.firstthingsfirst.org/early-childhood-matters/brain-development/#:~:text=90%25%20of%20Brain%20Growth%20Happens%20Before%20Kindergarten&text=It%20keeps%20growing%20to%20about,center%20of%20the%20human%20body

Fitzpatrick, E. M., Thibert, J., Grandpierre, V., & Johnston, J. C. (2014). How HANDy are baby signs? A systematic review of the impact of gestural communication on typically developing, hearing infants under the age of 36 months. *First Language, 34*(6), 486–509. https://doi.org/10.1177/0142723714562864

Foorman, B. R. (2007). Primary prevention in classroom reading instruction. *Teaching Exceptional Children, 39*(5), 24–30. https://www.cehd.umn.edu/EdPsych/RIPS/Documents/TieredServiceDelivery/MultitieredArticle4PrimaryPrevention.pdf

Foreman, J. (2002). The evidence speaks well of bilingualism's effect on kids. *The Brain in the News, 9*(19), 3.

Forestell, C. A., & Mennella, J. A. (2017, June 6). The relationship between infant facial expressions and food acceptance. *Current Nutrition Reports, 6,* 141–147. https://doi.org/10.1007/s13668-017-0205-y

Georgiu, G. K., Parrila, R., Cui, Y., & Papado, T. C. (2013, May). Why is rapid automatized naming related to reading? *Journal of Experimental Child Psychology, 115*(1), 218–225.

Goldberg, M. (2022, March 10). *Getting reading right: Why California overhauled the way literacy is taught.* Right to Read Project. https://righttoreadproject.com/

Gopnik, A., Meltzoff, A., & Kuhl, P. (2000). *The scientist in the crib.* William Morrow.

Goswami, U. (2020). *Cognitive development and cognitive neuroscience: The learning brain* (2nd ed.). Routledge.

Graham, J., & Forstadt, L. A. (2011). *Children and brain development: What we know about how children learn.* Bulletin #4356. Cooperative Extension Publications, University of Maine Cooperative Extension. https://extension.umaine.edu/publications/4356e/

Great Schools. (2022). *Cn u rd ths? A guide to invented spelling.* https://www.greatschools.org/gk/articles/invented-spelling/

Green, B., Schlichting, S., & Thomas, M. E. (2003). *Five-minute warm-ups* (Rev. ed.). Incentive Publications.

Hall, S. L., & Moats, L. C. (1999). *Straight talk about reading: How parents can make a difference during the early years.* NTC/Contemporary.

Hasbrouck, J. (2022). We know HOW to teach children to read: Let's DO it! [Audio podcast episode]. In *EDVIEW360* [Audio podcast series]. Voyager Sopris. https://www.voyagersopris.com/podcast/2022/we-know-how-to-teach-children-to-read-let's-do-it!

Hasbrouck, J., & Tindal, G. (2017). *An update to compiled ORF norms* (Technical Report No. 1702). Behavioral Research and Teaching, University of Oregon.

Help Me Grow, Minnesota. (2022). *Cognitive milestones.* https://helpmegrowmn.org/HMG/DevelopMilestone/CognitiveMilestones/index.html

Hill, B. (2022). *5 simple steps to help children overcome learning struggles and become capable, confident, learners.* Brainware Safari. https://parenttraining.mybrainware.com/a/AStBV4?id=zxqXQe_

Hill, H. C., Papay, J. P., & Schwartz, N. (2022, February 15). Dispelling the myths: What the research says about teacher professional learning. Research

Partnerships for Professional Learning. https://annenberg.brown.edu/sites/default/files/rppl-dispelling-myths.pdf

Hirsh-Pasek, K. (2017, October). *The power of play: How play motivates children's academic and social development* [Seminar presentation]. The Educated Brain Seminar Series, University of Cambridge.

Hogenboon, M. (2022, March 1). *What is the best age to learn to read?* BBC News. https://www.bbc.com/future/article/20220228-the-best-age-for-learning--to-read?utm_source=pocket-newtab

Honig, B., Diamond, L., & Gutlohn, L. (2018). *Teaching reading sourcebook* (3rd ed.). CORE & Arena Press. https://www.corelearn.com/wp-content/uploads/2020/05/teaching-reading-sourcebook--sampler-202006.pdf

Hope Abilitation Medical Center. (2019, February 1). *Importance of language development and literacy in children.* https://www.hope-amc.com/importance-of-language-development-and-literacy-in-children/

Hudson, R. F., High, L., & Al Otaiba, S. (2007). Dyslexia and the brain: What does current research tell us? *Reading Teacher, 6,* 506–515.

Human Physiology Academy. (2020). Images of somatosensory function. https://humanphysiology.academy/Neurosciences%202015/Images/3/somatosensory%20hounculus%20rcl.rutgers.edu%20.jpg

Hutton, J. S., Huang, G., Sahay, R. D., DeWitt, T., & Ittenbach, R. F. (2020). A novel, composite measure of screen-based media use in young children (ScreenQ) and associations with parenting practices and cognitive abilities. *Pediatric Research, 87,* 1211–1218. https://doi.org/10.1038/s41390-020-0765-1

Hyerle, D. (2004). *Student successes with thinking maps, school-based research, results, and models for achievement using visual tools.* Corwin.

Johnson, J., & Newport, E. (1989). Critical period effects in second language learning: The influence of maturation state on the acquisition of English as a second language. *Cognitive Psychology, 21,* 60–99.

Johnson, K. (2019, April 2). *Holy cow your toddler probably knows way more words than you realize.* Romper. Retrieved from https://www.romper.com/p/how-many-words-do-toddlers-learn-a-day-they-understand-a-lot-more-than-you-may-realize-16954479

Jusczyk, P. W. (1999). How infants begin to extract words from speech. *Trends in Cognitive Science, 3,* 323–328.

Kirk, E., Howlett, N., Pine, K. J., & Fletcher, B. C. (2012). To sign or not to sign? The impact of encouraging infants to gesture on infant language and maternal mind-mindedness. *Child Development, 84*(2), 574–590.

Koontz, D. (Author), & Parks, P. (Illustrator). (2001). *The paper doorway: Funny verse and nothing worse.* HarperCollins.

Kotulak, R. (1997). *Inside the brain: Revolutionary discoveries of how the mind works.* Andrews McMeel.

Krashen, S. (1999). Training in phonemic awareness: Greater on tests of phonemic awareness. *Perceptual and Motor Skills, 89*(2). https://doi.org/10.2466/pms.1999.89.2.412

Kristanto, D., Liu, M., Sommers, W., & Zhou, C. (2020, September). Predicting reading ability from brain anatomy and function: From areas to connections. *NeuroImage, 218,* 116966. https://www.sciencedirect.com/science/article/pii/S1053811920304523

Kuhl, P. K. (2012). Early language learning and literacy: Neuroscience implications for education. *Mind, Brain, and Education, 5*(3), 128–142. https://www.ncbi.nlm.nih.gov/pmc/articles/PMC3164118/

Liebbrand, J. A., & Watson, B. H. (2010). *The road less traveled: How the developmental sciences can prepare educators to improve student achievement: Policy recommendations.* National Expert Panel of the National Council for Accreditation of Teacher Education. https://files.eric.ed.gov/fulltext/ED550407.pdf

Lindamood, P. C., Bell, N., & Lindamood, P. D. (1997). Sensory-cognitive factors in the controversy over reading instruction.

*Journal of Developmental and Learning Disorders, 1*(1), 143–182.

Lindamood, P. C., Bell, N., & Lindamood, P. D. (2020). *Lindamood Phoneme Sequencing® Program for Reading, Spelling, and Speech (LiPS®)*. https://lindamoodbell.com/program/lindamood-phoneme-sequencing-program

Liversedge, S. P., & Blythe, H. I. (2007). Lexical and sublexical influences on eye movements during reading. *Language and Linguistics Compass, 1*(1/2), 17–31.

Loewus, L. (2017, May 5). Invented spelling leads to better reading, study says. *Education Week.* https://www.edweek.org/teaching-learning/invented-spelling-leads-to-better-reading-study-says/2017/05#:~:text=The%20researchers'%20recent%20study%20followed,literacy%20skills%20after%20a%20year

Lynch, G. H. (2012, May 16). *The importance of art in child development.* PBS Kids for Parents. https://www.pbs.org/parents/thrive/the-importance-of-art-in-child-development

Mader, J. (2022, February 2). *Behind the findings of the Tennessee pre-K study that found negative effects for graduates.* The Hechinger Report. https://hechingerreport.org/behind-the-findings-of-the-tennessee-pre-k-study-that-found-negative-effects-for-graduates/

Manley, R. J., & Hawkins, R. J. (2013). *Making the Common Core standards work: Using professional development to build world-class schools.* Corwin.

Martin, B., Jr. (Author), & Carle, E. (Illustrator). (1967). *Brown bear, brown bear, what do you see?* Doubleday.

Mathes, P. (2003, May). *The Tallahassee and Houston first grade intervention studies* [Presentation]. International Reading Association, Orlando, FL.

Mayo Clinic Staff. (2022a, February 10). *Screen time and children: How to guide your child.* https://www.mayoclinic.org/healthy-lifestyle/childrens-health/in-depth/screen-time/art-20047952#:~:text=If%20you%20introduce%20digital%20media,doesn't%20work%20as%20well

Mayo Clinic Staff. (2022b, June 3). *Pregnancy week by week.* Retrieved from https://www.mayoclinic.org/healthy-lifestyle/pregnancy-week-by-week/in-depth/prenatal-care/art-20045302#:~:text=The%20baby's%20brain%20and%20spinal,that%20will%20soon%20become%20arms

McBride-Chang, C. (2010). The development of invented spelling. *Early Education and Development, 9*(2), 147–160. https://www.tandfonline.com/doi/abs/10.1207/s15566935eed0902_3

McCandliss, B. D., Cohen, L., & Dehaene, S. (2003). The visual word form area: Expertise for reading in the fusiform gyrus. *Trends in Cognitive Sciences, 7*(7), 293–299.

McGee, M. G., & Wilson, D. W. (1984). *Psychology: Science and application.* West.

McPherson, K. (2023). *Should I be correcting my toddler's language? The answer might surprise you.* CHOC. Retrieved from https://www.choc.org/news/should-i-be-correcting-my-toddlers-language-the-answer-might-surprise-you/#:~:text=While%20letting%20your%20toddler%20use,recommends%20discouraging%20your%20child's%20speech

McTighe, J., & Wiggins, G. (2013). *Essential questions: Opening doors to student understanding.* ASCD.

MindTools. (n.d.). *Ebbinghaus's Forgetting Curve: Why we keep forgetting and what we can do about it.* https://www.mindtools.com/pages/article/forgetting-curve.htm

Moats, L. (2000). *Speech to print.* Paul H. Brookes.

Moats, L.C. (2004). *Speech to print workbook: Language exercises for teachers.* Paul H. Brookes.

Moats, L. C. (2022). *Why every educator needs to understand the science of reading* [Interview]. Lexia Learning. https://www.lexialearning.com/user_area/content_media/raw/Why-Every-Educator-Needs-to-Understand-the-Science-of-Reading.pdf

Moats, L. C., Furry, A. R., & Brownell, N. (1998). *Learning to read: Components of beginning reading instruction, K–8.* Sacramento County Office of Education.

Morgan, P. L., Woods, A. D., Wang, Y., Farkas, G., Hillemeier, M. M., & Mitchell, C. (2022, May 28). Which Students With Disabilities are Placed Primarily Outside of U.S. Elementary School General Education Classrooms? *Journal of Learning Disabilities.* Advance online publication. https://doi.org/10.1177/00222194221094019

Murre, J. M. J., & Dros, J. (2015, July 6). Replication and analysis of Ebbinghaus' Forgetting Curve. *PLoS ONE,* 10(7), e0120644. https://doi.org/10.1371/journal.pone.0120644.

Nation's Report Card. (2022). *NAEP long-term trend assessment results: Reading and mathematics—Reading and mathematics scores decline during COVID-19 pandemic.* https://www.nationsreportcard.gov/highlights/ltt/2022/

Nation's Report Card: Reading. (2022). *State achievement-level results.* https://www.nationsreportcard.gov/reading/states/achievement/?grade=4

National Academy of Sciences. (1992). The development and shaping of the brain. In S. Ackerman (Ed.), *Discovering the brain* (Chapter 6, based on presentations by Pasko Rakic). https://www.ncbi.nlm.nih.gov/books/NBK234146/#:~:text=To%20arrive%20at%20the%20more,throughout%20the%20course%20of%20pregnancy

National Association for the Education of Young Children. (1998). Learning to read and write: Developmentally appropriate practices for young children. A joint position statement of the International Reading Association and the National Association for the Education of Young Children. *Young Children,* 53(4), 30–46.

National Center for Education Statistics. (2007). *The condition of education 2007.* U.S. Department of Education NCES 2007-064. https://nces.ed.gov/pubs2007/2007064.pdf

National Center for Education Statistics. (2022). English learners in public schools. *Condition of Education.* U.S. Department of Education, Institute of Education Sciences. https://nces.ed.gov/programs/coe/indicator/cgf

National Early Literacy Panel. (2009). *Developing early literacy: A scientific synthesis of early literacy development and implications for intervention.* National Institute for Literacy.

National Institute of Child Health and Human Development. (2019). *Report of the National Reading Panel.* https://www.nichd.nih.gov/publications/pubs/nrp/method

National Reading Panel. (2000). *Teaching children to read: An evidence-based assessment of the scientific research literature on reading and its implications for reading instruction.* https://www.nichd.nih.gov/sites/default/files/publications/pubs/nrp/Documents/report.pdf

Nevills, P. (2011). *Build the brain for reading, grades 4–12.* Corwin.

Nevills, P. (2014). *Build the brain the Common Core way.* Corwin.

Nevills, P., & Wolfe, P. (2009). *Building the reading brain, prek–3* (2nd ed.). Corwin.

Noland, T., Wiederstein, H., & Ness, M. (2022). *Using the read-aloud, think-aloud as a way to model metacognition for students* [edWebinar]. Sponsored by Learning Ally. https://home.edweb.net/webinar/readers20220210/

Nold, J., De Jong, D., & Aderhold, F. (2021, April 22). Early childhood education: Academic and behavioral effects of prekindergarten educational programming. *SAGE Open.* Advance online publication. https://doi.org/10.1177/21582440211010154

Nursery Rhymes. (2022). *There was an old lady who swallowed a fly.* https://allnurseryrhymes.com/there-was-an-old-lady-who-swallowed-a-fly/

O'Connor, R. E., White, A., & Swanson, H. L. (2007). Repeated reading versus continuous reading: Influences on reading fluency and comprehension. *Exceptional Children,* 74(1), 31–46. https://doi.org/10.1177/001440290707400102

O'Sullivan, C. (2022, April 18). *Pre-K is still the place for play* [edWebinar]. Sponsored by

Gryphon House. https://home.edweb.net/webinar/bookchats20220418/

Oxford University Press. (2023). *Learning.* OxfordLanguages. https://languages.oup.com/google-dictionary-en/

Parker, S. (Author), & West, D. (Illustrator). (1988). *Brain surgery for beginners and other operations for minors: A scalpel-free guide to your insides.* Scholastic.

Pashler, H., Bain, P. M., Bottge, B. A., Graesser, A., Koedinger, K., McDaniel, M., & Metcalfe, J. (2007, September). *Organizing instruction and study to improve student learning (NCER 2007-2004).* National Center for Education Research, Institute of Education Sciences, U.S. Department of Education. https://files.eric.ed.gov/fulltext/ED498555.pdf

Pathways to Reading. (2021, May 12). *What is the difference between phonological awareness and phonemic awareness?* https://pathwaystoreadinghomeschool.com/difference-between-phonological-awareness-and-phonemic-awareness/#:~:text=Basic%20phonological%20awareness%20develops%20from,as%20phonemes)%20in%20spoken%20language

Pence, K. L., & Justice, L. M. (2008). *Language development from theory to practice.* Pearson, Merrill Prentice Hall.

Petrilli, M. J., Davidson, B., & Carroll, K. (2022). *Follow the science to school: Evidence-based practices for elementary education.* John Catt Educational.

Phillips, R. D., Gorton, R. L., Pinciotti, P., & Sachdev, A. (2010). Promising findings on preschoolers' emergent literacy and school readiness in arts-integrated early childhood settings. *Early Childhood Education Journal, 38,* 111–122.

Pica, R. (2015). *What if everybody understood child development? Straight talk about bettering education and children's lives.* Corwin.

Pilgreen, J. L. (2000). *The sustained silent reading handbook.* Heinemann.

Polikoff, M., Wang, E. L., Haderlein, S. K., Kaufman, J. H., Woo, A., Silver, D., & Opfer, D. (2020). *Exploring coherence in English language arts instructional systems in the Common Core era.* RAND Corporation. https://www.rand.org/pubs/research_reports/RRA279-1.html

Pugh, K. R., Mencl, W. E., Shaywitz, B. E., Shaywitz, S. E., Fulbright, R. K., Constable, R. T., Skudlarski, P., Marchione, K. E., Jenner, A. R., Fletcher, J. M., Liberman, A. M., Shankweiler, D. P., Katz, L., Lacadie, C., & Gore, J. C. (2000). The angular gyrus in developmental dyslexia: Task-Specific differences in functional connectivity within posterior cortex. *Psychological Science, 11*(1). https://journals.sagepub.com/doi/pdf/10.1111/1467-9280.00214

Ramirez, N. F., Lytle, S. R., & Kuhl, P. D. (2020). Parent coaching increases conversational turns and advances infant language development. *PNAS, 117*(7), 3484–3491. https://www.pnas.org/doi/10.1073/pnas.1921653117

Read Naturally. (2023). *Hasbrouck-Tindal oral reading fluency chart.* https://www.readnaturally.com/article/hasbrouck-tindal-oral-reading-fluency-chart

Reading Rockets. (2007). *Nursery rhymes: Not just for babies!* https://www.readingrockets.org/article/nursery-rhymes-not-just-babies

Reading Rockets. (2019, January 23). *What are some misconceptions about dyslexia* [Video]. YouTube. https://www.youtube.com/watch?v=GgtHVDWbHH4&list=PLLxDwKxHx1yJy65BdMRGpV6TCeeiLIhBZ&t=2s

Really Great Reading. (2015). *Scarborough's Reading Rope.* https://www.reallygreatreading.com/content/scarboroughs-reading-rope#:~:text=In%202001%2C%20Dr.,complexity%20of%20learning%20to%20read

Reeves, D. (2008). You know what to do, teachers. Now do it [Speech at the Achievement Gap Summit, Sacramento, CA]. *The Special Edge, 21*(2), 3–4.

Reid, K. (Host). (2022, February 2). Defining play with Peter Gray (No. 18) [Audio podcast episode]. In *The DEY Podcast.* Defending the Early Years. https://dey.org/podcast/defining-play-with-peter-gray/

Reutzel, D. R. (2015). Early literacy research: Findings primary-grade teachers will want to know. *The Reading Teacher, 69*(1), 14–24. https://www.uwyo.edu/wsup/_files/docs/esl_conference/reutzel--2015-the_reading_teacher.pdf

Reynolds, G. D., Courage, M. L., & Richards, J. E. (2010). Infant attention and visual preferences: Converging evidence from behavior, event-related potentials, and cortical source localization. *Developmental Psychology*, 46(4), 886–904. http://dx.doi.org/10.1037/a0019670

Ricci, D. (2022, February 10). *Special feature on vision and brain development in children*. Reported by the International Agency for the Prevention of Blindness. https://iapb.it/special-feature-on-vision-and-brain-development-in-children/

Risley, T. R., Ramey, S. L., & Washington, J. (2022). *From babbling to books: Building pre-reading skills* [Webcast]. Reading Rockets. https://www.readingrockets.org/webcasts/1002

Ritter, M. (2007, March 19). New research is mind-wandering. *North County Times*, p. H8.

Rizzolatti, G., Fogassi, L., & V. Gallese. (2006). Mirrors in the mind. *Scientific American*, 295(5), 54–61.

Rogers, L. (2021). *When do kids start coloring and scribbling?* What to Expect. https://www.whattoexpect.com/toddler/scribble/#:~:text=Most%20toddlers%20are%20ready%20to,process%20that%20happens%20in%

Scheer, J. (Author), & Bileck, M. (Illustrator). (1964). *Rain makes apple sauce*. Holiday House.

Seal, B. & Depaolis, R. (2014). Manual activity and onset of first words in babies exposed and not exposed to baby signing. *Sign Language Studies*, 14, 444–465. 10.1353/sls.2014.0015.

Sequeira, K. (2002, April 1). *LAUSD ahead of California timeline on expanded TK rollout*. EdSource. https://edsource.org/2022/lausd-teachers-hesitant-but-hopeful-as-tk-expansion-set-to-roll-out/669620

Shaywitz, S. E. (2003). *Overcoming dyslexia: A new and complete science-based program for reading problems at any level*. Alfred A. Knopf.

Shaywitz, S. E., Shaywitz, B. A., Pugh, K. R., Mencl, W. E., Fulbright, R. K., Skudlarski, P., Fletcher, J. M., Katz, L., Marchione, K. E., Lacadie, C., Gatenby, C., & Gore, J. C. (2002). Functional disruption in the organization of the brain for reading in dyslexia. *Biological Psychiatry*, 52, 101–110.

Skene, K., O'Farrelly, C., Byren, E. M., Kirby, N., Stevens, E. C., & Ramchandani, P. G. (2022). Can guidance during play enhance children's learning and development in educational contexts? A systematic review and meta-analysis. *Child Development*, 93(4), 1162–1180. https://doi.org/10.1111/cdev.13730

Snow, P. C. (2021). SOLAR: The Science of Language and Reading. *Child Language Teaching and Therapy*, 37(3), 222–233. https://doi.org/10.1177/0265659020947817

Snowling, M. J., & Hulme, C. (Eds.). (2005). *The science of reading: A handbook*. Blackwell.

Stahl, S. A. (2003, Spring). How words are learned incrementally over multiple exposures. *American Educator*, 18–19.

Stanford Medicine Children's Health. (2023a). *Newborn reflexes*. https://www.stanfordchildrens.org/en/topic/default?id=newborn-reflexes-90-P02630

Stanford Medicine Children's Health. (2023b). *Newborn senses*. Retrieved from https://www.stanfordchildrens.org/en/topic/default?id=newborn-senses-90-P02631

Starnes, L. (2021, October 13). *Big conversations with little children: Addressing questions, worries, and fears* [Webinar]. Sponsored by Early Childhood Investigations. Early Childhood Investigations Webinars. https://www.earlychildhoodwebinars.com/webinars/big-questions-worries-and-fears-how-to-have-hard-conversations-with-little-children-by-dr-lauren-starnes/

Stoppler, M. C. (2022, February 8). *Stages of pregnancy: Week by week*. OnHealth. https://www.onhealth.com/content/1/pregnancy_stages_trimesters

Strauss, V. (2014, February 6). A very scary headline about kindergartners. *The Washington Post*. https://www.washingtonpost.com/news/answer-sheet/wp/2014/02/06/a-really-scary-headline-about-kindergarteners/

Targonskaya, A. (2020, April 14). Fetal brain development stages: When does a fetus develop a brain? *Flo Health*. Retrieved from https://flo.health/pregnancy/pregnancy-health/fetal-develop

ment/fetal-brain-development#: ~:text=In%20the%20first%20trimester %2C%20the,won't%20feel%20any%20 movement

Taylor, J. (2016, July 15). *Mirror neurons after a quarter century: New light, new cracks*. Harvard University, the Graduate School of Arts and Sciences. https://sitn.hms.harvard.edu/flash/ 2016/mirror-neurons-quarter-century-new-light-new-cracks/

Terada, Y. (2022). We drastically underestimate the importance of brain breaks, when it comes to optimizing learning, we don't value breaks enough, neuroscientists suggest in a new study. Edutopia. https://www.edutopia.org/ article/we-drastically-underestimate-importance-brain-breaks

Thomas, M. R., Tutschek, B., Frost, A., Rodeck, C. H., Yazdani, N., Craft, I., & Williamson, R. (1995, July 15). The time of appearance and disappearance of fetal DNA from the maternal circulation. *Prenatal Diagnosis, 15*(7), 641–646. https://doi.org10.1002/pd.1970150709

Torgesen, J. K., Wagner, R. K., & Rashotte, C. A. (1994). Longitudinal studies of phonological processing and reading. *Journal of Learning Disabilities, 27*, 276–286.

Treays, R. (Author), & Fox, C. (Illustrator). (2004). *Understanding your brain (Science for beginners)*. Usborne Pub.

Turkeltaub, P. E., Weisberg, J., Flowers, D. L., Basu, D., & Eden, G. F. (2005). The neurobiological basis of reading: A special case of skill acquisition. In W. Catts & A. G. Kamhi (Eds.), *The connections between language and reading disabilities* (pp. 103–129). Lawrence Erlbaum Associates.

Turnbull, K. L. P., & Justice, L. M. (2017). *Language development from theory to practice* (3rd ed.). Pearson.

University of California–Los Angeles. (2009, November 19). Blindness causes structural brain changes, implying brain can re-organize itself to adapt. *Science Daily*. https://www.sciencedaily.com/relea ses/2009/11/091118143259.htm#:~:text= 2-,Blindness%20causes%20structural %20brain%20changes%2C%20implying %20brain,re%2Dorganize%20itself%20

to%20adapt&text=Summary%3A,a%20 loss%20in%20sensory%20inputs

U.S. Department of Education, Office of Special Education and Rehabilitative Services, Office of Special Education Programs. (2022, January). *43rd annual report to Congress on the implementation of the Individuals with Disabilities Education Act*. https://sites.ed.gov/idea/files/ 43rd-arc-for-idea.pdf

Van Hekken, A., & Bottari, M. (2022). *The #1 reading skill your students are missing* [edWebinar]. Heggerty. https://media .edweb.net/edWebinar/?view=2022 0519edwebnet15

Vander Stappen, C., & Reybroeck, M. V. (2018). Phonological awareness and rapid automatized naming are independent phonological competencies with specific impacts on word reading and spelling: An intervention study. *Frontiers in Psychology, 13*(9), 320. https:// doi.org/10.3389/fpsyg.2018.00320

Walsh, J. A., & Sattes, B. D. (2005). *Quality questioning, research-based practice to engage every learner*. Corwin.

Waterford.org. (2019). *Why bilingual students have a cognitive advantage for learning to read*. https://www.waterford.org/edu cation/why-bilingual-students-have-a-cognitive-advantage-for-learning-to-read/

WebMD Editorial Contributors. (2021, June 28). *When do you stop swaddling a baby?* Grow by WebMD. https://www.webmd. com/baby/when-do-you-stop-swadd ling-baby#:~:text=%E2%80%8CYou%20 should%20stop%20swaddling%20your, raise%20their%20risk%20of%20SIDs

What Works Clearinghouse. (2007). *Intervention report*. https://ies.ed.gov/ncee/ wwc/Docs/InterventionReports/WWC_ Kaplan_Spellread_070907.pdf

What Works Clearinghouse. (2022). *Preparing young children for school*. https://ies .ed.gov/ncee/wwc/PracticeGuide/30

Whitehurst, G. J. (2002). *Dialogic reading: An effective way to read aloud with young children*. Reading Rockets. https://www. readingrockets.org/article/dialogic-reading-effective-way-read-aloud-young-children

Wikipedia. (2021, September 10). *Motor cortex.* https://en.wikipedia.org/wiki/Motor_ cortex#/media/File:Figure_35_03_04 .jpg

Wikipedia. (2022, August). *Manual babbling.* https://en.wikipedia.org/wiki/Manual_ babbling#:~:text=Deaf%20infants%2C %20like%20hearing%20infants,of%20 deaf%20children%20decreases%20 dramatically

Williams, C. P. (2020, October 13). *New research ignites debate on the "30 million word gap."* Edutopia. https://www.edu topia.org/article/new-research-ignites- debate-30-million-word-gap#:~:text= After%20analyzing%20the%20resulting %201%2C300,assistance%20heard%20 closer%20to%20600

Wolf, M. (2007). *Proust and the squid: The story and science of the reading brain.* HarperCollins.

Wolf, M., Bowers, P., & Biddle, K. (2000). RAVE-O: A comprehensive fluency- based reading intervention program. *Journal of Learning Disabilities, 33*(4).

Wood, A. (Author), & Wood, D. (Illustrator). (2009). *The napping house.* Clarion Books.

Woolfolk, A. (2008). *Educational psychology, active learning edition.* Pearson Education.

Worth, B. (Author), & Ruiz, A. (Illustrator). (2001). *Oh say can you seed? All about flowering plants* (Illustrated ed.). Ran- dom House Books for Young Readers.

Yolen, J. (Author), & Teague, M. (Illustrator). (2000). *How do dinosaurs say goodnight?* Blue Sky Press.

# Index

**Helping educators make the greatest impact**

**CORWIN HAS ONE MISSION:** to enhance education through intentional professional learning.

We build long-term relationships with our authors, educators, clients, and associations who partner with us to develop and continuously improve the best evidence-based practices that establish and support lifelong learning.